Advocating, Building, and Collaborating
A Resource Toolkit to Sustain Secondary School Writing Centers

Edited by

Renee Brown
Peters Township Middle School, Pennsylvania

Stacey Waldrup
Meridian High School, Idaho

Copyright © 2018 by SSWCA PRESS

Copyright © 2018 by SSWCA PRESS
This work is designed to be used solely by the purchaser and may not be sold or redistributed, in part or in full, without the written permission of SSWCA.

sswca.org
Washington, DC

Cover design by Michelle and Jeffrey Austin

The editors have made all reasonable efforts to contact original resource creators for permission and apologize for any omissions or errors in the form of credits given.

Paperback ISBN: 978-0-692-04092-8

Contents

Preface — 6
by Renee Brown and Stacey Waldrup

Introduction — 8
by Kate Hutton and Amber Jensen

Chapter 1: Defining the Work of the Secondary School Writing Center Director — 15
by Amber Jensen

Chapter 2: Planning and Proposing — 27
by Seth Czarnecki and Stacey Waldrup

- Mission Statement
- Proposal to Administration
- PowerPoint Proposal
- Budget Breakdown
- Grant Application
- Writing Center History

Chapter 3: Tutor Recruitment and Selection — 41
by Kate Hutton

- Tutor Recruitment Timeline
- Tutor Selection Criteria
- Seeking Faculty Nominations
- Teacher Recommendation Form
- Invitation for Recommended Students
- New Tutor Application
- Writing Sample
- Returning Tutor Application
- Invitation to Interview
- Interview Questions
- Acceptance Letter
- Denial Letter

Chapter 4: Tutor Training — 55
by Stephanie Passino

- Tutor Agreement Form
- Tutoring Class Syllabus
- Tutor Training Schedule
- Virtual Writing Lab Training
- The Seven Priorities of Tutoring
- Tips from Experienced Tutors
- Sample Tutoring Questions
- Visualizing Steps of the Tutoring Process
- Fish Bowl and Tutor Checklist
- Case Study Analysis
- Asking Useful Questions
- Sandwiching
- Using Sample Texts
- Role Playing
- Read More Than You Write
- Reviewing Tutoring Logs
- Writing Assignments
- Journaling
- Tutor Observation Reflection
- Observation Outline
- Self-Evaluation
- Director Observation Form
- Giving Tutors Choice
- Tutor Mentoring Prospectus
- Senior Tutor Legacy Project

Chapter 5: Outreach and Promotion
by Renee Brown and Stacey Waldrup

87

    Logo and Slogan
    Staff Outreach Guide
    Student Outreach Guide
    Bookmarks
    Classroom Presentations
    Videos

    Posters
    Promotional Contests
    Blog Posts and Website
    Social Media
    Community Outreach

Chapter 6: Gathering Evidence for Success: Data and Evaluation
by Trisha Callihan

107

    Session Form
    Tutoring Evaluation Form
    Tutoring Reflection

    Monthly Data Report
    Yearlong and Historical Data

Chapter 7: School-Wide Writing Initiatives
by Joe Golimowski

123

    Non-English Faculty Collaboration
     Invitation
    Workshop Planning
    College Essay Workshop

    Writing Process Breakdown
    Written Response Questions
    Involving Writing in Athletics

Chapter 8: Middle School Writing Centers
by Susan Frenck

139

    Writing Tutor Job Description
    Client Description and Needs
    Tutoring Session Outline

    The Five Coach-Mandments
    "What if..." Troubleshooting
    Role Play

Chapter 9: University Partnerships
by Jeffrey Austin and Christine Modey

153

    Email of Introduction
    Planning Timeline and Field
     Trip Communication
    Student Visit Worksheet

    Agenda for a University Visit
    Conference Proposal
    Professional Learning Network
     Expansion

Appendix A: All-Subject Peer Tutoring Centers
by Heather Barton

171

Appendix B: About the Contributors

177

Preface

The mission of the Secondary School Writing Centers Association (SSWCA) inspired us to further develop secondary school writing center toolkit resources:

> The Secondary School Writing Centers Association (SSWCA) exists to build community among secondary school writing and learning center directors, tutors, and partners; promote advocacy for peer-driven programs that transform schools by empowering student leaders; and support development and sharing of resources for new and existing centers across the United States.

The toolkit you are about to peruse has been a true collaborative labor of love from people dedicated to and passionate about that mission. In May of 2018, we volunteered to take the existing Capital Area Peer Tutoring Association (CAPTA) resource toolkit and work with our board to modify, update, and expand it. That task quickly blossomed into a comprehensive re-imagining beyond anything we could have hoped! The two of us worked with a team of ten other authors to review resources submitted from 22 writing center directors and partners from across the country to contextualize, highlight, and share best practices.

We wanted to create a resource for teachers. And, being teachers and writing center directors, we understand time constraints. Thinking like busy teachers, we tried to format and organize this book in an easy-to-use fashion. Towards that end, each resource is on a separate page when possible to make them easier to find and read. We also tried to streamline our word choice; for example, the word 'tutor' is mainly used instead of 'consultant,' 'coach,' or other writing center titles. (We realize that different centers use different semantics, so where possible, you will see references to both client and tutee.) Furthermore, you can either read the toolkit sequentially or jump to a specific chapter. You'll find reference notes to other chapters as you read.

Being first-time publishers, in the middle of working on this project, we were told that most people don't start their publishing careers as editors. And while we now understand the reason behind that, we have enjoyed helping to craft the individual voices and experiences of our colleagues, and we have undeniably learned much about ourselves and writing center pedagogy in the process.

Just like all writing, editing this toolkit has been a process of planning, drafting, and revising; but ultimately of growth. And, just like all writing center work, editing this toolkit has been mentally, emotionally, professionally, and physically exhausting; but ultimately rewarding. We invite you - no matter if you're a high school or middle school student or teacher, a pre-service teacher, a writing center director or director hopeful, or interested in continuing to grow the work of SSWCs - to read this toolkit, mark up pages, change resources, share your thoughts and ideas, and, most importantly, contribute to future editions to keep expanding the great work of writing centers.

This toolkit would not have been possible without the determination of our entire team and the contributions of writing center professionals across the country. We are grateful to each contributor, chapter author, and supporter who has had a hand in helping this come to press. Thank you for your tireless work streamlining forms, breaking down your experience and process, creating discussion questions, and working through the revision process with us.

We are proud to present the 2018 version of the SSWC toolkit: *Advocating, Building, and Collaborating: A Resource Toolkit to Sustain Secondary School Writing Centers*.

-Renee Brown and Stacey Waldrup

Advocating, Building, and Collaborating
A Resource Toolkit to Sustain Secondary School Writing Centers

Introduction

By Kate Hutton and Amber Jensen

Dear Secondary School Writing Center Director (or future director),

Welcome! If you're anything like either of us, you have embarked upon this journey with a mind full of ideas and possibilities as you envision a secondary school writing center (SSWC) that accomplishes the vision you have of the most meaningful kind of peer-centered writing and learning. Maybe you are already the director of a SSWC and you're looking for fresh perspectives, or maybe you are cracking open this toolkit as a first step to laying the groundwork of the SSWC you're just starting to develop. Either way, you are likely eager to see how the advice, strategies, models, and templates in this resource toolkit will inspire your next steps. And we think they will!

In order to understand this toolkit and how you'll want to use it, we'd like to tell you a little bit about the people and the history behind it. With nearly 20 combined years of working with SSWC directors, there's one thing the two of us have noticed to be true about (almost) all of us: We live and work by the collaborative model that writing center pedagogy exemplifies. Just as we know that good writing doesn't happen in isolation, we know that successful writing centers and directors can't exist in isolation. That's why the SSWC directors we've met and worked with are eager to try new approaches, share them, revise them, and learn from each other as we implement them in various settings. This toolkit has been built through grassroots efforts by SSWC directors whose contributions reflect their unique institutional situations, affordances, and complications of running writing centers in secondary schools. Most of us are the only writing center professionals in our building, if not in our district or in our whole region. This is why finding this community and sharing the resources we have built with each other is the cornerstone of our vision for the professionalism and progress of SSWCs.

It is our goal to help inspire and support new and continuing SSWC directors in establishing and sustaining successful writing centers. This toolkit is meant to be accessible to SSWC practitioners who may not live in the world of academia but whose work is no less significant. As you read through the toolkit and imagine what will work at your center, keep in mind that, in your particular situation, some things are going to work, and others won't. That's why we envision this toolkit as a living resource; we hope that with each version, we'll be able to tell more of the stories and include an ever-expanding range of resources from different schools to deepen and widen our professional repertoire.

History of SSWCA

SSWCA began in 2010 as a small and informal regional network of secondary school writing centers and peer tutoring centers concentrated primarily in Fairfax County, Virginia. Inspired by the work of SSWC directors who pioneered and advocated for peer-driven programs before us, including Rich Kent, Pamela Childers, Jennifer Wells, Dawn Fels, Andrew Jeter and many, many others, and in recognition of the value of and need for student-centered approaches to the teaching of writing, teachers began to establish SSWCs throughout our region. Our close proximity to one another and the support of our district resulted in an organic network of fledgling centers that was built on a culture of sharing resources, experimenting with different models of implementation, advocating for our programs, and supporting and celebrating the work we and our centers were doing.

After organizing three secondary school writing center conferences in 2011, 2012, and 2013 via this informal network with the support of the University of Maryland and George Mason University, five directors (Amber Jensen of Edison High School; Beth Blankenship of Oakton High School; Jenny Goransson of West Springfield High School; Alison Hughes of Centreville High School; Kate Hutton of Herndon High School) formally founded the Capital Area Peer Tutoring Association (CAPTA) as a 501(c)3 nonprofit organization in 2014 with 12 member schools.

CAPTA hosted three additional secondary school writing center conferences, and by early 2017, membership grew to include 35 member schools from up and down the East Coast. Attendance at the annual conferences was a clear indicator of the growing interest in and professionalization around best practices and research in secondary school writing centers. As depicted by Figures 1-3 below, each conference between 2011 and 2017 drew a greater number of attendees (up to the 475 attendee maximum capacity allowed by the venue) from an increasing set of secondary and postsecondary institutions, welcoming a wider and more diverse set of tutor and director presenters at each conference. The network seemed to be both serving existing SSWCs and creating a forum for learning about and developing new centers in a wide range of schools far beyond CAPTA's original regional focus.

Figure 1. Number of Attendees at Annual SSWC/CAPTA Conferences, 2011 - 2017

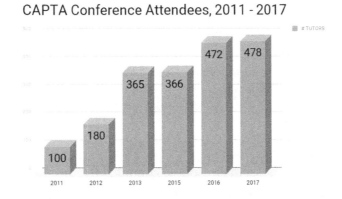

Figure 2. Numbers and Types of Institutions Attending Annual SSWC/CAPTA Conferences, 2011 - 2017

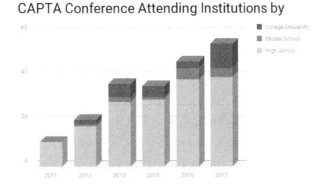

Figure 3. Numbers of Tutor Presenters, Tutor Presentations, and Tutor Schools Represented at Annual SSWC/CAPTA Conferences, 2011 - 2017

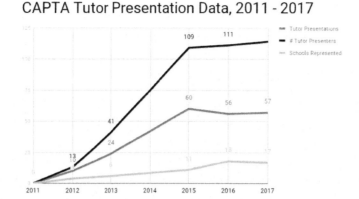

By 2017, the need for a national SSWC organization had become abundantly clear. The national SSWC network was mapped over time on a Google Map maintained by Hannah Baran, through the 2017 census of SSWCs led by IWCA Secondary Schools Representative Jeffrey Austin, and through the ongoing communications via SSWC directors via a longstanding, independently-run SSWC listserv. Furthermore, CAPTA members and leaders had developed relationships with current and prospective directors outside of the Capital Area who had learned about CAPTA through the organization's website, CAPTA conference materials, and SSWC directors' presentations at national conferences. At CAPTA 2017, the sixth annual conference for secondary peer tutors and writing center directors, CAPTA formally announced the exciting news of our expansion into a national organization for SSWCs. In January 2018, we officially transitioned into the Secondary School Writing Centers Association (SSWCA), a national organization dedicated to promoting scholarship, community, and sustainability for secondary school writing centers, their directors, and their tutors. By July 2018, SSWCA membership included over 60 middle and high school writing and peer tutoring centers from 22 states.

History of the SSWC Toolkit

This toolkit is the fifth iteration of the original resource compiled in 2010. With each update, emergent and experienced directors alike have contributed new perspectives, ideas, and resources; and we've all drawn upon these materials as we've visioned and revisioned our centers, advocated for them, weathered change, and clung to the principles that inspired us in the first place. In large part, the diversity of contributors and the range of replicabile and adaptable artifacts is what makes this toolkit so rich. SSWC directors have worked to develop these resources or artifacts from the ground up, and this work represents an approach that is rooted in theory and vetted by practice. The timeline below depicts each of the versions of the toolkit, acknowledging the ways it has improved and expanded with each update.

2010	**Fairfax County Public Schools (FCPS) English Teacher Inservice** Distributed to nearly 100 English teacher attendees at a countywide inservice day in January 2010, the original toolkit was a bound booklet of artifacts Amber Jensen had developed as she proposed and

	implemented the Edison Writing Center, the first SSWC in FCPS. Organized around a framework with guiding questions, the toolkit later became a resource for developing the county's program of studies for Advanced Composition, a credit-bearing elective course for high school writing center tutors and a model for eventually over 20 FCPS SSWCs.
2011	**Regional SSWC Tutor Conference, George Mason University (GMU)** In preparation for the first regional SSWC tutor conference held at GMU in partnership with the Northern Virginia Writing Project (NVWP), four conference planners and FCPS writing center directors (Amber Jensen, Jenny Goransson, Beth Blankenship, and Allison Hughes) collaborated to build upon the original toolkit by adding a wider range of resources across all implementation phases. The booklet was printed, bound, and distributed to SSWC directors attending from 11 different high schools in the Northern Virginia region.
2015	**CAPTA Resource Toolkit: CAPTA Connects Conference, GMU** The toolkit was once again moderately adapted and rebranded as a resource published by the Capital Area Peer Tutoring Association, a newly-established independent non-profit organization of SSWC directors, tutors, and administrators. Nearly 50 toolkits were published and distributed at the 2015 conference to directors of over 37 attending institutions. The 4th annual regional conference – officially the first under the new CAPTA organization – welcomed 365 attendees and featured 109 student presenters from 11 secondary schools.
2017	**CAPTA Digital Toolkit: People, Passion, and Purpose Conference, GMU** This iteration of the toolkit was edited by CAPTA's Middle School Representative Renee Brown. In the interest of making the toolkit easier to distribute to our growing membership, many of whom were from outside the immediate CAPTA region, we published the toolkit digitally. Resources included in this toolkit were submitted by current and former CAPTA board members and were presented as they were without context. Renee removed institutional references and synthesized resources so that the artifacts included in the toolkit could serve as templates for other directors to map their work onto and make their own. Chapters were organized by phases of implementation. The toolkit was included as a benefit of CAPTA/SSWCA membership, and it was distributed digitally to over 60 member schools.
2018	**SSWCA Toolkit: Process and Progress Conference, GMU** As SSWCA transitioned into a national organization, we decided to publish a more robust print version of the toolkit to be included as a benefit of SSWCA membership and also to be available for purchase by those outside of the SSWCA network. Under the mentorship of Dr. Richard Kent, SSWCA Vice-President Renee Brown and Member At-Large Stacey Waldrup co-edited the toolkit, which now includes introductions to each section written by SSWCA Board Members. Section authors have also contextualized each of the nearly 100 artifacts. For the first time, we have also included sections with resources specifically geared toward middle school centers, post-secondary partnerships, and an appendix for all-subject peer tutoring centers.

Navigating this Toolkit

This toolkit features nine chapters, each designed to be helpful to directors in any phase of writing center implementation and in any context. Section authors have drawn on their experiences as SSWC directors to identify overarching themes for each section, offer first-hand accounts of their experiences, and frame ways of thinking about the many roles you fulfill as an SSWC director. Following that "discussion" found at the start of each chapter, you will find a collection of resources. When presenting these artifacts, our intent is not to say that one way of doing something is better than another, but rather to offer examples of several models that have worked in different contexts. Those of you just starting out will find that each chapter focuses on a different phase of implementation that you can move through chronologically, while those of you whose centers are well-established will find that you can easily jump from chapter to chapter depending on your needs.

In "**Defining the Work of the Secondary School Writing Center Director: Leadership and Advocacy on the Frontier**," Amber Jensen, founder of the Edison Writing Center in Alexandria, VA, explores the kinds of labor and tasks writing center directors often take on and the range of the roles you'll want to think through strategically as you navigate your role as SSWC director.

In "**Planning and Proposing**," Seth Czarnecki of the Algonquin Writing Center in Northboro, MA and Stacey Waldrup formerly of the Raider Writing Center in Corvallis, OR encourage you to consider the story you want your center to tell and to recognize that in many contexts, the process of planning, proposing, and establishing your center is often a revolutionary act. They offer strategies and resources for starting a peaceful writing center revolution.

Kate Hutton of the Herndon Writing Center in Herndon, VA offers strategies for organizing a strong, dedicated staff in "**Tutor Recruitment and Selection**." Tutors are perhaps the most essential part of your center; after all, you can't have a peer-driven tutoring center without tutors! She offers suggestions for identifying potential tutors, selecting strong tutors, and involving faculty and staff outside of the center in the tutor recruitment process.

In "**Tutor Training**," Stephanie Passino of the Hawk Writing Center in Alexandria, VA guides you through the tutor training process. She reminds us that the training our tutors need will vary depending on their experience and the context in which your center operates, and she examines strategies and activities to help best prepare your tutors.

After establishing a center and finding tutors, how do we promote our center to our students and our colleagues? In "**Outreach and Promotion**," Renee Brown of the Peters Township Middle School Writing Lab in Pittsburgh, PA and Stacey Waldrup formerly of the Raider Writing Center in Corvallis, OR offer techniques for getting our school communities to buy into the potential of our centers.

Trisha Callihan of the Eagle Writing Center in Manassas, VA offers strategies for analyzing and presenting data from your center in "**Gathering Evidence of Success: Data and Evaluation**." She examines the many ways you can collect data in your center, why you might want to collect it, and how to interpret it for a variety of audiences.

In "**School-Wide Writing Initiatives**," Joe Golimowski of the Kettle Run Writing Center in Nokesville, VA invites directors to consider the ways in which the center can support writing across disciplines and encourage students to see themselves as writers. Joe provides examples of partnerships and initiatives that you might try in your center.

Susan Frenck of the Irving Writing Center in Springfield, VA, argues that middle school writing centers benefit younger writers by introducing them to collaboration and peer-centered learning earlier in their education in her chapter "**Middle School Writing Centers**." While many of the artifacts included in other sections are translatable to a middle school context, middle school directors should consider the specifics and the degree.

Jeffrey Austin of the Skyline Writing Center and Christine Modey of the Sweetland Center for Writing, both in Ann Arbor, MI, examine one model of forming partnerships between secondary and postsecondary writing centers in "**University Partnerships**." They emphasize the importance of both centers recognizing one another as equals and seeing the partnership as mutually-beneficial.

Realizing that many centers have a wider scope, there is an appendix for directors of peer tutoring centers. In "**All-Subject Peer Tutoring Centers**," Heather Barton of Etowah's East WING Tutoring Center in Woodstock, GA reflects on her center's transition from a Writing Across the Curriculum Center into an All-Subject Center and offers an example of how that transition occurred.

Over 20 directors contributed their resources to this toolkit. If you are interested in learning more about or connecting with our contributors, review their biographies in the "**About the Contributors**" appendix.

Conclusion and Invitation

While our core mission to build community among, promote advocacy for, and support the development of SSWCs remains the same as it was in 2010, our transition into a national organization and the publication of this toolkit represent the beginning of an exciting new era in the world of SSWCs. Our intent is to republish this toolkit at regular intervals, so we hope that if you modify or adapt these resources, or create new ones, you will consider submitting them to the next iteration of this publication as a way of contributing to the living, breathing nature of the field of SSWCs and the exciting prospects of its future. We also encourage you to join our organization at SSWCA.org and attend our annual conference.

Whether you are a well-established center or a brand-new center, we hope that you will find the resources in this toolkit to be practical, accessible, and useful.

Write on!

Amber Jensen, CAPTA Founder and SSWCA Past President
Kate Hutton, SSWCA President and Herndon Writing Center Director

Chapter 1
Defining the Work of the Secondary School Writing Center Director: Leadership and Advocacy on the Frontier

By Amber Jensen

At the 2015 International Writing Centers Association (IWCA) conference in Pittsburgh, I welcomed more than 20 writing center directors to the Special Interest Group (SIG) for secondary school writing centers (SSWC). The diversity of attendees at this session represented an exciting cross-section of programs on the frontier of an expanding and fluctuating network of SSWCs worldwide. They included a university director from Lebanon preparing to report back to eager high school teachers in her country, directors from middle schools in Texas and Pennsylvania, and school administrators and teacher-directors from urban, suburban, and rural, public, private, and charter high schools across America. We had a rich, practice-oriented, scholarship-informed discussion on the work of directing a writing center. When one attendee tentatively raised her hand to ask, "Is there a job description for secondary school directors that I can give to my principal to define my role more clearly?" heads nodded eagerly. It was a smart and strategic question, one that is likely very familiar to writing center directors at all levels and at most institutions.

Defining the work of the secondary school writing center director is a crucial step, one that many of us – new and veteran writing center directors included – continue to grapple with. Understanding what our work is, what it isn't, and what it can be is essential to answering a few key questions we should all consider. How do we make our work visible to and valued by our institutions? How do we define and occupy our roles in ways that ensure their sustainability and our own success within them? What tasks should we be prepared to accomplish and what roles should we assume as program administrators? How do we develop and grow within our positions to meet our own professional goals as well as to serve the missions of the institutions where we work? What kinds of resources, partnerships, and networks are available to support us in defining, establishing, and sustaining these roles, particularly in precarious situations? I wrote this chapter to address these questions. In it, I draw on literature from writing center research and writing program administration (WPA) scholarship to provide useful frameworks that help SSWC directors consider and clarify their roles with the organization and empower them to advocate for their own positions and, ultimately, their centers' success.

The State of the SSWC Director

The demand for a clearer definition around the role of a SSWC director is evident. In a 2016-2017 census of Secondary School Writing Center directors, the IWCA Census Committee reported that there has been considerable growth among SSWCs in recent years: 67% of 115 census respondents started their writing center in the last five years, while 40% of the respondents opened their writing centers in the last two years (Austin & Roche, 2017). This speaks to the excitement around this work and to a strong groundswell of interest in building these kinds of programs that we know can make a tremendous impact on learning and writing in our schools. It is important to understand that many of the directors of these centers are coming to this work from a variety of backgrounds, mostly without much, if any, formal training in writing center theory and/or program administration. In fact, 32% of census respondents reported that their training consisted of reading books and articles on writing center pedagogy and practice, 21% were trained by attending a conference, 15% considered their own college writing center tutoring experience their training, and 32% were trained by other means (Austin & Roche, 2017). Unlike their counterparts at the postsecondary level, most SSWC directors come to the work having been hired to do something else: teachers, librarians, instructional coaches, school administrators. This is likely one factor for 40% of census respondents reporting that they were uncompensated for the work they do as the writing center director. While others are compensated with a course release, relief from other expected duties, or a monetary stipend, few writing center directors at the secondary level are hired exclusively for that job and are paid sufficiently for their work. Work that is unrecognized and uncompensated is unsustainable in the long term; this is one reason this chapter aims to frame the work of the writing center director in a way that will help make it more visible to directors themselves, institutional stakeholders, and the field at large.

Understanding where SSWC directors come from and who we are is an important step in acknowledging our specific challenges in defining our positions and advocating for support in these roles. Here are some things the research and our experiences tell us many of us have in common:
- SSWC directors are typically self-selected for our roles, which we are also tasked with defining.
- SSWC directors may receive course releases, stipends, or reassignment of duties, but we are often not compensated for the full amount of work we perform.
- SSWC directors are usually new to writing program administration.
- SSWC directors often downplay our roles and needs, particularly in the initial stages of proposing a writing center, in order to get buy-in for our programs.

Although many SSWC directors may be, indeed, "called" to the position and passionate about the work, as Kent (2006), in his book *A Guide to Creating Student-Staffed Writing Centers, Grades 6-12*, suggested, if we do not articulate our work as program administrators—not just club advisors, activity sponsors, or any other support role expected in a secondary school setting—it will remain hidden and our positions marginalized. We must be cautious about allowing passion for our work and willingness to sacrifice for the program to undermine our own sustainability and success as well as that of our programs. If we downplay our roles as directors when negotiating for our centers, we may inadvertently allow our work to remain invisible and, thus, unvalued by school administration, and ultimately, unsustainable.

Finding a balance between personal humility, professional value, and institutional expectations in a resource-constrained environment demands that we not only understand but also articulate and advocate for our work. Though it may push us out of our comfort zones, the success of our centers requires it. In the sections of this chapter that follow, we will look to scholarship and models from the field to examine what a job description for a SSWC director may entail ("Defining the Work of Writing Center Directors") as well as the roles directors take on as they move into a new position as a writing program administrator ("SSWC Directors as Program Administrators"). As you read these sections, I hope you will consider how you can frame and articulate your work in ways that will empower and sustain you in that work moving forward.

Defining the Work of Writing Center Directors

Defining the work of SSWC directors begins by examining scholarship on the work of (almost exclusively postsecondary) writing center directors. In the introduction to *The Writing Center Director's Resource Book*, Murphy & Stay (2006) "envision writing center professionals as enacting multiple complex roles in being teachers, administrators, scholars, budget officers, technology coordinators, tutor trainers, mentors, and academic colleagues" (p. xiii). These roles are not context-exclusive; they apply to directors at four-year universities, two-year colleges, high schools, and middle schools, yet it's important to remember that they are context-dependent.

We know that no two institutions are alike, and thus, secondary school writing center directors must translate scholarship and transfer principles into their context with flexibility and creativity. You have probably thought about how you can adapt your center and your job description from others you've become familiar with in the field. As one writing center director in an international private high school said, "thinking creatively about what to draw from other writing centers and what to leave behind," allows her to "open the cage of orthodoxy . . . and give herself a little bit of room to explore and play as she takes her writing center to the next stage" (Caswell, McKinney & Jackson, 2016, p. 199). By considering frameworks of director positions, we can accept, challenge, adapt, and yes, even play with how local context and institutional priorities define a director's responsibilities. So where do we begin when defining our roles?

As a starting point, the table below lists the job responsibilities reported by two important studies in writing center and writing program administration. The National Census of Writing (2015) profiled program administrators of writing programs at 680 four-year universities and 220 two-year colleges, compiling a list of the common job functions and responsibilities of these directors. As a complement to this study, Caswell et al.'s (2016) book, *The Working Lives of New Writing Center Directors*, used a qualitative research methodology to answer similar questions: Who are writing center directors, and what is their work?

Consider the kinds of responsibilities outlined in the table as you begin to build your own job description. Which tasks are you already aware that you do? Which tasks might be invisible to others? Which tasks are included in your job description – and which would you like to add that might clarify your role for yourself, your administrators, etc.? The first section of the table depicts the tasks that were reported in both the WPA Census (2015) and in the Caswell et al. (2016) study; the second section shows tasks reported by directors in one study, but not the other. The types of work indicated in the table can be categorized into four types of labor: administrative labor, disciplinary labor, everyday labor, and emotional labor.

Table 1. The Work of Writing Center Directors

Findings from both National Census of Writing (2015) and Caswell et al. (2016)	
Administrative Labor: • Hire and recruit tutors • Train tutors • Create and execute assessment plans • Market the writing center *Everyday Labor:* • Consult with faculty; educate faculty about the center • Maintain a budget; request funding • Attend university/school meetings and/or serve on committees	
National Census of Writing (2015) 392 survey respondents	**Caswell et al.** (2016) 9 case studies
Administrative Labor: • Offer student workshops • Oversee curriculum development • Plan events *Everyday Labor:* • Maintain website • Create tutoring schedule • Serve as academic advisor • Supervise staff and tutors • Teach courses • Tutor students	*Administrative Labor:* • Establish new initiatives; change or drop existing initiatives • Establish or change writing center policies *Disciplinary Labor:* • Attend and/or present at academic conferences *Emotional Labor:* • Mediate conflicts • Discipline/dismiss team members • Mentor team members

Administrative Labor

Both studies indicated that directors are responsible for the work of hiring, recruiting, and training tutors, as well as overseeing the long-term vision and strategy of the center the way an administrator would. They write proposals to establish new initiatives or secure funding, conduct program assessment and evaluation, and meet with other faculty and administrators to secure the resources necessary for running the center. This kind of administrative work, alongside managing the daily functions of the center (considered everyday labor, and described below) are the factors most likely to show up on writing center directors' job descriptions across most institutions. These are some of the most visible aspects of a writing center director's job; but even so, they are aspects of the position SSWC directors new to administrative work may not completely be able to predict or account for in the early stages of proposing their center and/or writing their own job descriptions.

Everyday Labor

Caswell et al. (2016) considered the kinds of tasks required to keep the day-to-day operations of the center open in a category of its own, which they called "everyday labor." These tasks were included in both the WPA census (2015) and in Caswell et al.'s (2016) case studies; they include responsibilities like attending meetings, requesting funding, creating the tutoring schedule, managing tutor attendance, and maintaining a website or social media presence. While these daily tasks go hand-in-hand with the bigger administrative vision and priorities, the amount of time spent on this kind of work is often difficult to quantify or make visible to administrators when defining and defending the position. The work of the center would be impossible, however, without these kinds of duties being accomplished with regularity. Some university and secondary writing centers have had success with creating roles for tutor leaders to take on some of these daily jobs, such as collecting attendance data or managing the center's Twitter account, which can preserve some of the director's time for the bigger-picture administrative functions. However, it is important to recognize that outsourcing these tasks requires extra training, supervision, and evaluation of the tutor leaders assigned to these responsibilities, which then becomes an additional burden on the director.

Emotional Labor

Caswell et al.'s (2016) study identified a third, and often unrecognized, category of director responsibilities, those that they refer to as "emotional labor." Emotional labor takes shape in the form of mentoring, mediating, and disciplining. This is the dimension of the job that is most invisible and most difficult to identify or name in a census-like study, which is why it is unsurprising that it showed up only in the case study. Much of the work SSWC directors end up thinking about and focusing on is connected to their emotional labor. The relationships and connections with student tutors can be one of the most rewarding aspects of the job; however, this work can be some of the most draining as well. It is the kind of work those who define or determine the value of a job may not see, but it is essential to a director's role, and important to take into consideration as you conceptualize a new role.

Disciplinary Labor

Finally, another set of expectations related to contributing to the profession overall is considered "disciplinary labor." This might include attending and presenting at academic conferences, conducting research and contributing to the knowledge of the field, or publishing about your writing center's research and practices. It is an expectation that tenure-track postsecondary directors engage within their field by conducting, publishing, and presenting research. However, most secondary school directors exist within positions and institutions where scholarship, or disciplinary labor, is not an expectation or a professional affordance. The lack of time and resources to devote to research, scholarship, and conference attendance may contribute to less overall knowledge about and awareness of how theories and practices are implemented in these particular contexts. Yet, the mentoring, collaboration, and ongoing professional growth made possible by attending conferences and networking with other writing center directors, particularly for those who work mostly in isolation, is essential to a director's sustainability. Contributions to the field in ways that enhance the knowledge about and practices of SSWCs is also important to building and sustaining a vibrant community of practice.

SSWC Directors as Program Administrators

More than thinking just of the kinds of *tasks* writing center directors are responsible for, it is important to understand the new *role* we are embracing: that of a program administrator. What follows is a working definition of the kinds of roles SSWC directors assume as part of their work, the ways in which SSWC directors take on the overlapping identities of visionaries, negotiators, collaborators, managers, and advocates, and how these roles are contextually shaped and challenged specifically within secondary school settings. How might you think of yourself embracing one or more of these roles as you embody your position as a writing program administrator?

SSWC Directors as Visionaries

Whether at the stage of proposing and planning a new writing center, evaluating next steps to sustain or improve an existing one, or facing a transition from one director to another, SSWC directors become the program's visionaries. This role demands a level of disciplinary knowledge – a familiarity with writing center theories and practices, at a minimum – in concert with a nuanced understanding of the institution itself – its culture, its practices, its people, its expectations. Crosby & Bryson (2005) noted that having a well-developed mission and a sound formative evaluation process to later assess and communicate the program's fulfillment of its stated goals is crucial at the outset of new programs; this will help the director not only gain buy-in from key decision makers early on, but also "identify obstacles and steer over, around, under, or through them to achieve policy [in this case, program] goals" (p. 315). Many prospective SSWC directors spend months and even years researching writing center theories and practices, seeking out other directors at similar institutions, and considering how to adapt what they learn to their local sites. As they draft action plans and present program proposals to department chairs, colleagues, and school administrators, they assume the role of entrepreneur, bidding for a chance to implement an innovative program in a setting where it is not the norm. Skillfully navigating obstacles and opportunities requires a director to have a clear vision of what the writing center aims to accomplish, who it will serve, and how it will impact the school community and its stakeholders.

> Toolkit resources that help you think like a VISIONARY:
> - Mission Statement (p. 32)
> - Proposal to Administration (p. 33)
> - Yearlong and Historical Data (p. 119)
> - PLN Expansion (p. 168)

Directors seeking to define a program's vision can begin by strategically connecting it to the institution's mission and priorities. Vander Lei & Pugh (2013) stated that, when program administrators do so, "they position the writing program to become a valued part of the [institution]" (p. 112). Andrew Jeter (2012), during his tenure as director of the Niles West High School Literacy Center, exemplified a visionary stance by inviting various stakeholders into the process of defining the center's mission statement: "It was a combination of this need for flexibility and a wariness about the ability of teachers to reach consensus with something like a mission statement that prompted us to adopt an *evolving* mission statement. With an annual review of our mission, we continue to address the current needs of our students and gain greater buy-in from teachers" (p. 42). Jeter warned, however, that directors should be careful not to allow a program's vision to be easily swept aside to accommodate new institutional initiatives, as a loosely-defined vision or constantly-changing mission can undermine a program and make it susceptible to obstruction or conscription by "other adult stakeholders (teachers, administrators, parents) who want to define . . . the role and mission of the center" (p. 41). A writing center director is both a collaborator with the larger institution and a protector of the program's vision.

As existing programs evolve, an effective SSWC director-as-visionary will use successes to highlight the program's achievement of and progress toward stated goals; Crosby & Bryson (2005) noted that embodying the role of entrepreneur means "weaving [successes] into a story" that connects to the program's mission, strategies, performance, and standards (p. 321). Being a visionary includes anticipating challenges and responding to unexpected demands while honoring the vision of the program itself. Directors who strategically develop, articulate, and maintain a program's vision are more likely to find success and gain credibility in their work. This is particularly important in secondary school settings, where little precedent exists for what a writing center will or will not achieve and how it will look; a visionary director can be authoritative, creative, and flexible as different situations require, especially when it comes to defining, and redefining as necessary, its goals and values.

SSWC Directors as Negotiators

Toolkit resources that help you think like a NEGOTIATOR:
- Budget Breakdown (p. 37)
- Grant Application (p. 38)
- Seeking Faculty Nominations (p. 47)
- Staff Outreach Guides (p. 93)

Not surprisingly, in the process of defining a vision, implementing a program, and asking for resources and support, SSWC directors often find themselves confronting conflict and, by necessity, stepping into the role of negotiator. Crosby & Bryson (2005) acknowledged that "change is typically a complex and messy process involving many actors and organizations with a host of complementary, competing, and often contradictory goals and interests" (p. 312). In the secondary school context, where new initiatives and policy measures are enacted regularly, teachers often feel powerless, expected to accept and respond to such changes without being invited into discussions or negotiations with administrators, policy makers, or other decision makers. New writing centers may be perceived by teachers and administrators as yet another threatening policy initiative or fleeting program; directors know, however, that these programs do have the power to institute significant change in a school community. Kent (2006) emphasized their change-making potential: "It is a fundamental truth that creating and maintaining a writing center is a political act. The presence of a writing center changes the landscape of a school and creates a paradigm shift" (p. 29). SSWC directors, whether invited or self-designated, will find themselves negotiating with students, teachers, administrators, and other school stakeholders about mission, policies, priorities, resources, and other factors intricately connected to the success of the program. Lerner (2013) reminded us that writing centers are sites of struggle, even in institutions where they have long-standing traditions. This may be even more true in the secondary school context, where writing centers are still fairly uncommon and may be seen as untested.

In the face of these struggles, directors may earn power – or lose it – based on how they negotiate through these tensions. Caswell et al. (2016) found that the writing center directors in their study all faced situations where "their superiors contradicted or complicated the visions the directors had articulated," and that, regardless of their institutional status or position, they were able to show "sophistication in navigating tricky administrative waters. They understood when issues carried a political significance and seemed always viscerally aware of where they stood in terms of power within the institution" (p. 261). Although secondary school directors may often occupy positions of relatively little power in decision making, they can assert influence and gain trust as they lead "by listening, learning, and finding common ground," by "understanding and empathizing," and by "invoking the personal with the professional" (Mirtz & Cullen, 2002, p. 99-100). Using these approaches will help directors more likely gain ground as leaders and find success as program administrators.

Katerina, a SSWC director in Caswell et al.'s (2016) study, modeled this leadership style when she perceived distrust, misunderstanding, and even resentment from her colleagues upon assuming the role of writing center director. In response to this tension, she "purposely attempt[ed] to reach her fellow teachers through personal, face-to-face communication, encouraging them to send students her way whenever the students [had] writing tasks or projects. She [did] this, she [said], because she [understood] the 'peculiarities of culture,' that it is 'better to communicate face-to-face, in a friendly chat and with everyone personally'" (Caswell, et al., 2016, p. 187). Katerina's sensitivity to her audience of colleagues and her willingness to take the time to connect with them in hopes of alleviating their fears and concerns demonstrates effective program leadership and awareness of the rhetorical demands of her school context. The inevitable tensions and negotiations SSWC directors will face call upon their interpersonal skills and professional expertise, kinds of work that Caswell et al. (2016) referred to as "emotional" and "disciplinary" labor. It is so important not to downplay or sweep aside this aspect of the job; the director's attention to the interpersonal can open or close pathways to future progress as a writing center.

SSWC Directors as Collaborators

Interactions with other people and other programs within the broader institution are not always marked by tension or conflict requiring strategic negotiation; writing center directors who find partners and collaborate effectively solidify their own roles and their program's place within the institution, prevent isolation, and generate critical and ongoing partnerships even when there is no crisis or resistance. Making connections with others is an effective way for directors to tie the work of the writing center, implicitly or explicitly, to the work and mission of the larger institution. This is particularly useful for SSWC directors because it helps to situate the writing center, in the minds of key stakeholders, as a necessary contributor to the overall mission of the school. By tying the writing center to key institutional goals and outcomes, directors will solidify its position at the school in the long term. When writing center directors make connections with what Crosby & Bryson (2005) termed "key implementers," they are acting strategically within a larger system.

> Toolkit resources that help you think like a COLLABORATOR:
> - Community Outreach (p. 105)
> - Faculty Collaboration Invite (p. 127)
> - Workshop Planning (p. 128)
> - Involving Writing in Athletics (p. 136)

Fortunately, collaboration and communication are already inherent to the ethos of the writing center community; just as Lerner (2013) reminded us that tutoring "implies shared responsibility, mutual turn-taking, and symmetric power relations" (p. 228), so also do writing center administrators when they collaborate with others in the institution. Wells (2012), in her chapter on directing her writing center at a private school in the Bay Area, chose to "use the pronoun *we* to describe what we do, because the success of any program depends on the collaborative efforts of those both directly and indirectly involved in it" (p. 80). In secondary school centers, partners may include librarians, career center specialists, department chairs, teachers, school counselors, special program coordinators, club sponsors, coaches, and parents. Program collaborations may include a wide range of activities such as research workshops in the library, student-athlete tutoring support, college preparation workshops, student essay competitions, and oral language practice with English Language Learners.

Caswell et al. (2016) noticed that "principled alliances can be built proactively or reactively" (p. 402). While new and veteran SSWC directors will likely forge relationships at times *in response* to a particular unexpected problem and at other times *in anticipation* of areas where programs' missions overlap or where an untapped opportunity emerges, it is an important survival strategy to "seek conversations with others on campus in order to find areas of common interest from which to build connections" (Caswell et al., 2016, p. 402). Directors should ask themselves where there are possible alliances in their institutions, which programs may have corresponding or overlapping purposes, and which initiatives seem to attract the gaze of decision makers and resources. Collaborating with these partners will not only strengthen the program but ensure its sustainability over time.

SSWC Directors as Managers

Toolkit resources that help you think like a MANAGER:
- Tutor Recruitment Timeline (p. 45)
- Tutoring Class Syllabus (p. 62)
- Session Forms (p. 112)
- Tutoring Evaluation Forms (p. 115)

While keeping in mind the big-picture role of visionary and the interpersonal roles of negotiator and collaborator, writing center directors in all institutions find that most of what they do is the daily kinds of work – what Caswell et al. (2016) called "everyday labor" – that make up the managerial job of administering a writing center. These include tasks like recruiting and training tutors; supervising tutoring sessions, workshops, and other events; maintaining a budget; and analyzing and reporting data. Unlike most postsecondary writing center director positions, roles that are at least somewhat defined in formal job descriptions, however, many SSWC directors are not typically hired into positions that articulate their roles as clearly as Caswell et al. (2016) assumed. This may be because, unlike long-standing, familiar secondary school positions such as teacher, librarian, counselor, or instructional assistant, the job of the writing center director is as of yet still largely unfamiliar and thus not institutionalized or clearly defined. As the SSWC directors in attendance at the IWCA SIG indicated, they are often working in absence of a formalized job description, which may lead to spending hours and hours on work that goes unnoticed and unacknowledged. For this reason, it is important for both prospective and current directors to first acknowledge for themselves, and then make visible to their administrators, the time they spend and the work they do managing the center and the kinds of work running a program demands. This move is essential to long-term positioning and the institutional buy-in of the program.

In the high school writing center he founded, Kent (2006) estimated that he spent "about one hundred and fifty hours a year on writing center work" (p. 31), although this number is likely to fluctuate greatly from site to site and director to director. Jeter (2012) described the frenetic nature of the daily work of a SSWC director: "Because I'm the coordinator of the program, my desk sees a never-ending flurry of memos, requests, board and usage reports, budget concerns, and ideas for potential extension programs" (p. 39). Despite what may appear from the outside to be behind-the-scenes work of program administration, the paperwork and daily tasks Jeter mentioned are just a sampling of the kinds of work that are required to keep the center in motion.

It is imperative that this work not remain in the shadows, unacknowledged and unaccounted for. Without clear definition and boundaries around the expectations of director's job, many SSWC directors might relate to how one of the participants in Caswell et al.'s (2016) study described a conflict in her roles: though she "leads the writing center, [she] is unable to focus all of her attention on it or even spend significant amounts of time in the writing center because of her other duties" (p. 216). For this reason, it is essential that we articulate and put limits on (or gain support for) these kinds of managerial tasks, given the rest of what we need to accomplish. Bringing our work out of the shadows is imperative to SSWCs gaining the kinds of institutional support they need to thrive and gain recognition.

SSWC Directors as Advocates

Underlying all of the other roles writing center directors take on, they must always consider themselves advocates – of both their programs and their own positions. Caswell et al. (2016) reported, "nearly all of our directors note needing resources – time, money, space, tutors, equipment, or administrative support. Many directors note feeling successful when obtaining even the smallest gain in resources" (p. 260-261). Identifying needs and advocating for resources is a constant part of the job of a program administrator. Especially for SSWC directors who often first advocate to establish a writing center, then propose and pilot tutor training programs or courses, and then continue to manage the daily work all while gathering data and highlighting the ways in which the writing center program supports the school's mission, advocacy is an essential and ongoing task.

Toolkit resources that help you think like an ADVOCATE:
- PowerPoint Proposal (p. 35)
- Budget Breakdown (p. 37)
- Grant Application (p. 38)
- Monthly Data Report (p. 118)

Yet SSWC directors are often uncomfortable advocating for the kinds of support they need to sustain their own work, especially alongside their other responsibilities at school. Often colleagues and administrators view these teachers' primary responsibilities to be teaching their assigned course loads, while also expecting that they can direct a successful school-wide writing center often without the recognition, the time, or a budget that values and sustains what it takes to do so effectively. What are the ways in which SSWC directors can elicit institutional support that validates and nurtures their work? How might such institutional support look in various settings? Caswell et al. (2016) suggested that staffing decisions can be a marker of an institution's understanding of and commitment to the intellectual and administrative work writing center directors take on. Even though it might be tempting for SSWC directors to situate their requests for institutional support around the *program's* needs without asking for an investment in themselves as its *director*, it is important for directors to acknowledge, articulate, and advocate for themselves as the primary facilitators and enablers of the programs the institutions are willing to support. Of course, this feels like a monumental task, particularly for fledgling centers or those not yet considered central to the school's mission or purpose. But that's also why the growing community of SSWCs is working to establish norms and help new and existing directors advocate for themselves in compelling ways. You don't have to go it alone!

Final Thoughts and an Invitation

I invite SSWC directors out of the margins and into the field in more visible ways. As we grow as a community and more explicitly define our own roles, there open many opportunities for new research about our work and within our sites. First, we must understand who SSWC directors are: What kinds of institutions do we represent? How are we prepared for our work? How do we and others at our institutions define our roles and measure our success? How are we compensated? How do we participate in scholarly communities? How does our work compare with and differ from that of our postsecondary counterparts? The IWCA Census on Secondary School Writing Center Directors (2017) was a start to mapping this landscape; additional opportunities for directors to collaborate at SSWCA conferences, to write and publish about their work, and to mentor and be mentored by their peers will all help to explore these questions.

A few months after meeting at the Pittsburgh IWCA Conference, I received an email from one of the SSWC SIG attendees, Paula Habre, who directs the writing center at the Lebanese American University in Beirut. Habre informed me that she had received a grant from the U.S. Embassy to conduct a series of writing center workshops for 40 teachers from urban and rural, public and private, secondary schools all over Lebanon. A few months later, I had the opportunity to meet these teachers through a virtual session I conducted for them on strategic planning and writing center administration. Most recently, I heard again from Habre, who reported, "The team and I went to Sidon today to one of the schools there that actually convinced their administration to launch a writing center. We conducted a training session for their future tutors and the follow up will carry on. I hope other schools will follow their path" (personal communication, September 8, 2015).

I am inspired by the power and promise of scholarship and collaboration in expanding the scope of our field and working together to make visible the meaningful work that is happening at all levels of writing center practice. I look forward to the annual Secondary School Writing Center Association conference, where the presence, research, and work of these practitioner-scholars will be even more visible and more vibrant. I am excited about the ways in which their work will continue to illuminate and enrich the work of our field as a whole.

References

Austin, J. & Roche, B. (2017). *The state of our centers: Preliminary findings from the SSWC census.* Special Interest Group Presentation, NCTE Annual Convention, St. Louis, Missouri.

Caswell, N.I., Grutsch McKinney, J. & Jackson, R. (2016). *The working lives of new writing center directors.* Logan, UT: Utah State University Press.

Crosby, B.C., & Bryson, J.M. (2005). Developing a proposal that can win in arenas. *Leadership for the Common Good* (pp. 267-289). San Francisco, CA: Josey-Bass.

Jeter, A. (2012). Building a peer tutoring program. In D. Fels & J. Wells (Eds.), *The successful high school writing center: Building the best program with your students* (pp. 39-50). New York, NY: Teachers College Press.

Kent, R. (2006). *A guide to creating student-staffed writing centers: Grades 6-12.* New York: Peter Lang.

Lerner, N. (2013). What is a writing center? In R. Malenczyk (Ed.), *A rhetoric for writing program administrators* (pp. 223-236). Anderson, SC: Parlor Press.

Mirtz, R.M., & Cullen, R.M. (2002). Beyond postmodernism: Leadership theories and writing program administration. In S.K. Rose & I. Weiser (Eds.), *The writing program administrator as theorist: Making knowledge work* (pp. 90-102). Portsmouth, NH: Boynton/Cook.

Murphy, C. & Stay, B.L. (2006). Introduction. *The writing center director's resource book* (pp.xiii-xviii). Mahwah, NJ: Lawrence Erlbaum.

National Census of Writing. (2015). Retrieved from http://writingcensus.swarthmore.edu/

Position Statement on Secondary School Writing Centers. (2014). International Writing Centers Association. Retrieved from http://writingcenters.org/wp-content/uploads/2008/06/IWCAPositionStatementonSecondarySchoolWritingCenters.pdf

"Secondary School Writing Centers Association" (2018). Retrieved from http://sswca.org/.

Vander Lei, E.A. & Pugh, M. (2013). What is institutional mission? In Malenczyk, R. (Ed.), *A rhetoric for writing program administrators* (pp.105-117). Anderson, SC: Parlor Press.

Wells, J. (2012). Integrating reading into the high school writing center. In D. Fels & J. Wells (Eds.), *The successful high school writing center: Building the best program with your students* (pp. 79-94). New York, NY: Teachers College Press.

Chapter 2
Planning and Proposing
By Seth Czarnecki and Stacey Waldrup

Guiding Questions

- What role might a writing center play in developing writing at your school?
- What is the purpose, objective, mission, and/or vision of a writing center?
- Who are the key stakeholders, supporters or allies, and beneficiaries?
- What resources, materials, and space are needed?
- What are the funding needs and funding sources?
- What are logistical concerns and options: location, time, and student staffing?
- What is the timeline for implementation and growth?

Resources

- Mission Statement
- Proposal to Administration
- PowerPoint Proposal
- Budget Breakdown
- Grant Application
- Writing Center History

Resource Contributors

- Renee Brown, PTMS Writing Lab at Peters Township Middle School, PA
- Seth Czarnecki, Algonquin Writing Center at Algonquin Regional High School, MA
- Kate Hutton, Herndon Writing Center at Herndon High School, VA
- Amber Jensen, George Mason University, VA; formerly of Edison Writing Center at Edison High School, VA
- Liz Reilly and Eric Weiss, Mariemont High School Writing Center at Mariemont High School, OH
- Stacey Waldrup, Raider Writing Center at Crescent Valley High School, OR

Discussion

Every SSWC has its unique origin story. My writing center began as a dream deferred. A variety of factors--being a new teacher, graduate school, the day-to-day demands of the job, procrastination – caused me to table the hard work of creating a writing center at our school. The dream, however, was always alive even if it was lingering on the edges of my priorities. It took a long conversation with a colleague, who's now my co-director, about why a student-run writing center holds more promise than one run by faculty to get the planning process started in earnest. A year and a half after that initial conversation, we opened the Algonquin Writing Center at Algonquin Regional High School in Northborough, Massachusetts.

Purpose

When starting to plan your writing center, it's best to think about it in terms of a revolution. After all, the existence of a student-run writing center disrupts the typical teacher-student hierarchy in which the teacher is the sole authority. So, where do you begin? All revolutions start with a purpose. The Sons of Liberty didn't dump hundreds of chests of tea into Boston Harbor for nothing. It's important to know exactly why you're beginning this process beyond the fact you enjoyed working at a writing center when you were an undergrad or because you saw an interesting presentation at a local conference (For information on what roles you'll have as a director, see chapter 1). Writing centers and revolutions stand on principles, so what are yours? What role might a writing center play in developing writing at your school? Who will it serve? For what purposes? My co-director and I wanted to endeavor upon this project for a variety of purposes. Personally, I have always been troubled by the authoritative role teachers tend to play when teaching writing. The student-run writing center, with its focus on conversation and peer-to-peer interaction, gives some of that power back to those who deserve it – the writers.

Regardless of what your purpose might be, it's essential to communicate it clearly if you're to be successful in moving the project forward. Though you may have your staff write their own mission statement (See Resources below), you may consider putting together a draft statement so that administrators, staff members, and potential sponsors know what your writing center stands for.

Allies

To continue the metaphor of revolution, a successful writing center needs allies. Cross-curricular support is essential if your center is going to a) survive and b) serve all writers (Information on writing across the curriculum can be found in chapter 7). Create a list of stakeholders (Who will be affected by your work?) as well as people who might support your purposes in creating a writing center (Who are your pedagogical kindred spirits?). Of course, you're likely to find allies within the humanities (although you shouldn't be surprised if a number of colleagues never end up being advocates for your work; some like the hierarchy as it is). You should also think about other members of the school community who may be interested in the project even if they've never heard of a writing center. Our center has benefitted from positive relationships with administration, members of the science department, the librarians, parent organizations, and the custodial staff among others.

Funding and Operation

At this point, you've identified the purpose of your revolution as well as potential allies. Now, the hard part – determining your resources. Some centers open with a veritable war chest of funds while others, like mine, function with no budget at all. To figure out your resources, it's essential to determine your funding needs as well as potential funding sources.

When my co-director and I began this stage of the process, we envisioned a sustainable version of our ideal center in its ideal location and worked backward from there. Our hope was to have a dedicated space in a neutral (e.g. not located in the English department wing), high-visibility setting. Sights were set on a seldom-used conference room adjacent to the library. I should pause here to say that many SSWCs begin in a classroom or in the library and grow from there. This is undoubtedly a viable option when there is no other space available. In an environment where room availability is increasingly limited due to rising class sizes, we count ourselves lucky to have the space we do.

We wanted the space to stand out from other spaces around the school. We wanted it to be a flexible and creative space which could be adapted to meet the evolving needs of the writing center staff and its clients. Furniture would need to be ordered. We also hoped that students would be able to use the space as a place to write as well as to be tutored. Laptops, writing references, and supplies would need to be purchased. While we anticipated starting with one-on-one after school tutoring, we envisioned expanding our services over time to include workshops, classroom presentations, and tutoring hours available during the school day. We realized that scheduling software would come in handy there (For more information on outreach and promotion, see chapter 5).

Things to consider:
- What's your ideal center?
- Where will your center be located?
- How many students will staff your center?
- During what hours will your center be staffed?
- Will you need to buy furniture, supplies, textbooks, or software?
- What does your center *need* to operate? What would be *nice to have*?
- Do you plan to include services beyond one-on-one tutoring, e.g. workshops, events, presentations?
- How will you, the director, be compensated for your time – monetarily, course or duty relief? (For a breakdown of your role, see chapter 1.)
- Will you reach out to writing center partners? (University partnership information is in chapter 9.)

Once you've determined your funding needs, you'll need to determine a source for funding. Ideally, you'd have a line item in your school's budget which will help take care of some, or most, of the cost. However, this isn't always a possibility; it wasn't for our center.

Things to consider:
- How will you ensure the financial sustainability of your center?
- Is your school able to provide funding? Will they be able to do so in the future?

- Will your center fundraise for its own purposes? If so, how?
- Are there local or national education foundations for which you could write a grant?
- Are there partnerships with the local business community which might be worth exploring?

While our center is not supported financially by our school (it supports us in myriad other ways), we have been lucky enough to receive generous grants from local education foundations. That seed money allowed us to purchase furniture and technology for our space. To maintain our other costs – supplies, scheduling software, seltzer for the fridge – we've also explored a variety of fundraising opportunities including, but not limited to, private sponsorships, car washes, and selling holiday candygrams and baked goods. Regardless of what your budget might be and how those funds might come in, you'll want to make sure that your center is sustainable over the long term. Funding sources tend to dry up over time. School budgets get cut. Plan accordingly.

Timeline

Writing centers take time to develop. If it were simply a matter of finding a space and hanging a sign declaring "Open for Tutoring" more secondary schools would have them. Instead, there are many benchmarks, both in the short and long term, which need to be mapped out and met if your writing center is to develop methodically and sustainably. Moreover, your administration will likely want to know your vision, the steps you've already taken, and what will need to happen to fully realize your project. Backwards design works brilliantly here. Go back to the ideal version of your writing center. What will it look like in five years? What are the steps you'll need to take in the next three months to get you closer to that goal? The next year? The next two?

Again, the vision for our writing center was to create a student-run space where writers could come to work as well as be tutored. With this in mind, my co-director and I focused on tutor recruitment first (See chapter 3). In hindsight, this might have been cart-before-the-horse thinking; however, we figured that if we had student buy-in then administrative buy-in would be all but inevitable. We recruited fifteen or so founding members based on teacher recommendations and gave them some initial training in the spring of 2016. We also wanted the new staff to have some sense of the work they'd be doing the following year, so we scheduled a soft opening. This was tremendously helpful not only to the founding members but for my co-director and I as well. We were able to get a sense of what kinks would need to be worked out over the summer for our formal opening the following school year.

Proposal

We tell our students that when writing for any purpose it's essential to consider their audience. Who will be reading this? Under what circumstances will they be reading? What is the best form to deliver your message to this audience? Writing your proposal to administration is no exception. As you'll note in the samples or resources below, proposals can come in a variety of forms with varying degrees of depth and detail. The administration which was in place when we drafted our proposal was more receptive to presentations and roundtable discussions than lengthy documents. Regardless of what form your proposal takes, be specific about the *what, why,* and *how*. When you've been immersed in months of planning, it's easy to forget that most people in your school community don't know what a writing center is let alone why they should support the creation of one. Be clear about the vision for your SSWC, why the school community as a whole would benefit from one, and how you plan to go about accomplishing your goals.

The Road to Revolution

Even though writing centers in their modern forms have been around for decades, they still hold transformative powers for the institutions where they exist. This is especially so at the secondary level, where writing centers are still somehow a new occurrence. Kudos to you for wanting to change that. Still, revolutions take time and careful planning to be successful. You may lose a few battles along the way. Our center certainly has. But once your blueprints are in order and you've rallied your allies, you'll be ready to take on the hard work ahead.

Resources

Mission Statement

Whether drafted by directors, student tutors, or with the input of staff, a mission statement is key. It will guide future decisions and represent your center to students, staff, and parents. The three samples below showcase a mission in one sentence, one more focused on the writing process, and one more focused on student empowerment. While writing the mission statement that best works for you, consider if a separate vision statement works better for your community. For vision statements, what are the values or beliefs that inform your work? And what would you ultimately hope to accomplish as a result of your efforts? For mission statements, how do you plan to work toward this vision? And for whose specific benefit does the organization exist? Once you have answers to these questions, you can write a statement that provides not only direction but also rejuvenation.

Sample 1

The [Name] Writing Center at [Name] High School contributes to conversations about writing in order to promote and support a collaborative community of competent and confident writers.

Sample 2

Our writing center is committed to providing students with honest and constructive feedback at any point in the writing process. As fellow writers, we understand that writing is a struggle and strive to address writers' specific concerns during our one-on-one sessions. We pledge to conduct these sessions in a respectful and professional manner and take pride in our efforts to guide our peers toward achieving a new perspective of their writing. Together, it is our mission to strengthen the writing community at our school.

Sample 3

The Writing Center is an organization run by students for students. We empower writers by creating opportunities to discuss and improve their academic writing, by creating a space for students to express themselves creatively through writing, and by teaching students how to become reflective writers, learners, and thinkers, regardless of academic ability or native language.

Proposal to Administration

You've done your research and are ready to propose your new center! The following samples show the types of information you want to include, showcasing your research and thorough planning. Although you might not include these in your proposal, brainstorm all possible objections and be ready with solutions. You can also adapt this to share with fellow teachers, students, the school board, and the community-at-large. Getting more people invested in your center will increase its success.

Sample 1

Dear [administrator],

I am proposing that our school start a writing center. [Explain what a WC is or use your mission statement to explain the WC's purpose.] As you consider establishing this type of opportunity for our students and school, please review my research and planning below for how this program could be run, potential problems, and benefits.

- Logistics
    - [How many tutors will you have in the writing center?
    - Summarize how these students will be selected/will apply.
    - How will these students be trained?
    - What is your implementation timeline for opening?
    - Any other logistics you have can be briefly summarized.]
- This writing center will be for ALL students to receive help with any writing.
    - Students seeking help would work with trained tutors to improve their writing.
    - Help would include all assessed areas on state tests, including focus, content, organization, conventions, and style in all disciplines.
- Potential Problems:
    - [If there are any glaring issues, be honest. What possible solutions have you thought of to solve these problems?]
- Benefits:
    - Writing center tutors would be enriched and challenged to think critically as they perform in a leadership role.
    - Struggling writers can get one-on-one feedback with a friendly writing peer.
    - Conversations about writing result in better thinking and writing for both the student seeking help and for the tutor leading the conversation.
    - [Document the support NCTE, IWCA, and SSWCA give to secondary school writing centers.]

The potential a writing center offers to our students and school cannot be understated, but it will take your support. I am happy to discuss my ideas with you further if you would like.

Thank you for considering this program,

Sample 2

Rationale

At [Name] High School, we pride ourselves on preparing our students to be "scholars of today, leaders of tomorrow." Indeed, our increasingly fast-paced and ever-changing world presents the opportunity to reexamine and fortify our efforts. As we know, no matter what field or discipline our students enter, they will need to be able to think critically and creatively and to problem-solve collaboratively. The engineer who develops and tests new aerospace technologies. The marketer who researches and adapts ad copy to best address a target market. The electrician who completes inspection reports, documenting compliance with building codes. The graphic designer who creates a fluid content strategy and features for a website. The science teacher who models proper completion of a lab report. Each will need to articulate their process to someone. Writing is the skill linking all of these needs.

Goals
1. Student-Led, Teacher-Supervised
   Our Writing Center will be primarily run by students, called student consultants, who will drive the day-to-day operations of the center, conducting writing consultations with students who have come for help: clients. The co-directors will only weigh in on larger initiatives. Our student consultants will certainly benefit from this challenge, and our clients will appreciate visiting a space that is informed and driven by their peers.
2. Writing as a Process
   Our Writing Center will emphasize the *process* of writing over the final product. Clients will not have their essays "fixed" for them. Rather, our student consultants will address areas of student need and assist the clients in improving those aspects of their writing. Any revisions or edits to the paper will be made by the client.

Initial Implementation
1. Timeline: [Provide details for your school: what will be done this semester, next semester, next year?]

2. Budget [Are you funded through a grant, etc.?]

3. Space [Are you in the library, a classroom, or another space? Why is this the ideal space for your center and how does it impact the current occupants?]

4. Student Consultants [How many? How are they trained?]

5. Scheduling [How will clients get an appointment?]

6. Feedback [How will teachers know their students used the WC?]

7. Supervisors [Who will monitor the space when open? How often will the director have time to meet with the consultants?]

Long-Term Vision
1. Regular Credit
   As there will be teaching and learning happening in multiple areas, addressing multiple skills, the Writing Center could serve the function of a regular elective credit through the English Department.
2. Supervisors
   Faculty and staff members across disciplines who have buy-in and who want to will assume a more supervisory role—training of student consultants, troubleshooting, planning, etc.—thereby making the writing center more of a school-wide initiative.
3. Dedicated Space
   Room dedicated solely to the writing center.
4. Budget
   With a dedicated space comes the opportunity to outfit the space with materials and tools to supplement the learning and writing process: computers set aside specifically for student consultants and clients, sets of books about the writing process (such as *The Bedford Guide for Writing Students*), boards to display student tutor profiles.

PowerPoint Proposal

Just as writers must be aware of their audience, while proposing a new center you must know your audience and present your plans accordingly. Administrators, staff, and interested community members might respond better to the visual aspects of a PowerPoint. It is a time-tested presentation tool although other programs like Prezi and Keynote also work great. When working with a co-director or needing easier sharing capabilities, consider Google Slides. A handout to go with your presentation can further provide takeaway information as well as a place to take notes. The sample below shows various areas to highlight when presenting.

OUR WRITING CENTER
Proposal and Implementation Plan

WHAT IS A WRITING CENTER?
- A dedicated space for students to work one-on-one with knowledgeable peers
- Run for students by students
- Feedback on all types of writing across the curriculum
- Provides assistance and insight at any stage of the writing process
- Works to create better writers—a place where the process is emphasized over the product

WHY A WRITING CENTER? BENEFITS FOR THE SCHOOL
- Refocuses the school around writing, something we all do and engage in
- Promotes social interaction, academic discourse, and community building
- Provides more opportunities for extra help on writing
- Centralizes resources
- Supports formative assessment
- A next step in promoting writing across the curriculum

WHY A WRITING CENTER? BENEFITS FOR STUDENTS
- Low-stakes environment for feedback on writing
- Authentic responses from an authentic audience
- Students become the authority, students at the center of the process
- Learning is conversational & collaborative--mirrors the 21st century work of business, government, and the professions (Bruffee, 1984)
- Use of the writing center is associated with higher satisfaction with the writing process and fewer procrastination behaviors (Fritzsche & Young, 2002)
- Reinforces good, life-long writing habits

WHY A WRITING CENTER? BENEFITS FOR TUTORS
- Tutor-in-training
  - Greater understanding of the writing process
  - Builds speaking, writing, and listening skills
  - Conducts research on types of writing across the curriculum
  - Creating & joining a community of knowledgeable peers
  - First cohort will design how the center operates and the services it will provide
- Tutor-in-the writing center
  - Engages in academic and professional discourse
  - Fosters authentic interaction between students of all skill levels
  - Encourages reciprocal teaching
  - Becoming adaptable to new working situations

WHAT WE'VE DONE SO FAR…
- Research
  - Writing pedagogy: Bruffee (1984), (Fritzsche & Young, 2002), Kent (2010), and more
  - Conferences with middle and high school writing centers
- Outreach
  - Connections with English and Guidance department heads, librarians, and principal
  - Connections with local writing project and college-level writing center directors
- Collaboration
  - Business and art departments at our school
  - Richard Kent PhD, University of Maine and Foxcroft Academy Writing Center

IMPLEMENTATION PLAN
- Spring 2016 - Recruit Founders
  - Recruit students who fit the model of the ideal tutor
  - Collaborate with tutors from local university
  - Draft writing center mission statement
  - Name the writing center
  - Soft opening in May/June
- Fall 2016 - Run Tutor Course
  - Run Advanced Writing Seminar (H)
  - Formally train tutors
  - Business department to brand writing center and create marketing materials
  - Expand the scope of the writing center
  - Collaborate with tutors from local
  - Begin Writing Fellows program with local

IMPLEMENTATION PLAN - CONT'D
- Spring 2017/Fall 2017 - Tutor Course Embedded Model
  - Run Advanced Writing Seminar (H) for new recruits
  - Writing Center expands hours to select periods & after school
    - Trained staff can take Writing Center Tutor 1 or 2 (H) to tutor during school hours
    - Can earn community service for after school hours
- Spring 2018 - Embedded Model cont'd
  - Run Advanced Writing Seminar (H) for new recruits
  - Writing Center expands hours to select periods & after school
    - Trained staff can take Writing Center Tutor 1, 2, or 3 (H) to tutor during school hours
    - Can earn community service for after school hours
  - Pilot rent-a-tutor program

FUTURE PLANS (beyond Spring 2016)

- Expand fellowship with local university
- Grants
- Rent-a-Tutor program
- College essay feedback clinic
- Workshops for parents
- District wide implementation
- Middle school model
- Attend Northeast Writing Center Association (NEWCA) and International Writing Center Association (IWCA) conferences

WORKS REFERENCED

Bruffee, Kenneth A.. "Collaborative Learning and the 'conversation of Mankind'". *College English* 46.7 (1984): 635–652. Web.

Fels, Dawn, and Jennifer Wells. The Successful High School Writing Center: Building the Best Program with Your Students. New York: Teachers College, Columbia U, 2011. Print.

Kent, Richard. A Guide to Creating Student-staffed Writing Centers, Grades 6-12. New York: P. Lang, 2006. Print.

North, Stephen M.. "The Idea of a Writing Center". *College English* 46.5 (1984): 433–446. Web

Sommers, Nancy. "Revision Strategies of Student Writers and Experienced Adult Writers". *College Composition and Communication* 31.4 (1980): 378–388. Web.

Young, Beth Rapp, and Barbara A. Fritzsche. "Writing Center Users Procrastinate Less: The Relationship Between Individual Differences in Procrastination, Peer Feedback, and Student Writing Success". *The Writing Center Journal* 23.1 (2002): 45–58. Web.

Budget Breakdown

Whether proposing to open a center or discussing options as it expands, budget breakdowns allow you to have honest conversations about your labor (See chapter 1 for breakdown of director labor) and the cost of running a writing center. As you grow, keeping past years' budgets will create precedent, especially in the case of administrative turnover. Decide if you want to ask for a labor stipend and what it will be (Is it equal to another school stipend such as a yearbook or student government advisor?). What supplies do you need to operate your center? Are these one-time items or will they require yearly replenishing? What other funding opportunities are there, including grants and fundraising? Keep in mind that your budget can include items/projects that don't require funding. This breakdown provides a list of what you want to consider budgeting for.

Director Stipend
Responsibilities beyond teaching Advanced Composition course:
- After School Tutoring
- Workshops
- Coordinate Rent-A-Tutor
- Writing Across the Curriculum (WAC) Liaison
- Schoolwide Communication
- Facilitate Teacher Training on Writing
- Monthly and Quarterly Reports
- Publish Yearly Student Guide to Writing in the Disciplines
- Professional Development

Writing Across the Curriculum Projects
Technology/Supplies
Promotion/Advertising/Publishing
- T-shirts
- Printing promotional signs
- Publishing tutors' work for teacher, student, and departmental use
- Promotional materials (pens, pencils, etc.)
- Monthly raffle prizes (small gift cards, etc.)
- Semester Lunchtime Celebrations of Writing
- Materials & Snacks for SAT/College Essay/IB Writing Workshops
- Senior Send Off Celebration/New Tutor Induction Ceremony

Conferences/Training
- SSWCA
- IWCA
- Regional associations

Grant Application

As schools will not always have funding sources for a writing center, grants are an excellent option. Check for grants from your local school district and community organizations as well as larger corporations and foundations. The following artifact is an example of typical sections of a grant application. Other sections include number of students/staff involved, connection to/enhancement of current curriculum, implementation timeline, sustainability beyond the grant cycle and internal evaluation. Read your grant carefully to tailor answers to both your school and center. Depending on your funding needs, breaking down items into different grants (e.g. computers, furniture, conferences) can help cover a larger budget, especially when furnishing a writing center in its first year(s).

Grant Application
Affiliated School(s)/Organization(s):
Project Title:
Project Overview:
[Name] High School is in the process of creating its first student-run writing center. The center will be a dedicated space for students to work one-on-one with knowledgeable peers on any piece of writing from across the curriculum at any stage of the writing process. The writing center will be staffed before and after school as well as during school hours. Clients will have the ability to sign up for a tutoring session by appointment. Walk-ins will also be welcome. Writing tutors will be able to accommodate the needs of all students--from the AP Chemistry student putting the final touches on a lab to the Freshman who is having trouble starting her history essay. Ultimately, the writing center will centralize writing resources for the entire school. It will promote cross-curricular conversation about writing and further encourage collaboration as the chief method to promote individual growth and academic achievement.

Primary Goals /Objectives:
1. To refocus the school conversation around writing and to centralize resources
2. To promote a process approach to writing and to encourage formative assessment
3. To promote writing across the curriculum

Budget:

Two 48" library tables	$648
Eight 19" student chairs	$832.88
Two lounge chairs	$1400
Two 36" bookshelves	$1104
One teacher desk	$600
Estimated shipping	$300
Charging cart/station for storage and security	$1049.15
10 chromebooks	$2276.40
10 license agreements required for chromebooks	$260.90
TOTAL AMOUNT	$8471.33

Writing Center History

When you're first planning and proposing your center, recording its history is not on your priority list. But, as with all successful (and not) revolutions, it's important to know how they started. Keep your planning and proposal notes. Jot down strategies used, thoughts mulled over, roadblocks encountered, and decisions made. Once your center is off the ground and there is some breathing room, start compiling these together and documenting your history - and add on as you go. You can include data, student or teacher quotes, location information, new programs, etc. Consider making this a special project for one or several tutors. Having a living document enables you to share information with new tutors and staff as well as provide background and guidance for a new writing center director should you leave your school (See chapter 6 resources for a bulleted breakdown of center history). The following is an excerpt from a writing center history.

During [director's name] time as director, she proposed and implemented numerous methods to promote and expand the center. These ideas included having copies of required reading for all classes and encouraging students to use the writing center to earn extra credit. Utilizing "Pass Oaks Writing [state test] Program" and allowing time for self-guided writing skills practice helped students prepare for writing assessments. [The director] also spent time getting tutors from [local university] to assist in the editing process, putting on mini writing workshops that teachers signed students up for, and emphasizing the need - through fliers and word of mouth - for students to seek one-on-one help over the paper drop-off option. She succeeded in recruiting more tutors, creating a Writing Center Assistant option (where students could help in the center one class period and receive elective credit), and developing a system to pre-schedule sessions. During the [year] school year, the yearbook even mentioned the writing center as a helpful resource for "when students wrote essays, they had the help of the Writing Center, which was open to students regularly. This resource helped contribute to better, more insightful and mechanically sound papers and essays" (Gupta, 2011).

Reference

Gupta, L. (Ed.). (2011). *Revolutionary* (Vol. 39). Logan, UT: Herff Jones.

Ryan, L., & Zimmerelli, L. (2016). *The Bedford guide for writing tutors* (6th ed.). Boston, MA: Bedford/St. Martin's.

Chapter 3
Tutor Recruitment and Selection
By Kate Hutton

Guiding Questions

- Why is tutor recruitment an important phase of writing center implementation?
- What criteria should be considered when selecting tutors?
- Should the tutor recruitment process be selective or open?
- How can school faculty be involved in the tutor selection process?

Resources

- Tutor Recruitment Timeline
- Tutor Selection Criteria
- Seeking Faculty Nominations
- Teacher Recommendation Form
- Invitation for Recommended Students
- New Tutor Application
- Writing Sample
- Returning Tutor Application
- Invitation to Interview
- Interview Questions
- Acceptance Letter
- Denial Letter

Resource Contributors

- Hannah Baran, Studio C at Albemarle High School, VA
- Kate Hutton, Herndon Writing Center at Herndon High School, VA
- Amber Jensen, George Mason University, VA; formerly of Edison Writing Center at Edison High School, VA
- Stacey Waldrup, Raider Writing Center at Crescent Valley High School, OR

Discussion

Perhaps what I have loved most about my seven years co-directing my writing center has been witnessing what can happen when we empower young people to take ownership over a space in their schools. Writing centers challenge the traditional notion that adults are the only experts in the building, and while your role as a director is an incredibly important one, ultimately, it is your tutors who have the greatest impact on the success and the sustainability of your center.

I became a writing center director because I happened to be in the right place at the right time. I began teaching at my current school just as a wave of high school and middle school writing centers opened in my very large suburban district. After starting our center as an after-school program in 2010, our founding director was given the greenlight to open during the school day in the 2011-2012 school year through an embedded tutoring and writing course with just five tutors.

Throughout the 2011-2012 school year, our original five tutors worked closely with our founding director to promote the center, reach out to staff and students (See chapter 5), and generate interest in the program. Their hard work paid off, and the next school year, we were able to expand the course to two sections with 23 tutors. In the interest of sustainability, our founding director decided that directing the writing center should be a shared responsibility, and I was invited to become the co-director and teach the second section of Advanced Composition, the advanced writing and tutor training elective that houses our school's writing center. While my co-director created the space for our writing center to grow, our tutors are the ones who made it possible for our center to survive and thrive in those early years.

For those of you just starting out, know that the relationships you develop with your first few groups of tutors will be unlike any others. Seven years later, I can still close my eyes and see exactly where Sam, Danny, Shelley Y., Annie, Sumayya, Rehan, Georgina, Cierra, Mariam, Shelly K., Lyndsay, Alicja, Laura, and Emily sat every day. As I transitioned into my role as co-director, I relied heavily on Annie, the only second-year tutor in my section, to help me learn and support the culture she and the other original five tutors had worked to develop. While many of the ideas and practices they helped to establish have evolved, their impact on the growth and sustainability of our center is undeniable. Whether you're a seasoned director or you're just planning to open your center, tutor recruitment and selection is a vital process.

You and your tutors will be in the trenches together advocating, planning, creating, training, strategizing, and problem-solving. Your tutors are your partners, collaborators, and cultural liaisons between faculty and students in your school. While you facilitate the work done in your center, your tutors are the ones doing much of the heavy lifting. Therefore, as you recruit your tutoring staff, there is much to consider.

The Tutor Recruitment Process

Tutor recruitment is truly a *process*, and it's a phase of writing center implementation that is worth spending a significant amount of time on. After all, you can't really have a student-staffed writing center if you don't have tutors!

Generally speaking, the tutor recruitment process includes seeking nominations of potential tutors from faculty and current tutors, an application process, an interview process, and the selection of tutors. Tutor recruitment is as much about growing and staffing your center as it is about marketing your center to your school. The tutor recruitment process introduces prospective tutors to the culture of your center and gives your colleagues a sense of involvement with the center. Your approach to nominating prospective tutors, conducting the application and interview process, and welcoming or declining prospective tutors all influence how your school perceives your center.

If you are planning to open your center at the very beginning of the upcoming school year, I encourage you to begin recruiting prospective tutors early in the second semester of the current school year. Whether your center will run through an embedded course or through an extracurricular organization, you will want to identify the tutors' start date and work backwards from there. In my center, new tutors will start tutor training on the first day of school in the upcoming year; therefore, we begin collecting nominations for prospective tutors in December, applications are due in mid-January, interviews take place in February, and new tutors are notified of their acceptance in early March. It is a busy and lengthy stretch of time in our center, but taking the time to carefully recruit, review applications, and interview prospective tutors has, I believe, contributed to the success of our center.

Identifying Potential Tutors

You will probably find that most students who are visiting your center for the first time feel a little nervous. By asking for help and sharing their writing, tutees are putting themselves in a vulnerable position, so you want to choose tutors who are empathetic, kind, and trustworthy. Therefore, I'd encourage you to be fairly selective with which students you invite to become tutors, especially if you are in the very early stages of implementation.

Writing centers need supportive allies in the form of faculty and staff in order to thrive. Therefore, it's a good idea to invite teachers and administrators to participate in the tutor recruitment process by asking them to nominate potential tutors. Involving your colleagues helps them to feel invested the center, even if they aren't directly involved in day-to-day operations. Furthermore, don't underestimate the power and importance of involving your current tutors in the nomination process. For a long time in our center, about one-third of our tutoring staff consisted of students heavily involved with our Robotics Club. These days, we have a significant number of band and orchestra students. Last year, four of our 39 tutors lived next door to one another on the same street! If you have strong, motivated tutors, encourage them to recruit their friends. It will help sustain and grow your center. I've found that my center runs more efficiently and our tutors are more effective when we have a smaller group of enthusiastic tutors than when we have a larger group of tutors; keep in mind that your tutoring staff should emphasize quality, not quantity.

While instinct might make you believe that high-achieving, straight-A students who write beautiful essays seemingly effortlessly might make the best tutors, in my experience, it's the students who've struggled a bit with writing and who've demonstrated a willingness to wrestle with their own work who have become the most effective tutors. When considering students to nominate from my sophomore English classes, I tend to nominate students who willingly engage with writing as a process, who seek feedback from me and their peers, and who demonstrate a growth mindset. I also seek out students whose peers trust and respect them or those who've shown an interest in writing and reading outside of the classroom. Some of my strongest tutors have been those who initially struggled in English class or those who applied to become tutors without being nominated by a teacher. Writing skills can be taught; however, training a person to approach working with others in a gentle, empathetic way can occasionally prove challenging. I've traditionally favored tutors with good writing skills and strong people skills over those with strong writing skills but mediocre people skills. Including an application and an interview as part of your recruitment process will help you to identify those potential tutors who may be diamonds in the rough.

You might also be wondering what grade levels of students to pursue as tutors. Inviting only upperclassmen to become tutors might make underclassmen feel more open to and confident in the feedback offered by their peers, while including rising ninth and tenth graders might help to develop a stronger culture of writing at all grade levels and sustain your center. If you're worried that freshmen graders are too young, you haven't seen a middle school writing center! Some of you may be very lucky to have a writing center in place at your feeder middle school; if so, you'll want to ensure that those students who already have experience with peer tutoring have the opportunity to continue in high school (See chapter 8 for more information about middle school centers).

My center has always recruited rising tenth, eleventh, and twelfth grade students to become tutors, although quite honestly, we've tended to favor sophomores and juniors because they can enroll in our course multiple times, and they tend to stay committed to their tutoring roles longer than senior first-year tutors who have their eyes trained on graduation. Including underclassmen in your staff also gives your tutors the opportunity to attend and present at SSWCA's annual conference multiple times. No matter what grades you recruit from, there are many right ways to approach this aspect of tutor recruitment, and what will work best for your center depends on your school culture.

As much as possible, your tutoring staff should reflect your school's population. Last year, one of my Honors tenth grade students interviewed to become a tutor. She had taken general education English 9, and her teacher hadn't encouraged students to work with writing center tutors on a regular basis. During her interview, she was asked about whether she had ever worked with a tutor before and what her experience was like, and the interviewers were shocked to hear that she never sought help as a freshman because she thought the center was only meant to be used by students in Honors English courses! In order to ensure that your center is perceived as a welcoming, friendly, and comfortable space, reach out to students of all academic abilities and from all social groups.

Finally, I encourage you to use some type of application and interview process because it communicates to prospective tutors that becoming a tutor is a commitment and it helps you get to know your future tutors. In our center, our current tutors review writing samples and interview prospective tutors, which gives them the opportunity to ensure that their legacy lives on in the new group of tutors. The resources included in this chapter will help you to determine how to navigate the tutor recruitment process and which components will work best for you as you implement or grow your center.

Resources

Tutor Recruitment Timeline

This sample timeline is used by a center run through an embedded tutor training course, so their timeline is based on their school's Student Services department's course registration deadline. Materials for each phase of the tutor recruitment process follow.

- December: Seek nominations for prospective tutors. Present information about the writing center and what makes a successful tutor at a faculty meeting. Collect nominations directly from English teachers at an English department meeting. Ask tutors to nominate classmates or friends.
- January 2: Applications and invitations to apply are distributed to nominated students and are made available to all students. Begin advertising the opportunity to apply on social media and school announcements.
- January 4: Tutor leaders host a session for interested students during the school-wide Electives Fair as part of recruitment.
- January 8: Invite teachers, administrators, and school counselors to participate in prospective tutor interviews.
- January 19: Applications due. As applications are received, each application is assigned a number and the student's basic contact information and interview availability is entered into a spreadsheet. *(Note: You may choose to offer digital applications only, which will save you time!)* Names and identifying information are redacted from writing samples so tutors can review them blindly.
- January 22- January 26: Directors review applications and writing samples. Tutors review and blindly rate writing samples.
- January 29-January 30: Directors identify list of applicants to interview and build interview schedule.
- January 31: Tutors prepare and deliver invitations to interview.
- February: Interview prospective tutors. *(Note: This center is open during their school's lunch block. They can interview up to four candidates each day. Depending on the number of applications you receive and your time constraints, you may lengthen or shorten the interview window.)*
- March 1: Course Registration ends. Notify prospective tutors of their application status. Counselors, administrators, and English department chair are notified of students accepted to enroll in tutor training course.
- April or May: Current tutors plan and host a community-building event welcoming new tutors.

Tutor Selection Criteria

The selection criteria listed below is synthesized from criteria provided by several centers. Ultimately, you want to select tutors who will help to support your center's mission and vision (See chapter 2 for mission and vision information). Suggested qualities include:

Academic Qualities	Personal Qualities
<ul><li>A dedicated learner</li><li>A strong (although not necessarily perfect) writer</li><li>Demonstrates a growth mindset (they are teachable)</li><li>Has an excellent attendance and behavior record</li><li>Engages with writing and learning as a process</li></ul>	<ul><li>Kind, helpful, patient, and reliable</li><li>Enjoys writing for fun or might enjoy writing if given the chance</li><li>Open-minded and enthusiastic</li><li>Works well as part of a team</li><li>Perhaps needs a "home" or a place to belong in our school</li><li>Is a "nerd" (not required, but definitely helpful)</li></ul>

Seeking Faculty Nominations

A great way to get your colleagues to buy into the work done in your center is to involve them throughout the tutor recruitment process. Seeking staff nominations not only ensures that your tutors are more representative of your student body, but that your colleagues feel that your tutors are trustworthy and competent. Depending on your school culture, you might seek nominations just from teachers within your department or from teachers in all content areas. If you're seeking nominations from teachers across content areas, you might consider contacting department chairs to pass information about nominating students along to their department members, or you might simply send a staff-wide email. Whichever way you choose, make it as easy as possible for your colleagues to nominate students. One effective way of gathering staff recommendations is to ask teachers to bring a copy of their class rosters to a department meeting. After you explain a bit about the recruitment process and the qualities you're seeking in your potential tutors, ask your colleagues to highlight the names of students on each roster who they think would make great tutors. Another approach is to provide them with a paper nomination form that they can easily return to you, or by creating a Google Form to easily collect student names. Below is an email request for students your colleagues would like to recommend.

Dear [Department Chair, Colleagues, etc.],

The time has come for the [Name] Writing Center to begin recruiting writing tutors for next year! One way we can best prepare our tutors to work with your students on papers from multiple disciplines is to staff the writing center with students who have shown excellence in writing in your class, not just in English class.

Therefore, we are looking for each [department, teacher, etc.] to nominate a list of students, who will then be invited to apply to become a tutor in the writing center and to [enroll in our tutor training course, join our organization, etc.] next year. We are specifically looking for students who embody the following characteristics:

- [Provide your tutor selection criteria - see previous chart of tutor qualities]

We are looking for rising [grade levels]. Please feel free to nominate as many as fit the above characteristics – students only need one teacher nomination to receive an application. I have attached a current list of the writing center tutors for your reference.

*Please [return your list to [directors] in [room]/complete this form, etc] no later than [date] so we can move forward with the application process.

Thank you for your support! Please direct any questions to [director's email].

Teacher Recommendation Form

If you do accept applications from students who haven't been nominated by a teacher (and many centers do), you might consider requiring them to ask a teacher of their choice to submit an easy-to-complete recommendation form.

Teachers,

Please use the scale below to provide general information about this student (5 = strongly agree, 1 = strongly disagree). Any feedback you can provide is greatly appreciated.

He/she is a hardworking student that is always prepared for class.	1	2	3	4	5
He/she works well with other students.	1	2	3	4	5
He/she possesses strong writing abilities.	1	2	3	4	5
He/she is a leader inside and outside of the classroom.	1	2	3	4	5
He/she is motivated to learn and practice a variety of writing forms.	1	2	3	4	5
He/she would be a strong peer tutor for students struggling with writing.	1	2	3	4	5
He/she is NOT frequently absent from school.	1	2	3	4	5
I would recommend this student to train as a writing center tutor.	1	2	3	4	5

Additional comments:

Teacher Signature: _____ Date: _____

Thank you for your time and feedback!

Invitation for Recommended Students

A letter inviting students to join the writing center, often called a nomination letter, is the first contact you have with your prospective tutors. Include information about their nomination, the qualities they possess that led to their nomination, information about their commitment, and, most importantly, how to apply! Depending on your school culture, you may choose to hand-deliver or email nomination letters. Personally, I prefer to have tutors hand deliver letters to students because then I know that the students have actually received them, whereas you can't guarantee that emails always make it to students.

Dear [Student],

Congratulations! You have been nominated by [teacher's name] at [school's name] to apply to become a tutor in the writing center! This nomination indicates that your teacher thinks you would be an excellent peer tutor because you possess the following qualities:

[List the criteria for selecting tutors here.]

It is an honor to have been nominated, and the next step is up to you! Please read [information you want them to know: the Writing Center FAQ on the back of this letter to understand the purpose of the writing center, the benefits of being a tutor, the level of commitment we are asking from you, etc.]. Please also plan to join us during the Electives Fair on [date], stop by the writing center when were open, or speak to [directors] in room [number].

Application Materials & Deadline: Please complete the [online or print] application by [date].

[If your writing center is run through an embedded course, include information about the course]. Tutor Training Course: Please note that enrollment in [course name], a full-year elective course where you will learn more about writing and tutoring, is required of all tutors. Please reserve your space in [the course] if you have applied for the writing center – when final staffing decisions are made, we will adjust your schedule accordingly, but it's easier to drop [the course] down the road than to add it in.

[If your writing center is run as an extracurricular activity, include information about the expectations for training and their time commitment.] Requirements: If you are invited to become a tutor in the writing center, you will be required to:
- Attend tutor training starting [date]
- Commit to help staff the center in one or more of the following ways:
  - As a Writing Center Assistant (for credit) working during a period of your choice
  - As a freelance tutor during a period of your choice for a majority of the semester
  - During lunch for a minimum of one lunch per week
  - During advisory for a minimum of two advisory periods per month

If you have any questions or concerns, please feel free to contact [the directors] or, even better, a current tutor – we would be more than happy to answer your questions!

We hope you will join us!

New Tutor Application

Generally, most new tutor applications require prospective tutors to submit a written or digital application (sample questions below), a writing sample, and a teacher recommendation either in the form of a nomination or a recommendation form (see previous artifacts). Below are sample questions that you might include on your application. In addition to these questions, collect the applicant's name, contact information, and interview availability if you choose to conduct interviews. Paper applications are easy to distribute to prospective tutors, while digital applications can be posted on social media and websites and eliminates the extra step of having to enter any information into a spreadsheet. For each response, you may choose to give students a length expectation of between 150-250 words, or you can simply evaluate the prospective tutor based on how thoroughly they respond without guidelines.

- Why do you want to become a tutor in the writing center?
- What is your previous experience as a tutee in the writing center?
- What are your strengths as a writer?
- Joseph Heller said, "Every writer I know has trouble writing." Where are your trouble spots or weaknesses with writing? What have you done to address them?
- What interpersonal communication skills do you have that you think will serve you well in serving as a tutor?
- What kinds of writing do you think you could be most helpful with with and why?
- The [Name] Writing Center is composed of a dynamic group of students that bring together their varied interests, areas of expertise, and personalities for the better interest of the WC. Why do you want to be a part of this group? What will your individual contribution be? (Consider personal interests, academic, social, and leadership strengths.)

Please rate yourself in the following areas (5 = strong, 1 = weak):
- Your enthusiasm about becoming a tutor
- Your perception of your writing compared to that of your peers
- Your ability to work well with others
- Your dependability
- Your understanding of how the writing center works

Writing Sample

Evaluating prospective tutors' writing gives you the opportunity to review your prospective tutors' writing skills. Asking applicants to explain why they submitted a piece also gives you insight into how the writer thinks about writing. If you ask current tutors to review and rate writing samples, be sure that no identifying information appears on the samples they review, and emphasize the importance of confidentiality. You might choose to rate writing samples holistically, or you might create a more thorough evaluation system that examines the writer's organization, style, flow, etc. Below is an example of directions for submitting a writing sample.

Writing Sample Directions: Please attach a writing sample of your best written work. It can be something you wrote for a class (English, history, or any other discipline) or a piece you have written/are working on independently. Remember, this piece should showcase your strengths as a writer AS WELL AS show evidence of thorough revision. It should be between 2 and 4 pages, typed and double-spaced.

Below your writing sample, please write a short paragraph explaining why you selected this piece for submission.

Returning Tutor Application

Once you've established your center, you may be in a position to welcome back experienced tutors multiple years in a row. In some centers, once a student has been invited to become a tutor, they are automatically invited back each year until they graduate. As the tutor recruitment process for the following school year begins, tutors might be asked to complete a simple form asking whether or not they intend to continue tutoring for the following school year. In other centers - and especially in centers with large numbers of tutors - students may be asked to reapply each year. Below are questions you might ask students who are re-applying to tutor.

- Do you intend to continue tutoring next school year? Yes/No
- If yes: Hooray! What do you like about tutoring?
- If no: We're sad to see you go! Please share what would have made you stay.
- What tutoring-related accomplishment are you most proud of this year?
- What have you found to be most challenging about tutoring this year?
- Second- and Third-Year tutors are expected to take on additional responsibility for running the center, mentoring the new tutors, connecting with programs throughout the school, and planning and executing projects/events. Why are you qualified to be a leader in the peer tutoring program?
- Returning tutors are expected to share their knowledge with the wider tutoring community by proposing a presentation for the annual SSWCA conference. What topic do you think you would want to present on?

Invitation to Interview

Depending on the number of applicants you receive, you may decide to interview all candidates regardless of how they performed on their initial application, or you may only invite a certain number of applicants to interview. If you don't automatically offer all students the opportunity to interview, below is a sample letter inviting prospective tutors to interview.

Dear [Student],

Congratulations! Your writing sample and application are strong enough that we would like to invite you to interview with us as the final portion of your application to enroll in [tutor training course] and become a tutor in the writing center. The following date, time and location have been assigned to you.

[Information on date, time, and location]

You will interview with two current writing center tutors and a teacher or administrator. The purpose of the interview is to evaluate your interpersonal strengths, learning style, and leadership capabilities, as well as to cover some scenarios that you might encounter as a tutor. Please feel free to bring your lunch!

If for some reason, you are unable to make this appointment, please contact one of us right away so we can reschedule.

Interview Questions

When possible, you should invite supportive stakeholders from your school community (administrators, teachers, school counselors, librarians, students, tutors, etc.) to participate in the interview process. Below are sample interview questions. As you select and prepare questions for interviews, make sure that they are reflective of the mission and vision of your center. Be sure to thank the interview panel for donating their time to support your center! Keep in mind that the interview is as much about you and your staff getting to know prospective tutors as it is about your prospective tutors getting to know a bit about the culture of your center. I like to emphasize that any scenarios or any questions about tutoring specifics are just an opportunity for us to see how the prospective tutor thinks on their feet and that they'll participate in plenty of training when they become a tutor (See chapter 4 for tutor training information).

PERSONAL
- Have you had an experience as a tutee in the writing center? What was it like?
- What makes you want to become a tutor in the writing center?
- What makes you nervous about being a writing center tutor?
- Are you comfortable talking to and working with people you don't know well?
- One of your close friends signs up to work with you. How would you make sure that you use your time effectively?

WRITING
- What do you like about the writing process?
- What about writing challenges you? What strategies have you learned to overcome these challenges?
- Would you consider yourself a writer? Why or why not? Why might it be helpful for writing center tutors to find some things about writing to be challenging?
- Do you write outside of school? Do you enjoy writing for fun?
- How do you handle constructive feedback about your own writing?

LEARNING STYLES
- How do you learn best? How might you bring this learning style or strategy into a tutoring session?
- What are some of the benefits of working with peers as tutors instead of teachers or other adults? (*Note: Somehow, I always end up being the one to ask this question during interviews! I emphasize to the interviewee that their answer won't offend me as a teacher.*)
- In your mind or experience, what is the difference between being a tutor and being an editor?
- A tutee comes in with a paper that is in really rough shape. How do you begin to offer constructive criticism?

LEADERSHIP
- What is one way you have demonstrated leadership in a challenging situation with your peers?
- How might you help to make the writing center more effective or more visible in the school?
- What leadership qualities should a tutor possess as a representative of the writing center?

SCENARIOS (Choose 2 or 3 as time permits)
- A student comes in to work on their literary analysis essay. You haven't read the book they're writing about. How do you help this student?
- A member of your sports team/club/band/etc. comes into the writing center and signs up to be tutored by you. You are really good friends and your friend wants to spend more time talking about last week's game/the upcoming trip/some other event. How do you help this student?
- An apathetic student was required to come to the writing center. He sits down next to you and is unresponsive despite all of your efforts to welcome him. You try to ask a couple questions but he remains unresponsive and uninterested. How do you help this student?
- An older student comes to the writing center with a really well-developed and well-written paper. You feel intimidated and can't think of any suggestions for improvement. How do you help this student?

- A student is required to come to the writing center, but he shows up late and forgot his draft at home. He tries to tell you about what his paper is on, and then he tries to get your signature as proof of his visit. How do you help this student?
- A student comes into the writing center, and she appears to be really nervous. She doesn't want to read her essay out loud, she isn't making eye contact with you, and she's only giving you one-word responses to the questions you ask. How do you help this student?
- A student who is willing to receive help comes to the writing center. Although his overall idea is clear, English is not his native language, and you notice that he struggles with grammar and sentence structure. How do you help this student?

Acceptance Letter

Congratulations! You've made it to the most exciting part of tutor recruitment: welcoming your new tutors. In my center, current tutors hand-deliver acceptance letters to our new tutors, and we announce the names of newly-accepted tutors to faculty via email. In other centers, the announcement comes via social media or an invitation to a new tutor celebration. Below is a sample letter that you might send to welcome a new tutor.

Dear [Tutor],

Congratulations! We are excited to offer you a position as a tutor in the [Name] Writing Center and the opportunity to [enroll in our tutor training course/become a part of an organization] for the upcoming school year. Your application, writing sample, and interview were all very impressive. Please confirm your intent to enroll in [the course] with your counselor as soon as possible.

We look forward to your contributions to our school community as a peer tutor and to helping you grow as a writer through the course. If you haven't yet had the chance, please stop by to be tutored at some point this school year so that you can learn a little bit more about how the writing center works.

Be sure to like us on Facebook, follow us on Twitter, and check out our blog!

Please let us know if you have questions or if any problems develop with your course registration.

Keep Writing!

Denial Letter

Unfortunately, not every student who applies to become a tutor is necessarily a good match for your center. Their application might have been underwhelming or incomplete, their writing sample may have been subpar, or they might not have made the best impression during their interview. In our center, we are wary of applicants who emphasize that they're interested in becoming a tutor primarily because it looks good on college applications. Whatever the reason, it is important to maintain confidentiality about which students were denied an invitation to become tutors. In my center, tutors hand-deliver acceptance and denial letters in sealed envelopes, so they do not know which type of letter they're delivering. In your letter, acknowledge their willingness to apply and/or interview and encourage them to keep writing. Remember: They may come in to be tutored in the future!

Dear [Student],

After evaluation of your application materials, we regret to inform you that we are unable to offer you a position in the [Name] Writing Center for the [school year]. We received a large number of applications this year, and unfortunately, we are unable to accept everyone. Though you were not admitted, your application and your writing sample demonstrate that you are a committed writer at our school. Please consider applying again in the future.

Thank you for your interest in the writing center, and keep writing!

Chapter 4
Tutor Training
By Stephanie Passino

Guiding Questions

- What do new tutors need to know in order to be effective?
- How can returning tutors continue to be trained and what supports do they need?
- How and when will training(s) occur? Who will run them?

Resources

- Training Courses
    - Tutor Agreement Form
    - Tutoring Class Syllabus
    - Tutor Training Schedule
    - Virtual Writing Lab Training and Protocols
- Tutor Cheat Sheets
    - The Seven Priorities of Tutoring
    - Tips from Experienced Tutors
    - Sample Tutoring Questions
- Individual Activities for Training
    - Visualizing Steps of the Tutoring Process
    - Fish Bowl and Tutor Checklist
    - Case Study Analysis
    - Asking Useful Questions
    - Sandwiching
    - Using Sample Texts
    - Role Playing
    - Read More Than You Write
    - Reviewing Tutoring Logs
    - Writing Assignments
- Ongoing Professional Development
    - Journaling
    - Tutor Observation Reflection
    - Observation Outline
    - Self-Evaluation
    - Director Observation Form
    - Giving Tutors Choice
    - Tutor Mentoring Prospectus
    - Senior Tutor Legacy Project

Resource Contributors

- Hannah Baran, Peer Tutoring Center at Albemarle High School, VA
- Renee Brown, PTMS Writing Lab at Peters Township Middle School, PA
- Trisha Callihan, Eagle Writing Center at Osbourn High School, VA
- Seth Czarnecki, Algonquin Writing Center at Algonquin Regional High School, MA
- Kate Hutton, Herndon Writing Center at Herndon High School, VA
- Amber Jensen, George Mason University, VA; formerly of Edison Writing Center at Edison High School, VA
- Jim LaBate, Writing and Research Center at Hudson Valley Community College, NY
- Stephanie Passino, Hawk Writing Center at Hayfield Secondary School, VA
- Kimberly Sloan, IAS Virtual Writing Lab at Interagency Alternative Schools, VA
- Stacey Waldrup, Raider Writing Center at Crescent Valley High School, OR

Discussion

So, you've found the best tutors, and it's time to train them, right? Almost. Training your tutors can be a very daunting task. Whether you find yourself beginning the school year with a group of seasoned tutors or novices, your tutor training plan will vary from year to year. Depending on your situation, you may have a full training course during your school day, or you may be squeezing in training sessions before and after school. Regardless of your setup, it is very important to get to know the tutors in your program during the first few weeks of school. Find out the students' strengths. Do you have a group of students that are strong writers but lack the ability to connect with their peers? Do you have kind students who don't possess the strongest writing stills? No matter what type of tutors you have, or how often you are meeting with them, your job is to consider their different levels of experience in writing and working with others and to help them develop into the best peer tutors possible.

Despite the fact that my center has been open for five years, our tutor training plan changes each year and continues to evolve. As the director, I've learned to use the many available tutor training resources (like you'll see in this chapter) and to lean on my veteran tutors to help with the training process. Before you begin thinking of your training plan for this year, consider a few things: Do you have returning tutors? What skills need to be further developed in these returning tutors? Will the returning tutors be put into leadership roles? What skills do your new tutors have and lack? As you get to know your new recruits, you will find yourself asking more questions, especially regarding what skills are most important to teach with your particular group.

Tutor training can be done in a variety of formats and will vary depending on the number of experienced tutors in the center as well as the setup of your center. Those of us with an elective tutoring course can approach training much differently than someone who sees their tutors once a month during staff meetings or in small groups throughout the day when the center is open. The training schedule detailed below narrates how my school's model functions - I have tutors in class every other day for 90 minute blocks - but I have tried to add to my experience other approaches and considerations so that you can adapt and make modifications to fit your center's needs.

First Days

Without putting pencil to paper, tutor training starts on the first day of school for my team. Through ice breakers and classroom community builders, I focus on creating a space where tutors feel they belong and can take risks. While this may not be in the pacing guide for our class, I find that spending time building trust in our center is invaluable. The tutors must have ample practice talking with people they don't know and working together to accomplish a variety of tasks in order to best work with their peers. Some examples of simple team building tasks include line up in order by birthdate/alphabetically by last name without talking, solve rebus puzzle brain teasers, scavenger hunts, etc. Consider what games and activities are appropriate for your school's culture and the age of your tutors. Even if those activities are seemingly unrelated to writing or tutoring, they will help to break down barriers that naturally resurrect themselves at the start of a new academic year. Without this time to get to know each other through games, interviewing, and monthly celebrations and recognition, the atmosphere in the center is not up to par.

Once this environment is established, let the writing portion of training begin. My tutors write several pieces about their own writing process and tutoring experiences, a writer's autobiography for example. Through this introspective work, tutors will identify traits they possess, which they can then look for and and use to connect with clients. By identifying the emotions and feelings they have towards the many types of writing assignments, they can better empathize with students who seek our help. When tutors reflect on and better understand their own writing process, they are able to ask questions to those they work with who might have a different process or approach. These personal narrative pieces are typically shared with the group to help everyone gain a deeper understanding of the tutoring process. Consider what other writing activities can be done during these first days of training that will help to build empathy, help to bring tutors into a close-knit community, and help new recruits to overcome their nerves. Even if you are in a situation with limited training time, invest in those writing moments because they do make an impact.

Diving In

Once you begin to know your tutors and have built rapport, you can shift the training focus to what we typically think of as writing center skills. Over the next few class periods, I share the purpose and vision of our center as well as the process of a typical tutor session. As an established writing center, one of the largest obstacles we faced was removing the stigma that the writing center is a place where tutors will simply proofread a paper for spelling and grammatical errors (See chapter 5 for outreach ideas). It is essential to reinforce to your tutors that this is not what the center is or does. It is often the responsibility of the tutors to communicate that to the clients, so a discussion on how to clarify that misconception should be part of the training you offer. How does a tenth grader explain politely to a classmate she cannot proofread the paper? Role playing a variety of scenarios such as this helps tutors find the words to help eliminate this stigma and allow a session to run smoothly. Returning tutors have an opportunity at this point to become leaders and guide the newer tutors through role playing or lead break-out groups to discuss what they felt while stepping into a certain role.

Once students understand the purpose of the center and the goal of a tutor session, the tutors view and critique videos of tutor sessions, role play a variety of scenarios, and participate in their own tutor sessions. If you have seasoned tutors, it might beneficial to have them create tutor training videos that can be used the following years. I typically ask my students to observe and reflect on a session that went well and one that went poorly. We discuss which strategies we want to replicate and which ones to avoid. As you'll see in the resources below, if you are a new director without returning tutors or a video, you can use a "fishbowl" approach to demonstrate both strong and weak sessions. Another good idea to help new tutors solidify their understanding of the tutoring process is to have them create a flowchart or other visual representation of how their time with a client should be spent.

Once students have a grasp of what they are to do with a client, it is time to dive in and try it. In my center, tutor training sessions consist of three people: the tutee, tutor, and observer. Each person has a specific role, and these practice sessions last about 20 minutes, but you can truncate that if you have tighter time constraints. Each trio should "rotate" to perform a different role so that all new tutors have a chance to wear the "tutor hat" and get their feet wet with a practice session. All three people should reflect on the session in a write-up, after which all three share out their observations to help each other grow. Another reason this is a helpful training technique is that it allows your tutors to feel what it is like to be a client, which they may have forgotten or never experienced. Observations like this should continue throughout the year if possible as a way to encourage tutors to reflect on best practices.

Final Details

During the third or fourth week of my school year, we shift to focus on the actual assignments that will come into the center and the writing skills tutors need to help those clients. Seasoned tutors and expert staff members lead specific-assignment training sessions (For information on reaching out to colleagues in other departments, see chapter 7). During these training sessions, tutors examine writing prompts, rubrics, and student samples. By asking subject-area teachers to train the tutors on specific writing assignments, we have seen an increase in student use and a gained sense of trust. This is a great way to get teacher buy-in and gain credibility in the school.

We know that creating a welcoming and inviting atmosphere is important to get students into the center. We also know that knowledgeable, trained tutors are essential for establishing credibility. This is why you will most likely find yourself spending a great deal of your allotted training time preparing the tutors to work with any client. We want to provide our tutoring services to all students in the school whether they are English Language Learners, receiving special education services, or taking all advanced placement courses. Tutor training is essential for tutors to learn the process, build confidence in their abilities, and ultimately, effectively run the center.

The artifacts shared in this section are a culmination of director-created resources that have been revised over the past decade. We recommend that in addition to the provided resources, directors refer to other publications for best training practices, specifically:

- Fels, D., & Wells, J. (2011). *The successful high school writing center: Building the best program with your students.* New York, NY: Teachers College Press.
- Kent, R.(2017). *A guide to creating student-staffed writing centers grades 6-12* (2nd ed.). New York, NY: Peter Lang.
- Ryan, L., & Zimmerelli, L. (2016). *The Bedford guide for writing tutors* (6th ed.). Boston, MA: Bedford/St. Martin's.

As you begin your tutor training journey, remember that it is similar to any writing task - it should be constantly evolving and rely heavily on peer/student feedback. The best tutor training plans are never static and use a culmination of resources. Now it is time to review what your director-peers have implemented and get out there and train!

Given the large quantity of resources offered in this chapter, they are separated into subcategories. "Training Courses" will provide materials that have been used by directors who have separate, designated class time to devote to training; however, many of the materials in that subsection can be adapted and used in other training situations. "Tutor Cheat Sheets" are handouts that many tutors will find helpful ass references. "Individual Lessons and Activities" are training ideas that do not necessarily connect to or build from each other, so they can be used in almost any center regardless of the logistics of when you train your tutors. "Ongoing Professional Development" speaks to how directors continue to build skills in tutors who are already working in the center, both throughout the year and as returning tutors.

Your tutor training program is going to make a difference in your tutors' lives by showing them the power of collaboration and revision. Good luck!

Resources

Training Courses

Tutor Agreement Form

Each year tutors review this agreement with the director at the beginning of the year. This agreement helps to provide clear expectations and clear up any questions for new tutors.

I. Mission Statement: The [name of writing center] contributes to conversations about writing in order to promote and support a collaborative community of competent and confident writers.
- Tutors focus on improving their peers as writers, not on improving an assignment.

II. Integrity
- Respect all students and staff.
- All session information is private. If there are questions, talk to the WC director, but do not share information with others.
- Academic dishonesty will not be tolerated and will result in dismissal from the WC team as well as referral to administration.

III. Tutor Behavior
- Respect the center environment and materials and use appropriate language.
- Be on time to all sessions.
- Work in the center according to previously given time commitment.
- Attend all training sessions.
- Attend all writing center team meetings and stay informed of team announcements.

I agree to abide by the standards and expectations of the [Name] Writing Center.

_____   _____   _____
Name   Signature   Date

Tutoring Class Syllabus

From the beginning of the school year, tutors need to know what the expectations are for the center and themselves as tutor leaders. Consider sharing the history of the center with new tutors and work together to create goals and expectations for the current school year (See chapter 6 for information about center history). This artifact provides sections from a sample syllabus for a tutor training course. The syllabus typically outlines the course description, writing assignments, and assessment criteria.

Description
Advanced Composition is a higher-level English elective course that works in tandem with the writing center and entails an in-depth study of writing across all disciplines (science, math, English, social studies, business, theatre, etc.). Other areas of focus are utilizing the writing process, understanding and applying Standard English, building advanced grammar and vocabulary skills, identifying components of advanced writing across genres and for varied audiences, and becoming an effective peer tutor of writing. This content is applied and assessed as students both produce independent writing and volunteer as a peer tutor in the writing center.

Course Objectives
- Read and analyze a variety of texts to understand writers' craft
- Write narrative, expository, informational, and persuasive essays
- Use readings, research, and personal experience to develop writing
- Collaborate to help peers improve writing
- Review, publish, and present writing
- Serve as a leader in the building and throughout the community by organizing and executing outreach programs and events for the writing center

Grading
- Written work: An assessment that measures student mastery of all indicators included in a unit or other instruction periods. These grades will constitute roughly 50% of a student's quarterly grade.
- WC event work/classwork: A form of classwork and active participation that is graded for completion and not for mastery. This includes but is not limited to attendance at WC events, after school sessions, wearing t-shirt on designated days, in class committee work. These grades will constitute roughly 30% of a student's quarterly grade.
- Tutor sessions: A form of classwork and participation that is graded for completion and not for mastery. Tutor logs should be kept up to date and students should expect random check- ins. These grades will constitute roughly 20% of a student's quarterly grade.

Student Expectations
Academic Dishonesty Policy:
The policy is based on the idea that we will treat behavior separately from academic achievement. Any student who has forged, cheated or plagiarized will be referred to their administrator so their actions can be addressed, documented, and parents contacted. As English student leaders in the building, any infraction may result in removal from the writing center.

Tutor Training Schedule

This schedule outlines the first month of class in regards to building a classroom community, practicing the recursive process through individual writing assignments, and learning the tutoring process through training. The class combines first year to third year tutors, so there are many leadership opportunities for second and third year tutors to assist with training. While practicing the tutoring process is very important, you can supplement by having experienced tutors and sometime core teachers lead training on types of history essays, college essays, and resumes.

Advanced Composition – Introduction to Writing and Tutoring

Date	Advanced Comp 1	Advanced Comp 2/3
Class 1	Welcome to the Advanced Comp/WC • Introductions and overview of the year • Go over course syllabus/expectations • What is your compass direction? • Chromebooks – join Google Classroom • Tutoring 101 PPT – WC history/brainstorm using Padlet HW: Bring in materials	Year Two: Welcome back! • Introductions and overview of the year • Go over course syllabus/expectations • What is your compass direction? • Chromebooks – join Google Classroom • Tutoring 101 PPT – WC history/brainstorm using Padlet HW: Bring in materials
Class 2	Writer and Center Identity • Question Game • Tutoring 101 PPT - Quick write • Read chapter 2 of *The Bedford Guide for Writing Tutors* • Begin writing "Reflecting on Writing" essay	Year Two: It begins – taking the lead • Question Game • Tutoring 101 PPT - Quick write • Begin writing: "Mentoring Prospectus" / assign mentoring groups • Prepare for role play next class Year Three: It begins – taking the lead and beyond! • Begin brainstorming/drafting newsletter • Create tutor role-play scenarios
Class 3	Our Tutoring Philosophy • Quick write: What should tutoring look like in our center? What should it feel like? • Tutoring 101 – view videos (the good, the bad, our mission) • Leadership Positions/Committees • Writing assignment	Our Tutoring Philosophy • Quick write: What should tutoring look like in our center? What should it feel like? • Tutoring 101 – view videos (the good, the bad, our mission) • Leadership Positions/Committees • Writing assignment
Class 4 & Class 5	Writing with a Purpose • Review types of writing assignments and real world writing • Continue writing draft of "Reflecting on Writing" essay Tutor Training – College Essay/Personal narrative • College Essay – tutor training	The Role of a Mentor • Create mentor/mentee groups/1st activity • Work on draft of "Mentoring Prospectus" Tutor Training - College Essay/Personal narrative • College Essay – tutor training
Class 6	Tutor Communication • Mentor Match-up and lesson • Leadership roles/committees • Tutoring Priorities/Top Questions • Finish "Reflecting on Writing"	Leadership Training • Lead mentor match-up and getting to know you activity • Leadership roles/committees • Continue working on "Mentoring Prospectus"
Class 7	Tutoring Training/Tutor Communication • Mentor Match-up and lesson • Leadership roles/committees – committee goal setting • Practice tutoring sessions using "Reflecting on Writing" essay	Responding to Student Writing • Lead mentor match-up and getting to know you activity • Continue working on "Mentoring Prospectus"/tutor

Class 8	Tutor Training Goals • Committees meet for goal setting and have time to work • College Essay Tutor Training • Tutoring Practice - round 2 • Finish "Reflecting on Writing" essay	Tutor Training Goals • College Essay Tutor Training • Committee Work HW: Finalize presentations and be prepared to share on Wednesday/Thursday for DBQ Tutor Training
Class 9	Tutor Training • Tutoring DBQs • Turn in final copy of "Reflecting on Writing" essay • Resume Overview	Presenting on Research • Share presentations for CAPTA Conference • Deliver Tutoring DBQs presentation
Class 10	Tutor Training • Watch/participate in role play • Tutor Hats • Committee work	Mastering the Craft of Tutoring • Lead role play • Reflection on Tutor Hats • Committee work

Virtual Writing Lab Training and Protocols

As not all schools will have classes in which to train tutors, the following resource outlines and describes the methodology one school uses with their virtual writing center, serving multiple sites. It details the collaborative structures used to train tutors and to prepare feedback as well as some specifics on collaborative structures for the actual virtual conferencing.

Collaborative Writing Center Protocols at the Virtual Writing Lab (VWL)

Collaborative Training and Feedback Sessions
Each week, the Literacy Resource Teacher leads the VWL tutors in a collaborative session. Each tutor is given a copy of the submitted piece, and it is discussed in the group. Tutor groups range in size from 5 to 20 students. The Literacy Resource Teacher collects the students' comments on chart paper for later reference.

Creative Writing: The students use the following questions (adapted from Donald Murray) to frame their feedback:
1. What possibilities do you see for this work?
2. What question(s) do you have?
3. What is your favorite line or part and why?

Content Writing: The students utilize a sheet submitted by the tutee that lists what the assignment requirements are, what he/she feels positively about the writing, and what areas he/she would like help revising (i.e.: transitions, clarity, support, conclusion, etc.).

Positivity Structure: Each session uses a positive structure to prepare for the upcoming feedback session. One student tutor takes notes gathering all the feedback collected collaboratively. The form begins with positive feedback and ends with positive feedback. The constructive feedback is strategically placed in between these positive comments.

Collaborative Videoconferencing
After the collaborative face-to-face meeting has ended and all comments are captured in an easy to refer to format (see above), one student tutor is chosen to prepare for and engage in the videoconference feedback session with the tutee. Since the VWL engages in all collaborative structures, a "whisper tutor" is also assigned. A whisper tutor sits off-camera and helps to remind the primary tutor of any points he/she may be forgetting or jumps in if the main tutor is struggling.

Collaborative Letter Writing
Sometimes the tutee prefers a feedback letter instead of a videoconference. If this is the case, a team of tutors uses the collected feedback on the form to write a comprehensive letter. The letter is sent to the tutee and a request to resubmit the revised paper is always added.

Tutor Cheat Sheets

The 7 Priorities of Tutoring

Students come to the writing center with varying abilities, and it can be rather overwhelming where to even begin. Tutors should keep these priorities in mind when working with clients. This list will help tutors avoid getting bogged down in fixing grammatical errors.

I. APPROPRIATENESS
- Does it meet assignment specifications? Does it have the necessary parts? Does it do everything that's asked?

II. FOCUS
- Does it have a central idea? Is the idea expressed, worthy of discussion, and limited enough to be discussed thoroughly?

III. ORGANIZATION
- Is each paragraph connected to the thesis? Are paragraphs connected to each other logically? Does each paragraph deal with only one idea? Are the paragraphs unified?

IV. DEVELOPMENT
- Are claims and statements supported by sufficient examples, details, and illustrations? What do you want to know more about?

V. INTRODUCTION/CONCLUSION
- Do they accurately reflect the body of the paper? Does the conclusion provide a sense of closure? Is it more than a repetition of the introduction?

VI. SURFACE FEATURES
- Does the paper use proper punctuation, grammar, spelling, and documentation?

VII. DICTION & STYLE
- Do word choice, sentence structure, and tone enhance the purposes of the paper?

Tips from Experienced Tutors

Students often learn best from their peers, so providing novice tutors with tips from their experienced counterparts is very helpful. The advice serves as gentle reminders to help each session go as smoothly as possible. Give your returning tutors the chance to showcase their knowledge and to be leaders by having them create a list like this one.

Top Twenty Tutoring Tips from Experienced Tutors

1. Be friendly but professional
2. Ask open-ended questions (questions that lead to discussion – more than "yes"/ "no")
3. Set goals
4. Focus on higher order writing concerns (assignment / main idea / organization)
5. Meet the tutee's needs (listen to what the tutee feels is important)
6. *Do not* write paper for the tutee – guide ideas but don't come up with ideas for them
7. Don't criticize – respect feelings, writing, and ideas
8. Be patient
9. Always be engaged
10. Be comfortable and casual; it will make the tutee feel comfortable and casual too
11. Ask the tutee what he or she would like to focus on during the session
12. Read the paper aloud – first ask the tutees to read it aloud; if they don't, then you can
13. Don't write on their papers – they should write on their papers
14. Always smile and be welcoming; make them feel comfortable before starting the session
15. Know your MLA format rules (or know where to find the rules if you forget them)
16. Help them understand the assignment if they appear to have any questions or concerns about the basics of the assignment
17. Give constructive criticism; don't be too critical
18. Be conversational and approachable
19. If you tutor a "difficult tutee," be patient and continue to work through the session if possible
20. Show up to tutor

Sample Tutoring Questions

Novice tutors will want to keep this document nearby as they role play sessions and begin tutoring clients. Using the suggested questions can help guide a session that may be awkward or tense. These questions may also challenge the writer and tutor to think differently about an assignment.

Beginning:
- What would you like to accomplish during this time?
- When is your assignment due?
- In your own words, what is the assignment?
- Where are you in the writing process?
- What is the most troubling part of this paper?
- What is interesting to you about this topic?
- Why did you choose this argument?
- How did you want to set this up?
- Why did you organize it this way?
- What are you trying to say in this piece of writing?
- What needs improvement?

Throughout:
- Does your thesis answer the question?
- Tell me how you set up your argument.
- What are you trying to say?
- What is your main point in the paragraph?
- How does this relate to/support your thesis?
- How does this idea relate to something you said before?
- How do you think you can make this better?
- Do you think this is the best way to phrase this?
- What supporting idea do you have the most information on to support your thesis?
- Do you understand the structure here?
- Why did you choose this example?
- How?
- So what?
- How can you make this flow better?
- Do you feel you can change the structure/diction to make it clearer?
- Do you think your essay reflects your best efforts?
- Why did you use this specific language/diction/syntax/etc?

End:
- What I understand you're saying is _____, do I have it right?
- As someone reads this paper, what do you think they should have learned?
- Have you met the necessary requirements for this assignment?
- Is there any part of your paper now that you are not satisfied with?

Individual Activities for Training

Visualizing Steps of the Tutoring Process

Many centers ask tutors-in-training to read foundational texts such as Stephen North's article "The Idea of a Writing Center," Jeff Brook's "Minimalist Tutoring: Making the Student Do All the Work," and the first few chapters of *The Bedford Guide for Writing Tutors*. After reading these articles, one activity to solidify learning and to give tutors ownership is to ask them to create a graphic organizer to visually display the steps of the tutoring process. Students can make it linear or nonlinear. Consider asking students to color-code their work. The group can then vote on which graphic organizer best represents their process, and that piece is photocopied/laminated/enlarged for use during the year. Below is an example of the final product students created in one school.

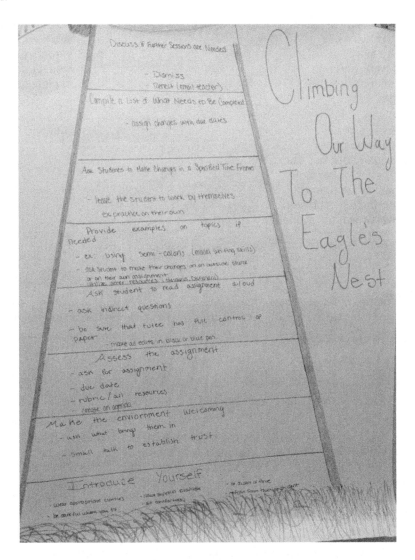

Fish Bowl and Tutor Checklist

The premise for this activity is that there is one tutoring session that the entire group of trainees observes and critiques. This could be done in several ways. The director may choose to participate in the role of client or tutor with another student acting in the other role. Or, returning tutors could play the two roles. While the mock tutoring session happens, as if in a fish bowl, the rest of the class observes, takes notes, provides feedback, and learns what to do and what not to do. Consider giving the students a checklist of "steps" or strategies to watch for, such as given here, especially if they are new to tutoring. Another way to use this checklist is to put tutors in groups of three: a tutor, a client, and an observer. The observer watches and checks off what the tutor is doing well. The observer can also make notes about what was weak if something on the checklist wasn't done well. Then the tutors switch roles. Afterward, they share their thoughts.

Tutoring Observation Checklist: *Put a check mark next to all the things that the tutor does correctly.*

1. Greets and Gathers Information
   a. Smiles and says hello _____
   b. Sits side-by-side _____
   c. Connects with writer _____
   d. Asks questions _____
   e. Don't judge _____

2. Coaches, Doesn't Correct
   a. Avoids writing on paper _____
   b. Student reads paper out loud _____
   c. Stops after each paragraph _____
   d. Sandwiches suggestions _____
   e. Focuses on the big problems _____
   f. Doesn't overwhelm the student _____

3. Says so Long and Gives Survey
   a. Gives 5 minute warning _____
   b. Summarizes suggestions _____
   c. Invites student back _____
   d. Completes survey _____

4. Thoughts and Comments:

Case Study Analysis

Building empathy and a connection with a client is sometimes a struggle for tutors because they often want to focus solely on the writing rather than the writer. Another training exercise is for the director to write some hypothetical clients with backstories and have tutors analyze why the client is struggling, what the client needs, and how best to help the person as well as the writing. You may choose to start this as a group activity and then ask students to do a case study on their own before comparing with other tutors.

Case Study A – Mary is a freshman who recently moved from Atlanta. She's had a difficult time making friends on account of her quiet manner. She's recently been assigned her first essay in English class. It's on the most important symbol in *Lord of the Flies*. She's read the book and taken ample notes. On Monday, she needs to have a draft prepared to peer workshop. In 8th grade, her English teacher put a lot of emphasis on a catchy hook, or first line, and she's having a difficult time getting started because she can't think of something unique to hook the reader. When she walks into the writing center, she's noticeably nervous. She's come to the WC for help getting started.

1. How do you go about making Mary feel comfortable in the writing center?
2. What are the major causes of Mary's inability to get started? How do you address those causes in the tutoring session?
3. After hearing about the assignment and Mary's problems getting started, you have thirty-minutes left before your next appointment. What are some reasonable goals you can set for the end of the session? What is your process for reaching those goals? What, if anything, do you suggest Mary do before Monday's peer workshop?

Asking Useful Questions

Consider the different types of open and closed questioning techniques explained below that tutors will need to utilize throughout a session. Introduce the trainees to these questioning methods. Once students understand the different ways questions are used, direct them to write 2-3 questions in each category and explain why that type of question would be used with a client.

Factual - These types of questions are used to gain the necessary information in order for a tutor to understand the writer, her rhetorical situation, and the circumstances for what brought her to the writing center. These types of questions are often closed.

Inquiry - When you ask a question about which you're genuinely curious, you respond as a reader. These types of questions may be used to gain more information about something related to the rhetorical situation or the writing itself. They may clarify something the writer said or wrote. These types of questions can be open or closed.

Divergent - Divergent questions are aimed at encouraging the writer to think more deeply about her writing. These types of questions often require writers to analyze, evaluate, or synthesize their own prior knowledge of the rhetorical situation or of the content, purpose, structure, or tone of the piece. Often these questions begin with "how" or "why." For the most part, divergent questions are open; however, in some cases, a simple, closed question may accomplish the same goals.

Instructive - During the course of a tutoring session, there will be times when you and the writer may need to make a decision—about the agenda, about what to do next, about what to do after the session. On occasion, you may need to tell the writer what to do; for the most part, it's best to offer these instructions in the form of a question as it puts the decision in the hands of the writer. These types of questions can be open or closed.

Sandwiching

As teachers, we often unconsciously give students positive feedback coupled with any criticism because we understand how much students need to hear compliments. Make sure tutors know they need to "sandwich" their constructive suggestions between positive feedback. This builds a stronger tutor-tutee rapport as long as the comments are genuine. Provide the students with some "sentence starters" for both positive and constructive comments. You can then ask trainees to write additional "sentence starters." You can also provide a sample piece of writing and ask them to sandwich their feedback for that pretend client.

- What an interesting/original topic!
- I can tell you've put a lot of work into this!
- This sentence/phrase/word/character/setting/example is very powerful/original.
- You might want to think about…
- I wonder if…
- I'm confused by…

Using Sample Texts

Nothing beats the power of repetition and practice. Tutors, especially new ones, may be tempted to focus on grammar. Spend time showing the trainees sample texts that are assigned in your school; ask your colleagues to send you both strong and weak copies of papers they receive, then change the names to protect the guilty and innocent. Consider fixing all grammatical errors so that the trainees can't fall back on those suggestions but are forced to think differently about the writing. Below are some sample handouts and examples to share as you train new tutors to focus on the writing rather than the proofreading.

Focus on the BIG Problems
- Did they do what the teacher assigned? Did they meet the requirements?
- Is there a thesis or main idea that is focused?
- Is there enough support, evidence, or detail? Is there unneeded information?
- Do you understand everything? Are there any confusing parts?
- Are their paragraph breaks at appropriate places?

Strong Example

*Individual **sports** were a very common pastime in the **Elizabethan Era**.* People used these sports as a source of entertainment when they were bored, and sports were even used as ways of relaxation. **Archery** was very popular in the Elizabethan Era, but it took loads of practice and patients. **Prizes** were given to the **most skilled shooters** in contests. Also, **bowling** was a very trendy activity. It was played often because it can be enjoyed throughout **all social classes.** It was played outside on **lanes** much like we have today called **bowling greens**. Furthermore, there were several versions such as "**Kayes**," which was played with **wooden pins and a wooden stick**, and "**loggets**," which was played by trying to knock down a pile of bones. Another sport that was frequently played was **tennis**. It was played differently throughout all the social classes. The **nobility** practiced on private courts made for the elite, the **commoners** played on public courts, and the **peasants** played in open fields in between villages. The ball was usually **stuffed with hair** and **hit with their bare hands**. *Individual sports played a large role in everyday Elizabethan life because they were played by all social classes, men, women, and children.*

*Starts with a topic sentence to introduce what the paragraph will discuss (italics)

*Gives specific examples of sports and details (bold/underlined)

*Meets the teacher's directions to research pastime activities in Shakespeare's time

* "Flows" by transitioning from one idea to the next (highlight)

*Ideas are in a logical order

*Ends with a sentence to summarize the paragraph (italics)

*No repeated info or off-topic info

Poor Example
(The assignment is to research diseases during the Elizabethan Era)

When getting The Black Death, the victim usually coughed up a bunch of blood, an immediate sign of being near death. Victims would also get flu-like symptoms such as, chills and a fever. Victims of the disease would not be able to move due to extremely weak limbs. When very close to death, large amounts of blood would gush from the nose. Also, the victims' lymph glands would swell severely. There wasn't much food available to the poor, so many people went hungry. If you were wealthy, this wasn't a problem. The worst part of the plague was Europe's population decrease. The Black Death killed countless people in Europe. The worst part was they ran out of graves so they floated bodies down rivers. They also dug large trenches and filled them with infected bodies. Non-infected plague survivors were not allowed near trenches.

Role Playing

This is a strategy recommended by several published resources, including the ones listed in the discussion. Here are some examples of "client" roles to assign so tutors-in-training can practice their responses to some "worst-case scenarios" (For more detailed role playing examples, refer to chapter 8).

- You only want help with grammar.
- Your assignment is due at the end of the period.
- Don't talk or give one-word answers.
- Keep asking if you will get an A.
- You don't want to talk about the paper but you want to gossip.
- You think you're smarter than your tutor.
- You just want the tutor to sign your paper so you can leave.

Read More Than You Write

One of the biggest temptations new writing tutors face is the desire to start fixing errors immediately just as they might do with their own writing. To overcome this temptation, tell tutors right from the start to read student essays without a pen or pencil in hand. We want tutors to focus primarily not on the local issues of spelling, punctuation, and grammar; but, instead, on the global issues of introduction, thesis, point of view, organization, transitions, and conclusion, among others. This particular article could easily be one of the first articles used in a training program or course. It was written by Jim LaBate.

Read More Than You Write

If you've ever looked through a magazine for writers, you may have noticed the classified pages in the back. There, various individuals and businesses offer to edit and/or proofread works by aspiring authors. Unfortunately, many students visit writing centers for that same type of writing assistance. However, the "assistance" that you provide as a writing tutor should not include editing or proofreading.

An editor or proofreader goes through a manuscript and corrects all errors in spelling, grammar, and punctuation. Naturally, struggling students would love for you to fix all the errors in their papers, so they can get better grades. In fact, some students would like to use the writing center as if it were a dry-cleaning operation: drop off the essay one day and pick it up all clean and ready to go to the teacher the next. And, as a novice tutor, you may be tempted to provide that type of service.

The temptation to grab a red pen and begin correcting errors is real because it's so easy and so appealing. If you attack a student's paper and start making changes, you immediately feel like you're helping, and you feel like an expert, a real professional. You can go through and mark words that are misspelled, you can point out the incorrect use of a homonym, you can show the lack of pronoun agreement, and you can even explain what a run-on sentence is and demonstrate how to fix it. Unfortunately, that type of correcting is like painting the side of the house when the foundation is cracking; the essay may look good but possess major flaws. So, instead of seeing yourself as a painter, try to imagine that you're a building inspector.

When you read a student's essay for the first time, just read it – with empty hands. Don't hold a pen or pencil because you may want to mark errors or make notes to yourself about problems in the essay. Even if the student encourages you to mark up the paper, don't give in. Simply say something like this: "I want to read the entire paper first, and, then, we can discuss it."

At that point, without a pen or pencil in hand, you can ignore all those minor errors and focus, instead, on the major components of the work. As you read, you should ask yourself the following questions (assuming the work is a standard essay):

- Does the essay have an interesting opening statement or introduction?
- Does the end of the first paragraph have a strong thesis, a thesis that indicates where the essay is headed?
- Does the essay have an organizational pattern, one that is strong, obvious, and unified?
- Does the essay offer support for the main points?
- Does the essay avoid errors in logic?
- Does the essay have a consistent point of view?
- Does the essay have transitions between paragraphs, transitions that move the reader smoothly through the essay?
- Does the essay have a strong conclusion, one that is both effective and memorable?

After you finish reading the essay, you may again be tempted to pick up a pen to write. You may want to circle sentences to be moved or deleted. You may want to mark spots where ideas are missing? Or you may want to write suggestions in the margin. Once again, however, you should resist that temptation. Instead, you should begin reading the essay a second time to, first, clarify your own thoughts, and, then, start asking questions:

- What are you trying to do in this introduction?
- Where's your thesis?
- Where's your support for this point?

In addition to asking questions, you may want to read a troublesome sentence or section aloud or, better yet, have the student read aloud. Often, the verbal reading makes it obvious that a word or phrase is missing or just doesn't sound right. While this conversation is going on, encourage the student to write notes about what needs to be done to make the essay stronger. When the student is writing, he or she is doing the actual work and is much more likely to remember what needs to be done when it's time to revise. If, however, you do the writing, the students may not quite understand what you've written or remember what you meant by a particular comment.

Can you resist the temptation to edit and proofread student essays? Of course you can. Sure, you may disappoint a few students at first when you explain that we don't edit or proofread entire essays; over the course of the semester, however, you'll find that helping students become stronger writers is so much more rewarding than editing or proofreading their essays for them.

Reviewing Tutoring Logs

It is essential to guide tutors through how to thoughtfully reflect on a session. By providing guiding questions, tutors must think more deeply about not only their experience but the tutees'. Tutors submit a complete list of their tutoring sessions and select two sessions upon which to reflect. The elements of the reflection here are Attitude, Work, Strategies, Impact.

Date: 1-2-14	Starting time: 8:15	Duration: 20 minutes
Client name: Pat Riot	Course: English 10	Teacher: Graham R. Nerd

Summary & Reflection:
  This was Pat's first visit to the writing center. He was required to bring in his 2 page analysis of the Bay of Pigs Invasion and it seemed like he didn't really want to be here. The essay was due later that day, so I didn't feel like I had much time to chat with him, but maybe I should have gotten to know him a little better. He had completed the essay, but some of the events were out of order and he hadn't provided much detail. I helped him to sketch a timeline of events and talked to him about supporting each claim with evidence. He wasn't too cooperative, and it was difficult not to just tell him how I would do it. By the end of the session, he seemed a little more confident and enthusiastic.

What to address in your summary & reflection:
- What did you notice about the student's *attitude*?
- What did the student *work* on?
- What tutoring *strategies* did you use? Were they effective? What might you change if you could?
- What *impact* did the session make on the assignment and/or the student's attitude?

What you would write on a receipt of this session:
Pat had a completed draft, so we worked on reorganizing his paragraphs in chronological order as well as adding more supporting evidence.

Sample logs -- What are they missing? (Attitude, Work, Strategies, Impact)

#1. Jane and I worked on her theater critique. It had to be 3 pages long but she didn't know what to write after the first two. When she came in, she was really frustrated, but by the end the paper was 3 pages and she was relieved!

What's missing? _____

#2. Boris was new to the writing center and was really nervous at first. He was also still learning English, so I think he was self-conscious about that. I spent some time getting to know him; we bonded over our mutual interest in soccer. I then helped him to organize his ideas into a web. He seemed a lot more confident when he left, and he scheduled a follow-up session for later in the week.

What's missing? _____

#3. I knew Ana from Key Club, so I was happy I got to work with her. She had written most of her lab report, but wanted someone to look it over. I noticed that she used "I" and "we" several times; when I pointed it out once, she caught the other examples as she read aloud. We also fixed a few minor grammar errors.

What's missing? _____

#4. Keena and Trey didn't have much time because they wanted to see another teacher before the end of CHAT. They hadn't begun writing their script for the commercial yet, so I showed them how to set up a storyboard. Then they bounced ideas off of each other; it didn't seem like they needed much input from me, so I mostly sat back and only spoke up when they asked me a question or were having trouble compromising. Is that okay? They didn't finish until right before the bell, but they did leave with a complete outline.

What's missing? _____

#5. Unfortunately, Gill was not excited about working in the writing center. He was required to come and his biography project on Abraham Lincoln was due later that day. I commiserate with him, since I had to write that paper last year. Then I suggested we read back through it and pretend to grade it like we were the teacher, using the rubric. It went okay, but I wish he had come in sooner.

What's missing? _____

Writing Assignments

Sample 1: Reflecting on Writing

This writing task, taken from *The Bedford Guide for Writing Tutors,* encourages students to reflect on their own writing journey. It provides an opportunity for first year tutors to think about what writing experiences have shaped them into who they are today and how writing can evoke a variety of emotions in a writer. Beginning the year with personal writing is an excellent way to instill a sense of community in your center because your tutors will use these pieces to learn the tutoring process.

PROMPT: Choose one of the following two topics to develop into a personal essay. (Further descriptions and prompting questions for these topics can be found on *The Bedford Guide for Writing Tutors* page numbers listed below.) Your final product should be 2-3 pages of size 12 Times New Roman font.
- How I Write (pages 14-15)
- Writing Autobiography (page 15)

We will use this essay to accomplish the following:
1. Reflect on our own writing processes and writing histories
2. Practice personal essay-writing (very useful for college application essays, improving voice)
3. Experience tutoring for the first time as both a tutor and a tutee
4. Reflect on the experience of tutoring and being tutored

During the next few classes, you will meet with a fellow tutor to conference about your paper. Each partner will have a chance to be the tutor as well as the tutee. For your tutoring session, bring any work you have done on the paper, including free-writes, outlines, drafts, etc. Please have at least a rough draft written by your first conference so that you can experience the tutoring session with a draft in hand. On the final due-date, you will pass in your final draft and a free-write about the tutoring experience.

Sample 2: My History with Writing

As part of tutor training, tutors can reflect on any vivid memories they have- positive or negative- surrounding writing. Then, they choose one moment to examine in detail. This exercise has many purposes: it helps tutors to examine their relationship with writing, it helps them to consider the experiences their peers have had with writing, it becomes incorporated into practice tutoring, and it serves as a community builder when tutors all share their narratives with the class.

Personal Narrative
Consider your Writer's Timeline. You probably had a high point in your writing experience and a low point. These moments stand out to you because they impacted you in some meaningful way – good or bad. Pick one of these moments to explore and reflect on it more fully.

Narratives tell a story, usually to some point, to illustrate some truth or insight. Craft a narrative about a writing experience, and make sure to connect it to some insight or truth you learned about the writing process and who you are as a writer.

Make sure your narrative has a beginning, a middle, and an end. There should be some clear background/exposition, rising action, climax, falling action, and an ending.

Ongoing Professional Development

Journaling

Most training happens when tutors are first hired and at the beginning of each academic year. However, as tutors begin to work, it is vital that the director continue the training so as to avoid bad habits and to address new issues tutors face. Consider having students keep a journal or log of their sessions in which they document what went well and what was a problem. Once a month, a grading period, or however frequently you can, have a roundtable discussion of "problem solving." Have students bring up situations that didn't go as they envisioned and discuss possible ways to approach similar situations in the future. Establish a safe environment of no judgment so tutors feel comfortable asking each other for help. If students are shy, you can have everyone write down a situation and submit it anonymously as a situation to discuss.

- What if I can tell they plagiarized?
- What if they are just coming for bonus and only have one question?
- What if they have problems with MLA but I don't want to seem nitpicky?
- What if everything is wrong and they haven't done what the teacher wanted? How do I tell them they need to start over?

Tutor Observation Reflection

One of the main ongoing training components of the writing center is tutor-to-tutor observations. The purpose is for tutors to get peer feedback from other tutors and for tutors to critically examine and learn from their peers' approaches to tutoring. The observing tutor needs to situation him/herself in a non-intrusive place where the client will not be uncomfortable, but where the observer can still see and hear how the session progresses. Depending on your situation, you may be able to have students do this once a month or quarter. Consider requiring that they always choose a different tutor to observe so that they learn new techniques. Tutors can then have a follow-up conversation about the session observed. (To use tutor observations as data, refer to chapter 6.)

Your Name: Assignment:
Tutor Observed: Date:
Tutee:

yes or no	
	Have you observed this person before? If yes, go find someone new!
	Did the tutor make an effective introduction?
	Did the tutor seem interested in the conference?
	Did the tutor do a good job of putting the student at ease?
	Did the tutor ask appropriate questions?
	Did the tutor check for understanding at the end of the session?

1. What were some good questions the tutor asked? (Give a few examples below!)

   -
   -
   -

2. How did the tutor engage the tutee in answering questions and being a part of the conversation?

3. What strategies did the tutor use to improve the tutee as a writer? (Instead of just the writing itself).

4. How effectively did the tutor manage time? What strategies did you notice about time management and transitions in the session?

5. What were some strengths of the tutor's tutoring?

6. What were some weaknesses of the tutor's tutoring?

7. What approaches or strategies did you observe that you can incorporate into your own tutoring?

8. Before your discussion with the tutor you observed, review the notes you made in the observation. Was there anything they did that you were curious about and/or did you have any suggestions for improvement?

9. After you have a discussion with the tutor you observed, write down some of the tutor's thoughts on his or her strengths and weaknesses you observed.

Observation Outline

This task provides another opportunity for tutors to learn from their peers through observation. This is extremely helpful for novice tutors to complete once per quarter as it challenges them to continually evaluate the tutoring strategies of their peers and themselves.

Reminders
- Have the mindset of a scientist making field notes. Observe as much as you can.
- It's fine to write in the first person voice. (I/me)
- Be sure to include both the tutor's name and the client's name.
- Your observation should be 450-525 words.

Contents of your reflection
- Identify the characteristics of the session:
    - Date & Time
    - Full names of tutor and client
        - If you don't catch the client's name, ask the tutor or me later.
    - Type of assignment
    - Phase - what has been done so far, what needs to be done today
- Setting up the session
    - What does the tutor do to connect with the client?
    - Describe the client's initial attitude.
    - What does the tutor do to learn about the assignment?
    - How do they set the agenda for the session?
- Tutoring: *This should be the most detailed/lengthy portion of your reflection. I strongly suggest you use dialogue (quotes) to provide examples of what you're observing.*
    - Which strategies do you observe the tutor using -- both for attitude and the work?
    - How does the tutor keep the client involved in the session and ensure that the decisions and the majority of the workload are remaining with the client?
    - What difficulties or areas of confusion is the client having? What understandings does the client reach as a result of the tutoring?
    - Do you see anything you might have done differently?
    - How does the tutor manage the session? When does the tutor seem most and least confident/effective?
- Closing the session
    - How does the tutor wrap up the session?
    - How do you perceive the impact on the client and/or assignment?
- Takeaways
  You are writing in a more reflective mode here. This is an <u>essential</u> part of your observation. Use these questions as guidance; you don't necessarily have to answer them all.
    - What were the best parts of the session?
    - What did you learn from observing this tutor?
    - What strategies might you try in the future?
    - If the tutor's style/strategies were very similar to your own, you can also write about that.

Self-Evaluation

Many of the resources in this section for ongoing training focus on reflection because students need time set aside to examine what is working and what is not if they are to grow. Determine a span of time - once a month, once a quarter - for students to review their tutor logs/portfolios/journals, any observations they wrote about their peers, the evaluations the tutees left them, and their other contribution to the writing center. Then, ask them to complete a self-evaluation.

At the end of each quarter, you should evaluate your contribution to the WC as well as your growth as a tutor. Using the information in your tutoring portfolios and the feedback on your tutees' evaluations, please answer these questions honestly and introspectively.

1. What is your biggest area of growth/awareness this semester AS A TUTOR?

2. What is your biggest area of growth/awareness this semester AS A WRITER?

3. In what area(s) would you like further training on TUTORING or WRITING?

4. TASK: Write a discussion board post prompt that addresses your area of weakness or interest in further training. These prompts will be the basis of our weekly online discussions next quarter, so think about what would be worthwhile hearing from your fellow tutors and/or doing research on!

5. How have you gone "above and beyond" to contribute to the writing center community?

6. Set 2-3 tutoring/writing goals for next quarter.

7. Considering all aspects of your tutee and self-evaluations, how would you rate your overall contribution to the WC and your fulfillment of your tutoring commitments? Justify your choice below.
    Exceptional   Very Good   Good   Fair   Poor

Director Observation Form

It's very important that you as a director have a grasp on your tutors' effectiveness. You can monitor your tutors' progress through observations and a form like this one. If possible, observe each tutor at least once per quarter. This observation form allows directors and tutors to conference with one another about tutoring best practices and encourages tutors to adopt a growth mindset and be reflective in their tutoring. (See chapter 6 for ideas about using these types of observation forms as data.)

Tutor Name: Assignment:
Tutee: Date:

Beginning the Session

Observed?	Best Practice	Glows	Grows
	The tutor introduces themselves to the tutee and asks the tutee their name.		
	The tutor creates a welcoming space for the tutee with positive, warm body language.		
	The tutor asks the tutee about their writing.		
	The tutor asks the tutee about their goals for the session.		

Session Content

Observed?	Best Practice	Glows	Grows
	The tutor focuses on the tutee's goals and higher order concerns throughout the session.		
	The tutor asks the tutee to read their writing aloud.		
	The tutor asks open-ended questions to help guide the tutee toward making strong decisions in their writing.		
	The tutor is positive, professional, focused, and supportive throughout the session.		
	If a challenging moment presents itself, the tutor handles it positively and professionally.		
	The tutor gives the tutee sound advice.		

Ending the Session

Observed?	Best Practice	Glows	Grows
	The tutor reviews the topics discussed during the session with the tutee.		
	The tutor checks to make sure that the tutee's concerns were addressed during the session.		
	The tutor asks the tutee to complete the post-conference evaluation.		
	The tutor thanks the tutee for their time, encourages them to return again, and offers the tutee a piece of candy.		

Giving Tutors Choice

If you have returning tutors for two or three years, you may find that keeping them motivated and providing opportunities for growth becomes more difficult. This tutor training document requires tutors to complete certain tasks (bold), and then to choose four additional tasks that they highlight and submit as part of a graded course.

DIRECTIONS:
In addition to the five tasks bolded below, you must choose an additional four tasks to complete by the end of year. Ideally, you will choose one task from each column; however, you may choose whatever combination appeals to you. Two of your chosen tasks must be completed by mid-quarter, and the remaining two must be completed by the end of the quarter. Highlight the tasks you intend to complete and submit your form by [date]. Once you have submitted the form, you are expected to complete the tasks you have chosen.

Tutor Training/Development	Tutor Leadership	Student + Staff Outreach	Writing
Implement your SSWCA/Legacy Project*	Plan and host a WC Workshop**	Plan and host a WC Workshop**	**Submit all drafts for required assignments on time***
Ensure on a weekly basis that Tutoring Logs are accurate and up-to-date.* Submit Self-Evaluation and Reflection at the end of the quarter.	Assist during a WC Workshop (Sign-up required during the first week of the quarter)	Meet with a teacher to discuss how they might use the WC during Q4	**Ensure that you have written at least two free-writes per week***
Read and review a scholarly article from *WLN, Writing Center Journal, Praxis,* or *The Peer Review*	Fulfill your Leadership Duties (Twitter person, Desk person, Statistics Person, + Paper Person Only)	Promote the WC by presenting at a Curriculum Team, Department, or Faculty Meeting	**Perform your Spoken Word piece in class***
Submit a post or create a podcast about a tutoring best practice to be posted on the WC blog/website	Build/maintain the WC Website	Secure an incentive or lead a WC fundraiser as part of our Incentives Program	Lead a Friday mini-lesson on a writing strategy or technique
Write and submit a tutor column or blog post to *WLN Journal****	Lead a mini-lesson (10-15 minutes) on a tutoring strategy	Emcee the Library's Poetry Cafe	Submit two or more pieces to the *Literary Magazine*

*Required for all tutors
**Workshops count twice: once in the Tutor Leadership Category and once in the Student + Staff Outreach category. You must receive approval to plan and host a workshop from WC Director during the first week of the quarter.
***Submitting a tutor column or blog post to *WLN* counts for two blocks.

Tutor Mentoring Prospectus

To build community within the center, you can create a mentor/mentee program, which pairs new and experienced tutors into "families". This paper provides second-year tutors with the opportunity to reflect on their own tutoring practices and share their advice with new tutors.

Remember back to when you were a new tutor: What questions/concerns did you have? What do you wish you could have known? What kind of lessons do you have to learn just by making mistakes and which ones could you have avoided altogether?

Now think about your new role as a mentor tutor. Consider the kind of relationship you want to have with your mentee – how is mentoring like tutoring? How is it different? What kind of feedback can you give that will be the most helpful? What do you hope to know from your mentee? How can a tutor measure his/her success? How can a mentor tutor measure his/her success?

Consider the types of things your mentee will want to know: Logistics of the WC? Adopting the persona of a tutor? Mechanics of writing assignments for Advanced Comp? Navigating the multiple expectations that teachers, students, fellow tutors, and your director have of a WC tutor? How to get the most out of your experience?

Your assignment:
In approximately 2 typed pages, write about what you think it means to be a mentor tutor. As you brainstorm, you might review your tutoring logs, comparing the older ones to your more recent one, read your quarter self-evaluations, and consider some of the best and worst tutoring sessions you had. It might be helpful to talk with other mentor tutors to see what ideas they have about how to make this role a successful one.
The genre of this assignment is up to you. Some ideas:
- Letter to yourself or to your mentee
- Job description (as if you were going to hire a tutor mentor. What are the expectations?)
- Comic strip
- Straightforward how-to guide
- Reflective essay
- Other: _____

*Your choice of how to approach this assignment will reflect the kinds of things you have thought about and want to say. Remember, FORM FITS FUNCTION!

Senior Tutor Legacy Project

Having senior tutors complete legacy projects helps grow the resources of your center. Ask senior tutors to identify a challenge that they want to address or an area of strength in the center that they want to make more sustainable. They then propose a "Legacy Project," which they must implement and present by the end of the school year. This document includes suggested dates/pacing to help guide students through the proposal writing process.

Final Project: Legacy Project Proposal and Presentation

Your contributions in the WC have shaped you and us and our school. This is already a significant gift. But hey, we want more! To ensure that a piece of your time in the writing center is truly left behind, you will work independently or in a pair or a group to create a sustainable program or tool that you leave for future WC students. As you plan your project, please consider the purpose of your project and your intended audience. In the 4th Quarter, you will begin the implementation of your Legacy Project as part of your Final Exam.

We'd like you to use SSWCA's Call for Proposals (CFP) as a guide for helping you plan your lesson or program. Please review the attached CFP from the Secondary School Writing Centers Association. You are welcome to work in groups or as an individual. WC directors are available to conference with you throughout this process.

Please adhere to the following deadlines to ensure that your proposal will be ready to submit on time! Each draft of your proposal must be tutored and must include evidence of revision.

Components
1. Genre Study of Successful SSWCA Proposals
2. Brainstorming, Conference with WC Director and Topic Selection
3. Rough Draft #1 (Must be tutored)
4. Rough Draft #2 (Must be tutored)
5. Final Proposal (Must be tutored and must show evidence of revision)
6. Proposals due to SSWCA

References

Brooks, J. (1991). Minimalist tutoring: Making the student do all the work. *The Writing Lab Newsletter, 15* (6), 1-4.

Fels, D., & Wells, J. (2011). *The successful high school writing center: Building the best program with your students.* New York, NY: Teachers College Press.

Kent, R. (2017). *A guide to creating student-staffed writing centers grades 6-12* (2nd ed.). New York, NY: Peter Lang.

LaBate, J. (n.d.). *Read more than you write.* Unpublished manuscript.

Murray, D. M. (2005). *Write to learn* (8th ed.). Boston, MA: Thomson/Wadsworth.

North, S. (1984). The idea of a writing center. *College English, 46*(5), 433-446. Retrieved from http://www.jstor.org/stable/377047

Ryan, L., & Zimmerelli, L. (2016). *The Bedford guide for writing tutors* (6th ed.). Boston, MA: Bedford/St. Martin's.

Chapter 5
Outreach and Promotion
By Renee Brown and Stacey Waldrup

Guiding Questions

- What is a process that is simple, effective, and enticing to encourage the most students in the school to use the writing center?
- What is a process that is simple, effective, and enticing to help teachers understand the way the writing center works?
- What role can/do student tutors play in promoting the center?
- What content needs to be shared with faculty and clients to best promote the center, and what is the best media to use?

Resources

- Logo and Slogan
- Staff Outreach Guide
- Student Outreach Guide
- Bookmarks
- Classroom Presentations
- Videos
- Posters
- Promotional Contests
- Blog Posts and Website
- Social Media
- Community Outreach

Resource Contributors

- Kyle Boswell, Lakeshore Writing Center at Lakeshore High School, MI
- Renee Brown, PTMS Writing Lab at Peters Township Middle School, PA
- Trisha Callihan, Eagle Writing Center at Osbourn High School, VA
- Alison Hughes, Wildcat Writing Center at Centreville High School, VA
- Kate Hutton, Herndon Writing Center at Herndon High School, VA
- Amber Jensen, George Mason University, VA; formerly of Edison Writing Center at Edison High School, VA
- Stacey Waldrup, Raider Writing Center at Crescent Valley High School, OR

Discussion

It's a fear we all have as writing center directors: I sold the idea of a writing center to my administration; I diligently sorted applications and interviewed candidates to find the best tutors; I spent weeks or even months building and implementing a curriculum to train those tutors in writing center theory and practice. But, when the doors open after such long anticipation, silence; no one comes to the center. Despite all our best efforts to construct a solid program, a writing center cannot be a success without clients, and how to attract those clients is yet another mountain the director must plan for and surmount. We need techniques to sell the writing center not only to students, but also to the faculty and even beyond the walls of the school into the community.

Important points to consider as you develop a promotional strategy: Who is the target audience? What are the best ways to reach that audience? What content should you share with that audience? And, what I would argue is the best place to start your strategizing, who is going to create these visible tools that will attract clients to your center? (Note: While outreach and promotion could be used interchangeably, I am using "promotions" to refer to what attracts student-clients while "outreach" is reserved for strategies to connect with other allies, such as the teaching staff or university partners as discussed in chapter 9.)

Who Are the Creators

I'd like to begin with the assertion that while directors are often experts in writing center work, many of us are no longer experts at being teenagers. The types of promotions teens notice seem to change yearly, but luckily, we work among students who are experts in this field. I teach in a middle school where I quickly realized that what I perceived as strong promotion of our center was ignored by the larger student body. It wasn't until I put the power of creation into the hands of my thirteen-year-old tutors that I began to see the result I desired: more students wanting to come to the writing center (See chapter 8 for more information specific to middle school centers). What works best for me in a middle school may not be ideal in other schools, however. The promotional needs of your center are highly dependent on your situation and client base.

If the writing center in question is student-staffed, it is necessary to consider how much voice those tutors have (a theme reiterated throughout this publication as a founding principle for writing center creation). Are you helping the tutors to channel their voices towards the promotional goals you are setting for the center? Some of the artifacts in this chapter were created by student-tutors, who are at times more innovative, willing to take bigger risks, and know their audience better than the adults around them. As directors, we can harness their enthusiasm and creativity as we create a strategy to attract visitors.

Audience and Medium

The primary audience for promotion is of course potential clients: the student-body. Tutors often connect best with their peer group and can create effective products to advertise the center. It's necessary to acknowledge several tried and true resources as first steps. Posters, flyers, t-shirts, and PSAs are often relatively easy to create, potentially reach a wide audience, and open a conversation in the center about what type of information to promote. When I asked my tutors to make promotional signs - and resisted the urge to add my input - they created hilarious and effective memes rather than simple informational posters. I like to think the humor, written by students, speaks more strongly to clients, who are consequently more likely to remember our center. A similar approach can be taken to school-wide announcements on the TV or intercom. At our school, the tutors told me, "No one listens to the announcements," so they decided to go into the study halls and speak directly to their clientele as a way to explain what the writing center is and the logistics of how it works. Doing this also created a space to "talk-back" to the tutors and ask questions, which can't be done through traditional school-wide announcements. If sending tutors into classrooms is not an option, classroom plugs by the director, the classroom teacher, or tutor-created video may be another way to spread the word to the student-body. (Note: As the director, you should always preview and vet everything your students create to make sure that materials reflect positively on your center.)

Thinking beyond those conventional approaches, writing centers are designing websites, blogs, social media accounts, and other technological ways to expand their reach. I initially resisted these digital platforms until I had an eighth-grade student ask if he could build our center a website, and the result was stunning. There are user-friendly templates available for almost every medium. Those digital forums are often an ideal space for writing center promotional contests; for example, the first 25 students to share an original acrostic poem/haiku/etc. and tag the writing center will receive candy when they next stop into the writing center. Social media is also ideal to begin outreach into the wider community, especially if there are school-wide accounts you can link with. (We also invite you to follow the SSWCA accounts to connect your tutors with other secondary centers around the country.)

It is vital to remember that there is another audience to whom directors must speak: the faculty. Having a staff that supports the writing center is a key factor in the success achieved in many schools, my own included. When your colleagues understand your mission (See chapter 2) and what occurs during a tutoring session (See chapter 4), they are more likely to encourage their students to use the center properly. Without reaching out to the faculty, you will find several extremes, such as teachers who send students to the writing center just for proofreading, and teachers who tell students not to go to the writing center because it is plagiarism. Continuing this outreach to your colleagues throughout the year helps to ensure that there's a common understanding of what the writing center is and how it functions. It's easy for teachers not engrossed in writing center work to forget the tutors are not a grammar service, and when the adults misunderstand the work you are doing, so will the clients.

A point to consider is the way your colleagues intend to "reward" students who visit the center. While some teachers may want to offer a bonus or an extension to students who work with a tutor, you as the director will have to balance those rewards with your mission. To what extent is improved writing and natural grade improvement its own reward? Since each school will have different policies and beliefs about this topic, it is something you will want to plan to discuss as you introduce or grow your center with staff outreach.

Consider how you or your tutors will disseminate information about the center to the school faculty: emails, flyers to hang in their rooms, lunchroom conversations, staff meeting presentations/announcements. Declaring "the writing center is open," will never be an effective way to help other teachers understand what work you and the tutors are doing, and what work you are not doing. In my case, I spoke to the administration about allotting time during a faculty meeting so that I could more fully and clearly explain how tutors were chosen and trained (See chapters 3 and 4), as well as what work I expected the tutors to do and not to do. When the high school in my district opened a writing center about four years later, the tutors were the ones who spoke to the entire high school staff during a faculty meeting to share similar information. Hearing students speak well about their work has a powerful impact, and I believe this contributed to teachers in that building supporting the center.

Content

What information needs to be shared in order to promote the writing center? Aside from essential information (e.g. how to schedule a session, location, times open, what to expect from the tutor, etc.), there's a rather large myth that is more than difficult to dispel. Regardless of age of the student - middle school, high school, or college - far too often there is a stigma attached to going to the writing center: only the struggling kids go there. Or, perhaps your school will have the opposite dilemma: the myth that the writing center is only for honors students. If examining client data (See chapter 6) isn't part of your current process, it should be, in part because it reveals how effective your promotional strategies are. Once you know the student-body's mindset, you can work to change or reinforce it. If there were a potion we could concoct to eliminate the mindset that the writing center is only "for" certain students, every director in the world would buy it in bulk. Sadly, however, overcoming this myth requires continuous labor on the director's part.

A good place to start is to examine what the promotions for your center imply as well as what they literally "say." What are teachers telling their classes about the writing center: Are they saying it is only for final edits, or do they understand it is a conversation and part of a process of revision? Are teachers requiring a visit to the center only after a poor grade? In what classes are the teachers encouraging writing center attendance: freshmen, ESL, honors, and AP? Are social media accounts speaking to students enrolled in the most rigorous classes? Are tutors advertising college essay help? Consider the physical advertisements as well. If your posters say, "Tired of getting a C," who is the real audience and how does this reflect the mission of your center? Attracting a handful of high achieving students in a visible way may lessen the fear in other potential clients that someone will think they are a "bad writer" if they sign up to see a tutor. At the same time, promoting a welcoming, judgment-free environment allows all learners to feel the center will benefit their work.

Having a clear mission to help all students in the school is easy to write but difficult to achieve without closely examining the center's outreach and promotional activities.

Word-of-Mouth

A final point to consider is that we should never underestimate the power of a positive experience with a tutor; the clients also promote your center. When students use the writing center and leave feeling it was time well-spent, they often tell their friends. Hearing positive feedback from a trusted classmate helps other students to feel more comfortable visiting the center. This is another time to utilize social media; encourage clients to post and tweet, tagging the center, after a productive session. It's worth pursuing any medium that spreads the message that your center is a welcoming space for all students to talk about their writing.

Similarly, when a student reports back to her teacher or guidance counselor that the tutor at the writing center really helped her writing for class or for the college essay, it has an impact. That teacher or counselor is more likely to recommend the center to other students after hearing such a testimonial.

While it's not a quick solution, clearly, word-of-mouth is one of the most powerful outreach and promotional tools. To harness it, we must let the tutors' work speak for itself. If you have the backing of the administration (See chapter 2), have hired quality tutors (See chapter 3), and have a solid curriculum in place (See chapter 4), trust in that framework to be a part of the promotional strategy you develop in addition to using the artifacts compiled here.

Resources

Logo

Logos are a great way to promote your center and give a visual component to all advertisements and documents - not to mention artwork for t-shirts! Use your tutors' creativity and design skills or run a school-wide contest. Choose the logo that best represents your center - whether that means including the school name, writing images, mascots, slogans, etc. - and revise as your center grows.

Slogan

Along with logos, slogans are a quick reminder of your center. Just like famous slogans that always seem to be stuck in our heads, your center's slogan can be a catchy phrase to remind students and staff of their connection to the center. You might go with a more serious or a more punny tone. Also consider the emotional resonance of your slogan: How does it make people feel when they read it? Have a brainstorming meeting with your tutors and see what they come up with!

- It's the "write" place to be.
- Do the "write" thing.
- "Write" this way.
- Get "centered."

A Resource Toolkit to Sustain Secondary School Writing Centers

Staff Outreach Guide

Student word-of-mouth is key but so is staff understanding. Even if you are lucky enough to be able to present to your entire staff, staff outreach guides are perfect for succinctly communicating what the writing center is, how it can help them and their students, how they can use it, hours of operation, and contact information for the director(s). To maximize teacher usage, email as well as print these on non-white paper and you'll often see them in classrooms throughout the school. This guide can also be shared with parents at a back-to-school night. The following artifacts provide two different examples of how to highlight your information.

Sample 1

How to Use the WC: A Guide for Teachers

What Is the Writing Center (WC)?
- The WC is a student-run, teacher-directed space where students across all content areas can get feedback on their writing.
- When students visit the WC, they spend 20-30 minutes discussing their writing and revising their ideas with a friendly highly-qualified peer tutor.
- Our tutors focus on how effectively and how clearly a writer communicates their ideas.
- We are NOT an editing service. A common misconception is that "revising" and "editing" are synonyms.
    - "Revising" means helping writers to "re-see" their ideas in a new way.
    - "Editing" means correcting grammar, punctuation, and sentence structure.

How Can Teachers Use the Writing Center?
- If your students are composing something for class (an essay, a lab report, a DBQ, a review, a reflection, a brief paragraph, a website, a resume, etc.- literally anything!), our tutors are here to provide feedback on how writers communicate their ideas.
- If you would like students to work with a tutor, email your assignment to [director name and email]. We will brief our tutors on your assignment and ask you any clarifying questions.
- Make a visit to the writing center an official part of your writing assignment. We've found that students are more likely to work with a tutor when a teacher recommends that they do so.
- We recommend identifying learning targets for the writing assignment somewhere in the directions so that your students and our tutors can provide quality, targeted feedback based on your goals for the assignment.
- Please share your rubric with us. If you'd like help developing a rubric or if you'd like to see sample rubrics, we're happy to work with you.
- Consider making a tutoring session part of the re-take policy for your written summative assessments.
- If you'd like to discuss anything writing-related, reach out to [director].

How Can Students Use the Writing Center?
- The WC is open [days/times].
- Sign up to work with one of our tutors on our sign-up sheets outside of room [#].
- Tutors are happy to help students in any stage of the writing process, whether they are brainstorming, organizing their ideas, writing an assertion or thesis statement, or refining their drafts.

Why Should I Encourage Students to Visit the Writing Center?
- The WC challenges the traditional notion that adults are the only experts in the building.
- We engage students with writing as a process by providing a space for them to discuss their ideas and by encouraging students to take ownership of their writing.
- Our tutors act as an authentic audience for your students' writing.
- We make the writing process visible.
- We support literacy across content areas.

Sample 2

Ways the Writing Center Can Support You
1. PROVIDE WRITING ASSISTANCE to your students. No matter the assignment, we can help with any stage of development, from brainstorming to polishing.
    a. One-on-one sessions: You are welcome to send a student down to the center any time during the day and can always call or email for confirmation of availability or student arrival.
    b. Online Writing Center: Students are able to submit papers to [name of website] and receive digital written feedback.

2. PROVIDE CLASSROOM ASSISTANCE. Any time you'd like help with writing in your classroom, send an email. Our tutors are available for modeling writing/assignments, circling and providing feedback to students, conferencing with students, working with groups, giving workshops, or anything that helps students receive guidance. Just email [director] to reserve the tutors!

3. PROVIDE PLANNING ASSISTANCE. We're also here to help you with planning writing. Stop by the WC or email [director] to have a conversation about what you want students to do and how to get students there. [Director] is happy to help you increase writing across the school!

4. PROVIDE TEACHER WRITING FEEDBACK. You are also welcome to use the center for any of your own writing: recommendation/college letters, grant applications, rubrics, assessment guidelines, model papers, etc.

5. PROVIDE AN ONLINE RESOURCE. If students cannot access the center, you can direct them to our website: [name]. There are various documents and links to resources.

Ways You Can Support the Writing Center
1. ADVERTISE THE CENTER ON YOUR SYLLABUS OR IN CLASS. Put up a writing center information sign (email for copies), add as a resource on your syllabus, or have an orientation (either in the center or in your classroom).

2. REQUIRE WRITING CONFERENCES in the WC for a particular assignment that is writing-intensive, or as a re-write opportunity for Mastery Learning. This will enhance the quality of what students turn in, and visits are verified with a signed WC session form.

3. OFFER EXTRA CREDIT when your students use the center for a particular assignment. Students receive session forms detailing what was worked on in the center. They will have more incentive to work ahead and go in-depth on your class assignments. It will make your grading easier!

4. PROVIDE CLASSROOM RESOURCES. These can be assignment sheets, grading rubrics and sample papers we will keep on file to ensure students are meeting your expectations. You can also come in and explain the assignment to the tutors!

5. RECOMMEND TUTORS. Recommend great writers and communicators to become trained peer tutors.

6. STOP BY THE WC during your lunch or prep period to see how your students are working with the tutors on your assignment and to offer your expertise.

Student Outreach Guide

Student outreach guides are written in student-friendly language and can be distributed to students as part of a back-to-school packet or when giving a WC orientation or classroom plug. You can also post this outside of your center door and on the school's website. Consider having this guide written in whatever languages are spoken at your school so that ELLs can learn about the center as well. To further lower the barriers to students visiting the center, you can make the guides double-sided and include information about how to make an appointment. This is especially helpful for new students just learning about the center.

Sample 1

No Wrongs. Just Write.
Visit the [Name] Writing Center in room [#]!

What is the WC?
The WC is a student-run space where all students in all classes can come to get writing help from a fellow student.

Where is the WC?
You can find us in room [#], which is [location details].

When is the WC open?
[days and times]

How do I sign up to work with a tutor?
You can sign up to work with any of our tutors on our sign-up sheets, which are at [location]. Be sure to pick up a cover sheet!

Does the WC only tutor English assignments?
No! You can bring any kind of writing for any class. Feel free to bring essays, PowerPoints, lab reports, DBQs, poems, etc. If your assignment involves writing, we are here to help! You can even bring your own personal writing!

What should I bring to the WC?
Bring a cover sheet, directions for the assignment you're working on, a printed copy of the writing you want help with, and a pen or pencil. We also have computers if you need.

Can I also bring my lunch?
Absolutely! You are welcome to eat your lunch while you work with your tutor.

We are excited to help you!
Visit our website: [name]   Follow us on Twitter: [handle]
Still have questions? See [director] in [location]

Sample 2

Need to make an appointment at the WC? Here's how!
1. Come to Rm. [#]
2. Find the clipboard and schedule outside on the wall
3. Choose the date and period (including lunch) you want to come
4. Sign up next to the tutor of your choice
5. Take an WC Cover Sheet from the folder on the wall
6. Note down your appointment time*
7. Come to your appointment with any and all materials you might need to work on your paper! Computers ARE available in the WC if you'd like to work on a digital copy or get help with formatting. Just let your tutor know. Printing your paper beforehand is advised.

*When you reserve an appointment, it is VERY important that you don't miss it. Tutors are waiting for you, and you may be taking an appointment slot from another student if you don't show up. Put a reminder in your planner, in your phone, on your hand, or sign up with a friend who will remind you!

*WC appointments are 20 minutes long. You can bring your lunch, but do not show up with less than 20 minutes left to work! We want to maximize our time to help you.

Let's plan:
My assignment is due _____
I can come to the WC on these dates: _____   _____   _____

Bookmarks

Depending on your school and students, bookmarks are a great alternative to guides. They are a quick (and smaller!) resource explaining the essentials of your center. Give bookmarks to students during writing center orientations and have them stick the bookmark in the front or back of binders. Some bookmarks have a coupon-like bottom, which students turn in for a prize when they come for their first appointment of the year. The following sample shows both the front and back sides.

What is a writing center?

A collaborative learning environment where students share and discuss their writing. Tutoring sessions are led by [name] High School students who are trained as peer tutors.

When should I go to the WC?

Sometimes your teacher will assign a visit; many proactive students go on their own for help on a class assignment. Extra credit is not the only reason to visit the WC!

What assignments can I bring?

You can bring your English essays, but we also love tutoring science lab reports, history essays, even speeches and PowerPoints for any class!

What should I expect?
- Thoughtful discussion about YOUR writing
- Friendly peer support
- Authentic feedback
- Tips from tutors who have taken your class & know your teacher's expectations
- A relaxed environment

[Name] Writing Center
[location]
[days, times]

We LOVE tutoring your:

- HOA Essays/Speeches
- College Applications
- History DBQs
- Persuasive Essays
- Creative Writing
- Lab Procedures
- Film Reviews
- Resumes for Jobs
- TOK/Extended Essays
- Research Papers
- PowerPoints
- Double Entry Journals

Classroom Presentations

Classroom presentations give students the opportunity to learn about the center as well as to put a face to the tutors. They can be a quick run-down of the center or a longer demonstration of what sessions look like, using a fish-bowl structure. Depending on your space, an alternative to classroom presentations is having a class gather in the writing center for an orientation.

The writing center would like to provide students from all disciplines with writing help, but in order to do that we need *your* help! We would like to know if you are interested in allowing our tutors to come into your classroom to deliver a brief presentation on the writing center. This "roadshow" will increase awareness that the writing center can help improve writing in all disciplines, not only English. We ask you to consider the road show if your students are struggling with any of the following:

- In math...
    - Word problems
    - AP Statistics help
- In history...
    - DBQs
    - Research papers
- In science...
    - Lab reports
    - Science fair
- Electives...
    - AP Psychology
    - AP European History
    - Creative Writing
    - Journalism
    - Debate
    - Speech Communication
    - World Religions

The roadshow presentation will be available during [time]. The length of presentation is up to you! We can be as brief as 5 minutes or we can go more in depth. If you are interested please email [director's name and email]. We really appreciate your flexibility and help, and we are certain your students will too!

Videos

When you cannot speak directly to students or faculty, videos provide an excellent medium for communicating information about your center. This can be shown to the entire staff and students in the fall and added to your center's website for viewing throughout the year. There are numerous examples of writing center informational videos online. Watch several and decide what aspects you want to include. Shorter time lengths work better, especially if you decide to make commercial-like videos to show on your school's broadcast. What aspect of writing do you want to promote in 30 seconds: generating ideas, providing clarity, working with commas? These quick bursts can target specific audiences or events at your school (e.g. workshops, college applications, athletes). Consider having your tutors work with the TV production teacher and gain credit for creating the videos.

Video Breakdown
- Scene Storyboard
    - General Idea:
    - Title:
    - Creators:
    - Due:
- Music & Images
    - Beginning image:
    - Beginning song:
    - Ending song:
    - Ending image:
- People & Materials Needed
    - Actors:
    - Videographer:
    - Materials (gathered by):
- Timeline
- Things to Do
    - Actor practice
    - Make/gather materials
    - Record principal's voiceover

Posters

Posters are a simple but effective way to promote the writing center. Your tutors will come up with some amazing ideas to spark interest. The artifact below is a meme created by tutors.

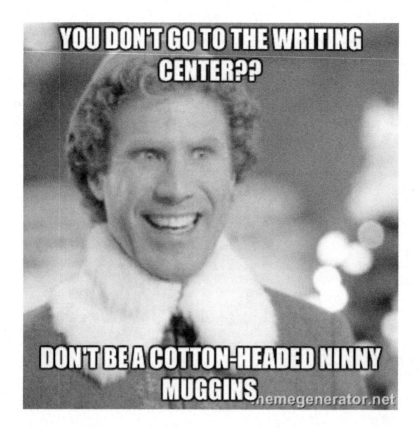

Promotional Contests

Throughout the school year, contests not only promote the center but also offer students a way to de-stress. There are a variety of writing contests - poetry, captioning images, short stories, grammar games, six-word memoirs - as well as those for creating logos, being the x# tutored, coloring pages, etc. Run a variety of different types to encourage student awareness and good feelings towards the center.

Acrostics for Airheads
Students/staff write an acrostic in order to receive an Airhead! The acrostic should reflect your ADVENTUROUS writing side. The student tutors will briefly review your writing to make sure you've successfully completed the theme for the day. They may even offer some additional feedback to improve your writing in the future!

What Is an Acrostic?
An acrostic poem is a poem that follows a list-like structure. The letters spell a phrase vertically, while horizontal words branch off from the phrase. This type of poem is used by many comedians, as well as motivational speakers.

Example:
Senior
Energetic
Nostalgic
Inspirational
Outstanding
Rivalries

How Do You Write an Acrostic?
-Brainstorm a word
-Attribute meaning to each letter
-Remember, be adventurous, be Original, be YOU
-Create a theme to write on
-Describe the theme in any (school appropriate) way
-Use verbs to make the acrostic connect into a sentence
-Most importantly, write in the list-like structure!

Blog Posts and Website

Blog posts can be a first step in giving your center a public and online presence. Tutors can decide and write relevant and informative content, and, as your center grows, can take on editorial roles as well. The following is a style guide to personalize to your school and blog platform. Below that is a picture of a writing center homepage on which the center provides logistical information as well as resources for student writers. Blog posts are often a portion of such a website. The website depicted here was created using Wix, a free platform, but there are many other free sites educators use such as Wordpress and Weebly. To see live samples of SSWC websites, go to the "About - Member Schools" page of the SSWCA website: http://sswca.org/about-us/capta-writing-centers/

The Writing Center Blog Style Guide

When Should You Make a Blog Post?
If you have done a workshop, you should update the blog with your workshop within a week. We also make blog posts at the start of every month on last month's statistics and raffle winners.

Content
We post a lot of things on our blog: statistics, reflections, creative writing, writing center conferences, WC special events, interesting writing assignments, and much more. If you're writing about a workshop you have done, you should include your Prezi and a synopsis of what you went over.

Accessing the Blog
Go to:
Username:
Password:

Titles
Come up with a creative title that informs the audience of what the post will be about and makes them want to read on. Always capitalize the first letter of each word. When we post a link to Twitter, your title will be published on the tweet along with a link to the post.

Style
When you write for the blog, remember to write in the style of a blog post. That means you don't have to be formal! Let your voice shine through. However, always check your grammar and use appropriate language. Basically, keep the audience of the blog in mind (parents, students, and other writing centers frequently view our blog). Reading past blog posts will give you an idea of the style to use in your own post. Tips:
  1. Don't use tabs. Posts should be written in journalistic block paragraphs with a space between each paragraph.
  2. Font is Times New Roman, "normal" size.

Hyperlinks
If you are writing about something that has a website (an article, another blog post, a high school or college, a conference, a writer with a web page, etc.), it is important to always include hyperlinks in your text. Highlight the text you want to link and then click on "Link" in the Menu bar. Copy and paste the URL from the webpage you want to attach, and the text you link should turn blue.

Images
Every blog post should have an image; ideally, you should have taken a photo that relates to the post (during the event if possible). How to insert an image:

Byline (Author Photo & Bio)
Give the post's author credit by including his or her picture and bio at the bottom of the post.

Tags/Label
Once you are done writing your post, add tags. Tags allow posts to be searchable. There are tags that you should always use:
1. Your first and last name.
2. A description of the post from this list of tags (use these only)

- [WC tag]
- [high school tag]
- College
- Workshop
- Conference
- Statistics
- Grammar
- Tutoring
- Writing
- Outreach
- Legacy

3. If you write about a workshop, include the title of the workshop as a tag.
4. Always capitalize the tags.

Back Dating or Future Dating your Post
Embedding a Prezi: HTML
Embedding a Power Point: HTML

Preview and Publish!
When you think you are finished with your post (and all of the important blog bells & whistles), click "Preview" on the top right corner. Make sure all of your formatting and photos look the way they should. Proofread your post for accuracy! When you think it looks great, click "Publish."
Congratulations, you are now a published author!

Troubleshooting
If you have any issues while composing or publishing your blog post, contact [name] at [email].

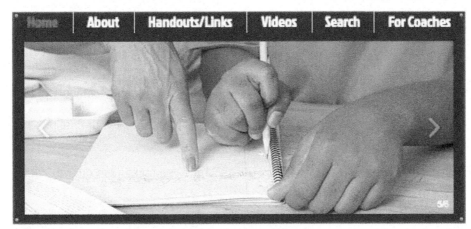

Social Media Posts

Whereas blog posts provide more in-depth information and allow tutors to grow as published authors, Facebook, Twitter, and Instagram, as common social media platforms, present quicker and shorter promotional use. In addition to brief updates and announcements, these posts can link to blog posts, educational opportunities, or interesting content. For better appeal, add visuals when posting. Using hashtags will increase the searchability of your posts and create a wider audience.

End of day huddle during our Fall Staff Development ... we're all in this together! #writingcenter #community #letsdothis

Language is fascinating! Here's some weekend reading to get primed for [school names's] upcoming rivalry game! #[school]rocks #go[mascot]

Today, we're greeting students during orientation! Whether you're a current or new student, stop by our table before 2:00 p.m. today for a bookmark and candy! #wcswag #backtoschool

Welcome to all students! We're looking forward to working with you! #writinghelp

AP students: Are you looking to put the final touches on your summer essays? You can do so at the Writing Center! Schedule an in-person or online consultation from our website: [name] Good luck to all! #[writingcentername] #firstimpressions

Looking for a podcast on the semicolon? Well, here it is. A good way to spend an hour. :)

Want to work in the writing center? Applications are now being accepted. Stop by [location] or talk to [director's name] to get a form! #[schoolname]community

This week we hosted our first-ever college essay workshop! Thanks [all who helped]! We look forward to hosting additional workshops this year! #workshop #[schoolname]

A huge thank you to our dedicated staff at [school name] and their support of the WC! #weloveteachers

"Righting Writing Workshop" is today during student success time! Come to [location] to develop strategies for beginning and working through assignments. For those who plan on attending, please bring something to write with and the prompt for an upcoming writing assignment. #workshop #writingtime #writinghelp #igotthis

We're nearing the end of the year. Stop in to see us this week for help with all of your final papers! #[writingcentername] #nearlydone

That's a wrap! We are officially closed for the year, and guess what? We conducted our 1,000th session of the year after school today! #celebration #writinghelprocks

Community Outreach

Outreach can happen beyond your school. More than just promotion, writing center tutors can go into the community to help improve writing skills, all the while spreading the word about what writing centers are and do. While your tutors can design and deliver writing lessons for elementary schoolers and community members, this is particularly helpful for introducing middle school students to the writing center, helping to bridge the gap between middle and high school writing, and opening up the conversation for writing centers in your district's middle schools! (See chapter 8 for resources specific to middle schools.) The following resource provides an overview of such a project, some mini-lessons as tutors develop their lessons, and two ways to promote student attendance.

Major League Writing (MLW) Day - Community Outreach

Part of what makes writing centers great is their ability to serve their surrounding communities. That begins with our high school community, but there are others in need of our services in our greater community. So, we will be taking part in a community outreach/problem-based learning project aimed at helping middle schoolers learn more about writing and get excited about it.

To do this, we will be working over the next few months to produce student-created, student-run sessions about various aspects of writing. Whether you decide to create a session about script writing, speaking, or poetry writing, you will share your excitement and skills with area middle schoolers. We will also focus on creating sessions specifically for 8th graders to prepare them for high school writing. Students will be in charge of promoting their sessions as well, though we will all take part in an overall promotional video. It's a great opportunity to work together to have a positive impact on our community!

EXPECTATION
- *Writing Center Comes First!*
  We will still have clients and workshops during this time! Don't forget that your job in the WC is to serve students-- I know it's tough when you're mid-outline or are just finishing your presentation. Have the client fill out the intake form and jot down your ideas so you don't lose them in while you help others with their own work.

GRADING (See rubrics for a more-detailed breakdown)
- Progress
- Session Workshop
- Participation

Mini-Lessons

Effective Starts

Task: To research how to create effective and engaging lesson starters and share this information with the class.

Engaging Activities

Task: To research how to create effective and engaging lesson activities that get students involved in what is happening during the lesson and share this information with the class.

Ending on a High Note

Task: To research how to create effective and engaging lesson closures that ensure students remember what they learned during the lesson and share this information with the class.

Generating an Audience

Individual Promo Video

Task: To create a promotional video for your Major League Writing Day session that discusses what your session is about, potential student outcomes, why they will have fun in that session.

How: Using the resources available (personal recording devices, iPads, etc.), create a video that is no more than 1 minute in length. It needs to include the following items:
- Session description
- Student outcomes (What are they going to walk away with?)
- Fun (Appropriate humor/content)
- Clean editing

Trifold Poster Assignment

Task: To create a trifold presentation for your Major League Writing Day session that will be on display during the event showcase. Using the resources available (trifolds, cardstock, other art materials, etc.), create a trifold poster that educates parents on your session. It needs to include the following items:
- Session description
- Student outcomes (What are they going to walk away with?)
- Colorful elements that engage the viewer
- Pictures
- Appropriate humor/content
- Clean and creative design

Chapter 6
Gathering Evidence for Success: Data and Evaluation
By Trisha Callihan

Guiding Questions

- What data is already being collected and what data is missing (qualitative/quantitative)?
- What are the most efficient methods to collect data and limit director labor?
- Who are the stakeholders who need to see the data, and what are the best ways to share it with them?
- What does the collected data reveal about the writing center, tutors, and clients?
- What improvements can be made in light of the data?

Resources

- Session Form
- Tutoring Evaluation Form
- Tutoring Reflection
- Monthly Data Report
- Yearlong and Historical Data

Resource Contributors

- Beth Blankenship, Oakton Writing Center at Oakton High School, VA
- Renee Brown, PTMS Writing Lab at Peters Township Middle School, PA
- Trisha Callihan, Eagle Writing Center at Obourn High School, VA
- Kate Hutton, Herndon Writing Center at Herndon High School in Herndon, VA
- Amber Jensen, George Mason University, VA; formerly of Edison Writing Center at Edison High School, VA
- Stacey Waldrup, Raider Writing Center at Crescent Valley High School, OR

Discussion

Day-to-day tasks at a secondary school writing center never seem to end, and yet, somehow directors are expected to seamlessly include data and evaluation into the already overwhelming to-do list. I have used data collection for a variety of purposes over the past four years, but the key is that, as a director, I used the data to take an honest look at my practices, so that I could ultimately go back and revise my work to improve for the following year. It also allowed me to develop stronger arguments to justify more support from administrators and school board members; and, finally, gathering and using data has allowed me to have larger conversations with other secondary school writing center directors about the writing center work narrative. So how do you start gathering or refine your use of data to improve your center?

During my first year as a writing center director, the idea of collecting data felt vast to me, as the thought of adding another task to focus on would be almost impossible with all of the other preps and extracurricular activities on my plate. Thankfully, I realized very quickly how many of my day-to-day procedures contained data, specifically my tutor report forms and all of the informal spreadsheets I logged. The impending write-up required for my grant, awarded to me by the local education foundation to support the writing center, was the driving force behind my initial collection, and so I didn't think beyond those requirements and questions to delve further into reflecting on my work at that point. However, as I began looking closer at numbers and anecdotal records, I found far more value beyond the simple task the grant required, and I began thinking about questions Schendel (2012) posed: "What patterns do [I] see that need to be explained? What piques the curiosity of [me] and [my] staff and makes [me] feel energized to answer via more focused or different kinds of research? What questions and concerns do[es] [my] data NOT speak to?" (p. 118).

Audience

My staff and I needed to consider our audience for the data and evaluation, and at the start, the grant reviewers included notable community members, the superintendent, administrators, school board members, among others. I knew, based on other presentations I had seen before, that I would need to reveal some type of growth in numbers whether in the center or in scores. And yet, even though I knew numbers would be the primary focus of the grant board, I asked my tutors to take some time to discuss their own experiences and the skills they learned from working in the center. The key in this was that I knew it was important to "be evaluated on our own terms," since many of the grant members had little knowledge of how the writing center functioned (Learner, 2001, p. 1). Additionally, since the tutors and I collected our own data, rather than leaving it in the hands of central office administrators, we were able to make strong arguments for whichever audience we selected after the first year. I recommend having control over your data whenever possible. In the first year of my center's implementation, when my work and results were tied directly to the School Improvement Plan, I had little voice as to what data to collect. Within my circumstance, my center was created "as [an] institutional band-aid" which tied itself directly to the hope for improved state assessment scores (Geller & Denny, 2013, p. 113). I was simply pleased that the writing center was finally taking root at my school, but allowing others to govern the desired results made my year frightening, since I wasn't sure if my work would meet the high expectations.

In the same vein, I had to consider what perspectives to include in the data collection: In addition to tutees' experiences or tutors' reflections from a session, should the tutee's teacher be asked about their perception of the tutee's skills? I thought about focus groups, such as ESOL, that I narrowed on, but I also thought about tutors, tutees, directors, and administrators. I began to look at my data and ask myself: Whose voices have not been heard in the data from my center? Is this accidental or on purpose? What other organizations or demographics in my school have already been collecting data? What other secondary schools have similar interests in data collection? Something else I considered was the narrative I possibly demonstrated in my data gathering and evaluation, as Grutsch McKinney (2013) advises directors to complicate the "grand narrative" (p. 11) which "shapes how we understand our work" (p. 82) since the narrative may perpetuate perspectives and problematic assumptions about writing center work. I certainly didn't want to advertise the center as a remedial, one-stop shop cure-all, so I constantly looked in data for instances that contradicted that narrative.

Trying to find a balance between qualitative and quantitative data was a little tricky for me at times, as it seemed to be easiest to collect the anecdotal evidence from day-to-day flow in the center. Tutors had an easy time discussing the skills and lessons they learned from tutoring, and students that attended the center relayed their positive experiences as well. However, administrators and school board members almost exclusively wanted to see how the writing center impacted grades or test scores, as in the past, they have asked me to sum up a year's work in 10-15 minutes. I've found that sharing the qualitative evidence, although much lengthier during presentations, allows the audience members to have a far richer understanding of writing center work.

Where to Find the Data

Tutoring session forms have been one of my primary sources for data compilation. The frequency of their usage in my own center has allowed my tutors and me to revise our form several times in order to meet the needs of the tutees, tutors, and other stakeholders. For example, the tutors have mentioned the need for check boxes to quicken the paperwork portion of the tutoring session, and we were able to make that adjustment. With my tutors, we focused on different groups based on what our sheets told us; specifically, due to our large ESOL population, we have been able to track the progress of those students, especially those that have used the center multiple times. Therefore, by gathering data we were able to make decisions in our center in regards to our forms, but multiple, evidence-based changes could be made depending on the data collected.

Additionally, I realized very quickly that the labor required to collect data should not remain in the hands of the director; rather, structuring the statistic work can and should be implemented as part of tutor leadership (Hutton, 2018) (See chapter 1 for more information about director labor). There are also platforms available online to assist in more effective data collection and analysis. For instance, my center has transitioned from the paper-copy tutoring forms to WCOnline, a web-based tutoring scheduler. It makes the data collection much cleaner. In the past, we also dabbled with Google Forms and Google Sheets since it is a free platform. It is important to note that without explicit training, tutors, who are the primary gatherers of data, may make mistakes. I've collected sheets in the past that have had "N/A" written for every box, or the tutor will simply forget to fill out a form. Making these expectations clear to tutors or any of the data-gatherers will be important for accurate collection and fewer headaches later (See chapter 4 for tutor training).

Beyond those tutoring report forms, I also took some time to see how the social media pages of my writing center held up in term of content as well as interaction throughout the year (See chapter 5 for social media ideas). I had done little research to determine the best times or the best content to engage possible tutees, so much of my information was haphazardly thrown together. I realized very quickly that many of the posts, especially on Twitter, were so isolated from other writing centers, as the content primarily focused on communicating awards or events to students at the high school. It is important to remember, though, that when first creating social media pages, content that is more reflective of writing center practice and collaborative in nature may improve the stats and overall hits on the pages.

What to Do with the Data

When I started gathering data, I had only thought of the grant board reading through my information, but there were plenty of other people that could benefit from hearing about the work: students, tutors, colleagues, administrators, school board members, parents, conference attendees, journal readers, etc. After I spent time pulling together all of the data, I had to decide what formats would work the best for each type of audience. When my center used Google Forms in the past, we very easily pulled the graphs and charts to place on presentations. As our documents began to grow, we had to find more helpful websites to organize the information. For instance, looking at all of the student goals listed on report forms worked perfectly as a Wordle, since it allowed us to see words used most often in that section of the form. My tutors also used the charts and data at the end of the year for more reflective work, as the information can elicit considerations about tutoring methods and can help tutors to make conscientious changes for future tutoring sessions. From those reflections and discussions, the tutors and I make regular and yearly changes to the forms and curriculum after reflecting on the data.

My hope is, after spending so much time collecting and organizing the data, that I can ultimately share some of what I've learned with other writing center professionals. In the past, it has been easiest to share my work with others through nearby conferences, SSWCA, and Twitter, specifically #wcchat. Ideally such data can eventually be published on a platform such as *The Writing Center Journal* or *WLN: A Journal of Writing Center Scholarship*. By breaking away from the lore that oftentimes traps directors, others can comment and provide feedback to some of the work that is already being completed. I wonder too the extent to which the published writing center work of secondary schools is valuable also to college writing centers or even broader literacy studies. Ultimately by sharing the conclusions and evaluations of your center, directors and other academic fields can learn about "our shared experiences, to find out how others have solved problems that we face," so that as a community, we can find solutions that sustain our work (Ede, 1989, p. 5).

Resources

Session Form

Session Forms or Tutor Report Forms are used to record session information for both students and the center. Students fill out the first part including identifying what area(s) they want help in. At the end of the session, tutors circle the areas actually worked on and write a session summary and list of tasks to complete. The tutor identification of areas covered is correlated with student requests to determine 1.) what students want help in the most, 2.) what students receive help in the most, and 3.) if tutors are helping with at least one area students requested. For the second sample form you'll see below, one could designate different colors or checks with the same purpose of signifying tutees' perceived needs and tutees' needs addressed. The form, if originally on paper, could be typed into a spreadsheet to collect data input. It can be used by the student as a reminder of the session and as proof of use of the writing center. You can also use carbon copy paper with the extra copy placed in the appropriate teacher's mailbox. The third sample form collects information through Google Forms. The session forms are malleable depending on the needs of the director and center in relation to data collection, as directors can add questions such as "How many times have you visited the center?"

Sample 1

Writing Center
Tutor Report Form

Writer's Name _____   Date _____
☐ FR ☐ SO ☐ JR ☐ SR   First Visit? ☐ Y ☐ N
English Language Learner (ESOL)? ☐ Y ☐ N   Would you like a bilingual tutor? ☐ Y ☐ N
Preferred Day of Appointment? _____   Date Assignment is Due _____
Tutor Name _____   Eagle Block Teacher _____
Teacher of Assignment _____   Class of Assignment _____
Assignment Type _____   Length of session _____
Reason for Attending: ☐ teacher required   ☐ teacher offered bonus
                          ☐ returning because it was helpful   ☐ heard about it, want to try it out
What is your writing/reading goal for the session? _____

What is your greatest concern/problem we can help you with? (Check no more than three items total)

DRAFTING	DEVELOPMENT	MECHANICS
☐ Understanding assignment	☐ Organization	☐ Documentation
☐ Generating ideas	☐ Paragraphing	☐ Punctuation
☐ Rough draft	☐ Thesis/Topic sentence	☐ Sentence structure
☐ Final draft	☐ Development/support	☐ Grammar
☐ Revision	☐ Transition	☐ Spelling
☐ Introduction	☐ Conclusion	☐ Other_____

To be completed by writing center tutor: Summary of writing tutor's strategy, suggestions offered for continued work.

Sample 2

**Writing Center
Session Form**

Date: _____ Name: _____ Fr. So. Jr. Sr.
Assignment: _____ Teacher: _____ Class: _____

Areas I'd like help in

Ideas & Content
- Brainstorming
- Thesis and topic sentences
- Supporting details (quotes)
- Clarity, Focus
- Content /details matching audience and purpose

Organization
- Introduction / Conclusion
- Paragraph order
- Detail placement
- Transitions

Voice
- Appropriate for topic and audience
- Expressive/engaging writing

Word Choice
- Strong and specific language
- Variety

Sentence Fluency
- Natural flow and rhythm
- Variation in sentence structure, length, beginnings

Conventions
- Punctuation
- Grammar
- Verb Tense
- Variety

Use of Sources
- Finding sources
- Integrating sources / in-text citation
- MLA Format / Works Cited

Session Summary:
Ideas & Content • Organization • Voice • Word Choice • Sentence Fluency • Conventions • Use of Sources

Next Steps:

Consultant: _____ Minutes: _____

Sample 3

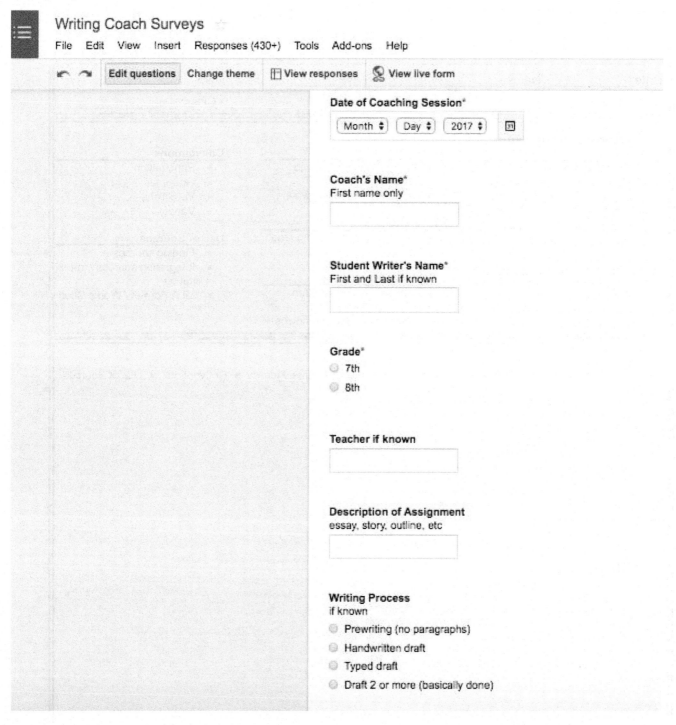

Tutoring Evaluation Form

After tutors have completed a tutoring session, clients, other tutors, and directors can provide constructive criticism for the tutors' performance. Directors may use these forms to track a tutor's performance in the center, or save them for tutors to complete larger-scale reflections of their work over time. The first two samples below show how you can add an evaluative part (italics) to your session form. (Note: There are additional samples of tutor observation forms in chapter 4.) The third sample presented here is for students to fill out independently of the session form, and the fourth sample is an evaluation by a teacher or director.

Sample 1

Evaluation on a Session Form

Student Name: _____
Where in the writing process are you?   Prewriting   Drafting   Revising   Re-writing
What is the writing assignment? _____
Who is your teacher? _____
When is it due? _____
What area(s) should I focus on during your conference? (Circle ONE or TWO)

Selecting a topic	Paragraphing	Grammar / Spelling
Research	Transitions	Voice / Style
Brainstorming	Introduction/Conclusion Commentary	
Supporting details/examples	Incorporating/Citing quotes	Other: _____

Date and Time In: _____ Tutor's Name: _____
Comments for the tutor after the session is complete:

Tutor signature: _____

Sample 2

Evaluation on a Session Form

Writing Center Log
Student: _____ Grave level: _____ Tutor: _____
Date: _____ Time: _____ First Visit?   Y   N
Class: _____ Teacher: _____
Assignment: _____

Stage of Writing:
Pre-writing   Drafting Revision   Editing   Re-Write
Areas of concern & Shared Goals/Focus of Session:
   1. _____
   2. _____
   3. _____
Tutee "Plan of Action"
I plan to revise / fix / change:
_____

Evaluation of Session
Great   Good / Okay   Poor/Bad

Session Summary and Comments:

Sample 3
Client Evaluation

Your Name (optional) _____   Grade Level _____
Your Tutor's Name _____   Date _____

1. What were your expectations of the WC before your first conference?

2. My tutor greeted me and explained what I could expect from the conference   YES   NO
3. My tutor addressed the areas of concern that I had   YES   NO
4. My tutor and I read the paper out loud together (at least portions of it)   YES   NO
5. My tutor asked me questions & encouraged me to talk about my paper   YES   NO
6. My tutor was knowledgeable about writing and gave me good input   YES   NO
7. I wrote down comments and took notes on my draft during the conference   YES   NO
8. I utilized the feedback of my tutor as I revised my assignment   YES   NO
9. I was satisfied; the WC conference met my expectations   YES   NO

10. Please evaluate your tutor, giving feedback (positive and negative) about his/her performance in the following areas: preparation, professionalism, knowledge about writing, listening skills, quality of feedback, communication skills with you.

11. Would you return to the WC if it were not required or your teacher did not offer extra credit?
    ____ Yes, I found it to be very useful
    ____ No, I would only go if my teacher required it

    I authorize my feedback to be given to my tutor   YES   NO

Sample 4
Teacher / Director Evaluation

Tutor Observed: Date:
Student Grade Level: Student Class:
Assignment:

      1=needs improvement   2=satisfactory   3=outstanding

1. What were your first impressions of the tutoring session? How did the tutor do introducing him/herself, putting the student at ease, and preparing for the conference?
   1   2   3   Comments:

2. What were your observations of the smoothness of the tutoring session?
   1   2   3   Comments:

3. How did the tutor do at asking good questions? Were the questions particularly meaningful or probing to engage the student?
   1   2   3   Comments:

4. What were your perceptions of the student's engagement in the conference? Do you think the student perceived the conference to be useful? Why or why not?
   1   2   3   Comments:

5. What were some of the main topics covered during the conference? Do you think these topics cover what the student most needed to work on?
   1   2   3   Comments:

6. Did the tutor have any tough situations? If so, how did he/she handle it? Any suggestions for improvement?
   1   2   3   Comments:

Overall suggestions for the tutor: _____

Tutoring Reflection

Using tutee evaluations and the session report forms provides tutors with ongoing tutor training and self-evaluation. After a singular tutoring session (sample 1) or at the end of semesters (sample 2), directors can give tutors an opportunity to review the tutoring practices and experiences they have completed thus far. The questions below can springboard discussions about what tutors are doing well and what their goals for improvement should be for following tutoring sessions. This type of data collection may be used more often for internal purposes only and would be pitched and tailored differently for an external audience (teachers, administrators, etc.).

Sample 1

1. Date
2. Client (name if you know, grade if you know)
3. Assignment (what was the paper "about")
4. How was this a successful tutoring session? What did you discuss or do that you believe was helpful to the writer? What did you do well?
5. How was this a challenging tutoring session? What questions or problems did the writer have that stumped you? What do you wish you did better?
6. Final thoughts you want to document for yourself about this session (For example, this was my first tutoring session, this was with my friend, this was for a paper I didn't write last year, I am also writing this paper right now, the student didn't have a full draft, we are super busy today, I worked with this student before, etc.)

Sample 2

- How many tutoring sessions did you complete over the past semester?
- What trends do you notice in your tutoring strengths or weaknesses?
- Compare your best and worst tutoring sessions and explain what made them so. Give as many explicit details as possible.
- How well do your reflections show the details of your sessions?
- Have your reflections evolved in their detailedness or analysis depth? If so, elaborate.
- Is there anything you could change about the way you approach your reflections in order to make them better suited to the purpose of tutoring reflections?
- In what ways have the reflection forms had an influence on your experience and performance as a tutor?
- What are your thoughts on the format of the reflection forms? Would you change anything about the format or even the idea of reflections overall?If you were to change the format of the reflection forms, how would you do so?
- How would these changes fit with your idea of the purpose of reflection forms?
- How would these changes fit with the way you've been writing your reflections?
- How have you contributed to the writing center this semester?
- What was your most valuable contribution? Explain in detail its value.

Monthly Data Report

A statistics manager, a possible leadership role for tutors in a center, may pull numbers from the primary sources of data. This may include Google Forms, hard-copy forms, WCOnline, or a handful of other online record-keeping platforms. The data may include the number of students who attended any writing center related event for the month (including tutoring sessions, online tutoring sessions, workshop attendance, rent-a-tutor attendance), and the tutor(s) can compile it into a one-page infographic to post in the writing center, send to administrators and teachers, or use to demonstrate the reach and impact of writing center initiatives school-wide. There are several websites that can support the creation of these infographics including Piktochart. These monthly data reports have the potential to become a touchstone to advocate for new programs, extra support, etc. with administration and elicit celebrations for the center's accomplishments.

Sample 1

Sample 2

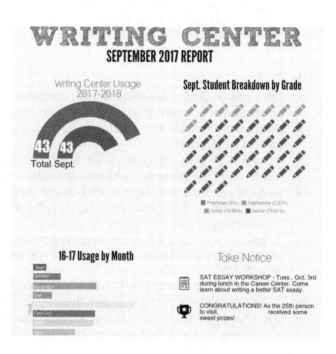

Yearlong and Historical Data

The first sample below outlines student retention over the course of the year broken down by semester. The second includes some of the most important historical data: information about the tutors and who they are; information about the clients and who they are; and conference presentations and publications. Centers can continually add to these types of information logs and present this information to key stakeholders: administrators, school board members, teachers, parents, and other interested parties (See chapter 2 resources for a sample on turning this into a narrative document).

Sample 1

School Year: _____ Semester 1: [#] visits by [#] students

- % of student body used the center
- # different assignments/topics
- # different teachers (including N/A and Unknown)
- # or % for each grade visiting
- # ELL/ESL sessions
- *Sessions In-House* _____ *Drop Off/ Online* _____
- Rate of Use

1 time	2-4 times	5-10 times	11-20 times	21+ times
%	%	%	%	%

Sample 2

Mission:
Vision:

Writing Center Historical Data

Who Do We Tutor?

	Year 1	Year 2	Year 3
Total Sessions	number	number	number
9th Grade	number/percentage	number/percentage	number/percentage
10th Grade	number/percentage	number/percentage	number/percentage
11th Grade	number/percentage	number/percentage	number/percentage
12th Grade	number/percentage	number/percentage	number/percentage
Honors/AP	number/percentage	number/percentage	number/percentage
Gen Ed/ SPED	number/percentage	number/percentage	number/percentage
ELL	number/percentage	number/percentage	number/percentage

*include any details of overlapping of organizations or changes in data collection methods

Who Are Our Tutors?

	Year 1	Year 2	Year 3
Total	number	number	number
10th Grade	number/percentage	number/percentage	number/percentage
11th Grade	number/percentage	number/percentage	number/percentage
12th Grade	number/percentage	number/percentage	number/percentage
Female	number/percentage	number/percentage	number/percentage
Male	number/percentage	number/percentage	number/percentage
Hispanic	number/percentage	number/percentage	number/percentage
White	number/percentage	number/percentage	number/percentage
Asian	number/percentage	number/percentage	number/percentage
Black	number/percentage	number/percentage	number/percentage
Other	number/percentage	number/percentage	number/percentage
FEL	number/percentage	number/percentage	number/percentage
SWD	number/percentage	number/percentage	number/percentage

Conference Sessions and Written Publications
Organization, Year: "Title of Conference" (Date, Location)
- "Title of Presentation" name (school name and location), name (school name and location), name (school name and location), name (school name and location), *any sponsorships*
- "Title of Presentation" name (school name and location), name (school name and location), name (school name and location), name (school name and location), *any sponsorships*

Writing Center Director Information
- name (dates as director)
    - Organization name, title, and years in title
- name (dates as director)
    - Organization name, title, and years in title

References

Ede, L. (1989). Writing as a social process: A theoretical foundation for writing centers? *The Writing Center Journal, 9*(2), 3-13. Retrieved from http://www.jstor.org/stable/43444122

Geller, A., & Denny, H. (2013). Of ladybugs, low status, and loving the job: Writing center professionals navigating their careers. *The Writing Center Journal, 33*(1), 96-129. Retrieved from http://www.jstor.org/stable/43442405

Grutsch McKinney, J. (2013). *Peripheral visions for writing centers.* Logan, UT: Utah State University Press.

Hutton, K. (2018). Always in beta: Incorporating choice and encouraging a sense of ownership by revamping tutor training in a secondary school writing center. Retrieved July 15, 2018, from http://www.wlnjournal.org/blog/2018/07/always-in-beta-incorporating-choice-and-encouraging-a-sense-of-ownership-by-revamping-tutor-training-in-a-secondary-school-writing-center/

Learner, N. (2001). Choosing beans wisely. *WLN: A Journal of Writing Center Scholarship, 26*(1), 1-5.

Schendel, E. (2012). Integrating assessment into your center's other work: Not your typical methods chapter. In E. Schendel & W. J. Macauley, Jr. (Eds.), *Building writing center assessments that matter* (pp. 140-161) Logan, UT: Utah State UP.

Advocating, Building, and Collaborating

Chapter 7
School-Wide Writing Initiatives
By Joe Golimowski

Guiding Questions

- What is already happening at the school involving writing across the curriculum?
- What other services can the writing center offer to students beyond one-on-one tutoring?
- How can the writing center prepare all students for writing beyond the humanities?
- How can the writing center help teachers incorporate more writing in their classes?
- How can non-English faculty contribute to the mission of the writing center?

Resources

- Non-English Faculty Collaboration Invitation
- Workshop Planning
- College Essay Workshop
- Writing Process Breakdown
- Written Response Questions
- Involving Writing in Athletics

Resource Contributors

- Renee Brown, PTMS Writing Lab at Peters Township Middle School, PA
- Kate Hutton, Herndon Writing Center at Herndon High School, VA
- Rich Kent, University of Maine, ME
- Stacey Waldrup, Raider Writing Center at Crescent Valley High School, OR

Discussion

To what extent should you consider school-wide writing initiatives for your center? Is not the writing center itself a school-wide writing initiative as centers are open to all students in all disciplines? Different schools use different buzz words for this concept; writing across the curriculum is one of the most common terms. At the center I direct, I believed for most of the first year of operation that we were automatically a school-wide writing initiative until I had a critical look at the statistics of where our clients came from (See chapter 6 for data and evaluation information). Most were referred or came from English classes with the occasional appearance of a social studies student. The center was successful based upon the number of visits and the feedback from clients, but was it achieving its goal of helping to create a school-wide writing culture that spanned all grade levels and disciplines? Were we preparing students to graduate and move into scientific fields ready for the types of writing required in those disciplines? Were we teaching the intricacies of business communication and not just the best way to write a persuasive essay? Apparently, I concluded sadly, not.

Writing centers can play a coordinating and facilitating role in the larger conversation about writing in the school. As directors, we are constantly thinking about how we can improve writers and their writing. In addition, we are familiar with the latest in composition research or know where we can find information about various questions which arise in the course of our daily work. This access to the latest research should place us at the center of the conversation as we can coordinate activities benefiting the entire school writing community.

Reaching Out to Other Departments

Consider how you will get the buy-in and support of other departments so that your center is reaching all subjects (The outreach and promotion ideas and resources in chapter 5 are a good place to start your movement). At my center, I realized one way of achieving this goal was taking the writing center "on the road" or offering a "rent-a-tutor" program. We needed to take the writing center to classrooms across the school or invite other departments to send their students to us for workshops. Luckily, one of my colleagues in the English department had a similar idea for her twelfth-grade classes. Rather than bring her entire class to the writing center, she "rented" the tutors for an entire study hall period. Each senior in her classes met with a tutor to work on their college essay. This class-wide focus on one assignment for one session engendered deeper and richer conversations about the essay because the entire class shared in the tutoring session.

Even more ambitious would be to partner with another department to develop joint workshops that help to develop competent writers in disciplines other than English. Consider how writing is different in lab reports or how citations outside the humanities are usually in APA style as examples of such workshops. These initiatives help to improve writing across the curriculum so that all faculty, not just from the English department, establish and maintain a writing culture. Once I made this breakthrough, I realized how the writing center could do its part to support a school wide-writing culture.

The writing center doesn't always have to expand out; faculty can also come in. Keeping focused on the purpose of the center to produce competent and creative writers, the possibilities arise to include faculty from other disciplines as writing center supervisors and experts. These faculty members bring their individual and discipline-specific perspectives to the writing center, thereby broadening the scope of the center's reach. By welcoming these faculty from outside the English department, we can develop a sense of shared ownership of the center, of helping each faculty member to reconceptualize their role in teaching writing specific to their discipline with the assistance of center tutors. Creating a space for non-English faculty to supervise and monitor the center does not mean the director ignores the role of student tutors in providing the bulk of the tutoring. On the contrary, it reinforces the idea of writing as essential to success in all disciplines. Both tutor and client benefit from subject-specific writing advice that helps them to refine their writing and to more clearly fulfill the requirements of each discipline.

Workshops and Cross-Curricular Projects

Within the center, workshops preparing students for an AP writing test, whether in English or social studies, offer a practical way for the center to reach out to other departments and engage them in the work of the writing center. Such a workshop would work particularly well with subjects, such as history, where a written product is expected from the test taker.

Another step on the road to a true school-wide writing culture is to partner with another department to sponsor a cross-department, high visibility project. One suggestion is to collaborate with the career counseling coach or guidance department to sponsor a mock senior interview program whereby employers from the community are invited to interview seniors for jobs as a way of helping students practice their job search skills before moving on to college or employment. Tutors within the center can offer help with resumes, cover letters, and interview techniques. Think about which local businesses would be interesting to your school's population. What time of day could this take place to attract the most clients? Consider how your center can expand its reach after-school and into the community.

In addition, the career counseling center offers the perfect partner to help students improve their college essay skills. With the career counselor offering the expertise of what colleges look for and the writing center helping applicants hone their approach, the center and its work become more than just the method to score well on the literary analysis essay; it's offering a practical, real life resource that students can use to create writing that has real life impact. Tutors can create a workshop that outlines the fundamental items to consider when writing a college application essay and then continue with targeted advice about the writing process related to the essay, tips regarding content, and ideas to help make the essay stand out from the avalanche received by many college admissions offices.

For many directors, it's easy to conceptualize writing assistance within the humanities, but we shouldn't overlook the other disciplines in our schools that also use writing to discover new knowledge and to communicate that knowledge to others in the field or to a general audience. Many teachers use writing-to-learn based strategies in the classroom to help students generate paper topics and to better understand the material. Sometimes we ask our students to reflect upon their performance to improve it, whether it be writing a paper or solving a mathematics problem. The depth of those reflections is based on the intellectual effort expended. The writing center can help students attain that deeper level all teachers want in reflections. Writing center directors should consider what services the center might provide to help improve student achievement in physical performance-based fields such as athletics or music by using writing. What school initiatives are tied to writing across the curriculum? Consider designing a professional development day for non-writing heavy subjects to support more writing in their classes. Is your school working towards the common core standard of writing in science, math, etc.? Use that to start conversations about writing. What common resources does your English department already use regarding writing (rubrics, outlines, common vocab, etc.) and how could you make those accessible to other departments?

As you peruse the sources below, I hope you take a moment to consider how we as directors can create school-wide writing initiatives that reach students in fields as varied as physical education and the sciences. If your experience is like mine, I am sure you have received the blank stares of faculty in mathematics and perhaps the sciences when we invite them to send their students to the writing center. What could their students possibly gain from such a visit? Yet, research reveals engineers write as much as other professionals regardless of the field. We have our built-in constituency in the humanities, and our efforts, if my experience is indicative, are successful at reaching this audience. However, expand your mission and take the writing center out to the sciences, business, and physical education classes. Our students will thank us when they start the professional careers of the future.

Resources

Non-English Faculty Collaboration Invitation

Soliciting support from non-English faculty needs a deft hand. The example below keeps in mind the partnership the writing center strives to create with all faculty. It asks for non-English faculty assistance with ideas for workshops and tutor assistance plus invites other faculty to collaborate with writing center staff to create programs which improve writing across the curriculum. Modify this sample to fit the needs and interdepartmental realities of your school.

Dear Colleagues,

The [Name] Writing Center is excited to announce that we are expanding our mission in order to better support students in writing throughout the disciplines. In aligning with the goals of Writing Across the Curriculum, the WC will be offering several new services to support you and the students in your classrooms. In the coming months, you will hear about our "rent-a-tutor" ["tutors-on-the-road," etc.] program and workshops. As the WC makes these shifts, we are eager to get both your input and your experience. This is your invitation to contribute to the WC as a content-area teacher. Please consider the following and let me know, via email or in person, in what way(s) you may be able to help the WC achieve these broader goals.

- Is there a workshop/lesson about writing in your discipline you would like your students to hear from the WC staff? If so, would you be willing to help our staff design that workshop?
- Would you be willing to invite a tutor or several tutors into your classroom to help students during in-class writing activities/assignments?
- Would you be willing to be a point person for a current tutor who is training to become a tutor specializing in your content area?
- In what other ways can we prepare and support students who are writing in your area of expertise?
- Would you like to join the WC staff as a content advisor/tutor?

Thank you in advance for your support as we work together to help our students write in all content areas. Please let me know if you have questions or are able to contribute to our growing writing initiatives.

Workshop Planning

One way to expand the services of the writing center outside the English department is to help tutors develop workshops assisting students from other disciplines to improve their writing process and product. Workshops can support the mission of the school and the center by appealing to different grade levels and content areas. They can either happen in the writing center or in a teacher's classroom. When creating a new workshop, a well-designed plan is essential to a successful workshop. Sample 1 is a template that helps students develop a detailed plan as it guides them in thinking about its design and ensures that the tutors have followed a workshop model. Writing center faculty provide additional support by reviewing the template well in advance of the workshop and offering advice as needed. Some sample topics include lab report missteps, MLA or APA, paraphrasing and in-text citations, improving style, finding digital sources for research, etc. Once the center director approves the workshop plan, tutors should create a handout (sample 2) to help participants remember critical elements of the presentation. This particular artifact highlights the main points of the workshop but is general enough that it can easily be adapted to various levels and disciplines. Sample 3 shows a more in-depth handout for a lesson on paraphrasing.

Sample 1

Workshop Planning Template
Generally speaking, a workshop is a brief session where attendees discuss and practice specific skills. When planning your workshop, you should be prepared to identify specific strategies and to offer small group work time to give attendees time to practice the skill. The majority of your workshop should focus on time for your attendees to practice the skill.

Please use the template below when planning your Writing Center Workshop, and please share this and any materials you create at least 24 hours in advance of your workshop. Writing center faculty are here to support you and to help you gather resources!

Welcome and Icebreaker (5-7 minutes)	
Definition of skill and identification of specific strategies (5-7 minutes)	
Small group practice time/ structured activity with tutor support (20-30 minutes)	
Debrief: What questions do attendees still have? Review or summarize the key points from the workshop. Plug the WC! (5 minutes)	

Tips for a Successful Workshop
- While some attendees might have come with their friends, others might not know anyone in the room. An icebreaker will help everyone to relax.
- Be willing to share with the workshop attendees your own challenges with the skill.
- While you might provide several strategies for tackling a skill, focus on 1-3 specific strategies for your attendees to focus on.
- Create a handout so your attendees can take something with them.

Sample 2
AP World History/US History Short Answer Question + Long Essay Question Workshop

SAQ Tips:
1. Answer the question being asked!
2. Use the stimulus to help you.
3. Annotate the prompt for big ideas.
4. Only write however much is necessary!
5. Leave nothing blank- but don't spend too much time brainstorming!

LEQ Tips:
1. Answer the question being asked!
2. Annotate the prompt for big ideas.
    a. Brainstorm 2-3 big ideas per event.
    b. Use the planning space provided!
3. Plan out what you write *before* you write it!
    a. Go with the idea you have the most evidence to argue.
    b. This *may not* be your personal opinion!
4. Format like an essay- long ESSAY question.
    a. Introductory paragraph + thesis
    b. Body paragraphs- as many as needed
    c. Concluding paragraph + thesis

AP Testing Tips:
1. It's only a few hours: a "One and Done" affair.
2. The objective: applying analytical skills with your historical knowledge.
3. Not the objective: gushing as much information as possible
    a. The College Board wants to see what you can do- show it off!
4. Don't psych yourself out!

As always, the Writing Center is here to help with any questions you have. Feel free to bring in prompts for brainstorming or some you already wrote!

Sample 3

Paraphrasing in a Research Paper

How do I make research sound like me?
The way I present facts and connect them together is all mine even if the facts are from other sources.

> Paraphrasing involves putting original material into your own words.

Steps to Effective Paraphrasing
1. _____ Read (and reread) the original passage until you understand its full meaning.
2. _____ Without looking at the original, write your paraphrase on a new sheet.
3. _____ Check your paraphrase with the original to make sure your version is correct.

How do I cite in-text?
Add what comes first in the works cited entry to one of two places:

- _____

Example: Kolata reports that South African researchers have created a database, Rhodis, with collected DNA from all available rhinoceroses.

- _____

Example: South African researchers have created a database, Rhodis, with collected DNA from all available rhinoceroses (Kolata).

Circle what information you'd use in the following examples:
"Stopping Poaching." *WWF International*, World Wide Fund for Nature, 5 Apr. 2011.

Paterniti, Michael. "Should We Kill Animals to Save Them?" *Poaching and Conservation*, National Geographic Society, 20 Sept. 2017.

Some ideas for introductory phrase citations

X states that . . .	X suggests that . . .	X concludes that . . .	X believes that . . .
X claims that . . .	X describes . . .	X maintains that . . .	X reports that . . .
X asserts that . . .	X observes that . . .	X concedes that . . .	According to X . . .
X agrees that . . .	X contends that . . .	X notes that . . .	As X states . . .
X strongly argues . . .	X writes that . . .	X argues that . . .	As identified by X . . .
X comments that . . .	X proposes that . . .	X warns that . . .	As reported by X . . .

Practice Paraphrasing and Citing

Their words As big game populations dwindle further under pressure from human encroachment, shifting climate norms, and widespread criminal poaching, there are hunters who argue that a thoughtfully regulated and expensive hunt for bull elephants in their waning [end] days makes a sustainable way to protect both species and habitat. Paterniti, Michael. "Should We Kill Animals to Save Them?" *Poaching and Conservation*, National Geographic Society, 20 Sept. 2017.
Your words
Introductory phrase citation
End citation

How can I get additional help with my writing?
Come in to the [Name] Writing Center in [location]!

College Essay Workshop

Each year, a significant percentage of seniors participate in the annual process of writing a college application essay. Often, I have seen seniors at my school struggle with the process until the English department intervenes and English 12 teachers provide assistance with the essay. To supplement the English department or to offer a standalone, consider offering a college application workshop. The college workshop slideshow below outlines the process, offers tips on content, and provides advice on the structure, diction, and syntax required to separate your students' applications from the hundreds many admissions office receive each year. (Note: This is a tutor-created slideshow workshop written in 2017; double check for updated requirements when presenting a workshop of your own.)

College Essay Workshop

Presented to you by the PTHS Writing Lab

Advantages of the Essay

- Strengthens your application
- May be an opportunity to explain past mistakes
- Universities appreciate strong writing
- If it's "recommended" or "optional," DO IT!

What are Colleges Looking For?

- Your Personality
- Analytical Skills
- Depth of Thought
- Clarity of Expression
- Sincerity
- Thoughtfulness
- Natural Vocabulary

Getting into the Nitty Gritty

General Prompt Topics

See Common App Essay Prompt 2018-19 handout

Prewriting

- The first stage of the writing process
- Should be informal and unstructured
- Get your ideas on paper!
  - Google Drive Voice Typing
  - Lists
  - Stream of consciousness
  - Think now, organize later

What to Write

- Answer the prompt.
- Showcase who you really are.
  - No such thing as an "ideal student"
  - Be honest
- What sets you apart from others?
  - Individualization is key... Stand out!
- Be specific.
  - Unique, specific details
  - Personal anecdotes
- Write about something you actually enjoy.
  - True passion will show through your writing!

Questions to Consider - Brainstorm!

- What interests, activities, travels, struggles, or situations are unique to you?
- What have been some challenges in your life?
- What are some of the failures or disappointments in your life?
- What are some of your best memories?
- Who has been influential in your life?
- How have you changed over the past four years?

Advocating, Building, and Collaborating

Narrowing the Topic

- Choose something that matters to you.
- Keep audience (adult admissions advisors) in mind.
- Be appropriate.

Show, Don't Tell

- Descriptive adjectives
- Be positive
- Convincing evidence
- Focus on your virtues/strengths

Describe Your Accomplishments

- Update Naviance Resume.
- Admissions officers know that you're only in high school!
  - No one expects you to have accomplished grand acts.
  - Significant events can be subtle moments.
- Include your reactions to these experiences.
- Be specific and reflective!
- Show how you will continue to learn and grow.

Voice – your writing style

- Includes diction, tone, syntax, punctuation, and development
- If there were a mess of essays on the floor, would they be able to pick out your personality and identity from your voice?
- Stay true to your original experiences!
- Accentuate your best qualities.

Guidelines if You are over the Word Limit...

- Get all ideas on paper first.
- Focus on the main ideas.
- Cut out small details.
- Keep background minimal.
- Do not repeat ideas.
- Focus on your reflection, not the small details.
- Replace "to be" conjugations with stronger verbs.

Remember... DO **NOT** PROCRASTINATE!

Senior Experiences and Advice

Common App Online

commonapp.org

Writing Process Breakdown

Teachers in non-English departments might not feel confident in teaching writing or might not feel they have the time to go into specifics about it. Just like in the workshops above, the writing center can help in breaking down the writing process and sharing or creating writing process resources. Think about the resources you already have as an English teacher and work with the requesting teacher to modify a resource for that class. The following artifact shows a peer review process broken down into the three steps the teacher wanted students to focus on, with additional specifics for the assignment and connections to the rubric.

Peer Review
Write Yes or No on the line for the following criteria.
STEP 1

MLA (This is a research paper. You need to be citing correctly!)
_____ Correct MLA formatting:

- Times New Roman Font (This is Times New Roman)   Y   N
- Size 12 (This is size 12)   Y   N
- Double-spaced   Y   N
- 1" margins   (1/2" header)   Y   N
- Header with last name and page number   Y   N
- Heading: Name, Teacher Name, Class Name, Date   Y   N
- Works Cited: Is the title Works Cited centered?   Y   N
- Is the page alphabetized by the first word of the entry?   Y   N
- Do all entries have a hanging indent?   Y   N

_____ Are all in-text citations correct? Check each citation. The first part of the works cited entry should match to the in-text citation.
Example: The number of people who are worried about students who cannot read at grade level has increased in the past five years (Staples). It is only through the dedicated efforts of those in education, along with the combined efforts of parents, administrators, the community, and the students themselves that this problem will be solved (Dolby). One solution is to read about current topics of national and local interest, such as global warming ("The Impact of Global Warming").
_____ Is there a period <u>after</u> the parentheses?

Works Cited

Dolby, Nadine. "Research in Youth Culture and Policy: Current Conditions and Future Directions." *Social Work and Society: The International Online-Only Journal* 6.2 (2008): Web. 20 May 2009.
"The Impact of Global Warming in North America." *GLOBAL WARMING: Early Signs*. (1999): Web. 23 Mar. 2009.
Staples, Suzanne F. "What Johnny Can't Read: Censorship in American Libraries." *The Alan Review* 23.2 (1999): Web. 12 Jan. 2012.

STEP 2

Ideas & Content
As you read through the entire paper, if you are confused, box the text and put a question mark in the margins.
Introduction
_____ Hook that makes you want to continue reading.
_____ A couple sentences of background information.
      Is this information cited? _____ If not, draw a huge circle around it and write: cite!
_____ Specific thesis that tells what the paper is about including problems and solutions.
      As you understand it, what is this paper going to give information about?

Body Paragraphs
_____ Underline each topic sentence.
      Does each topic sentence state what the paragraph will be about? _____
_____ Do all of the sentences relate to that paragraph's topic? If not, highlight them and put a ?
_____ Are there citations in the paragraphs? Do you *clearly* know where all the info comes from?

Conclusion
_____ Is the thesis restated?
_____ Does the author summarize the main points?
_____ Does the author give the So What? Do they say why this issue is important?
_____ Is there a final thought on this issue?
          After reading this, what are you thinking?

Organization
_____ Intro paragraph?
_____ Are there 2 problem paragraphs?
_____ Are there 2 perspective/solution paragraphs?
_____ Is there a paragraph saying what the author believes is the best solution?
_____ Conclusion?
_____ Are there transitions between the body paragraphs?
          If not, write in TRANSITION HERE at the end of the <u>body</u> paragraph.

STEP 3
For this step, read the paper paragraph by paragraph, and look for each area separately.
Voice
      This is a research paper. You should not be giving your opinion (except in the proposed solution).
_____ 3rd person throughout. No I, we, us, our, you, etc. If you see these, cross them out.

Word Choice
_____ Does the writer use a variety of different words?
      If you notice the writer using the same word/phrase several times, circle them and note: Word Choice.
_____ Is there any advanced word choice. Put a star on the top of any higher-level vocab. ☺

Sentence Fluency
_____ Are the sentences varied? (When you read the paper out loud, do the sentences start to sound the same or are they a combo of long and short?)
_____ Do sentences start in different ways? (If you notice the writer starting several sentences in a paragraph the same way, circle this and make a note: SENTENCE VARIETY.

Conventions
_____ Can you read the paper easily without getting lost in run-on sentence, punctuation errors, etc.?
          If you see any errors (capitalization, run-ons, sentence fragments) point them out.
Comments:
What are two areas that you think the paper is strong in?
MLA   Ideas&Content Organization   Voice   Word Choice   Sentence Fluency   Conventions

What are two areas you think the paper needs work in?
MLA   Ideas&Content Organization   Voice   Word Choice   Sentence Fluency   Conventions

Come in to the [Name] Writing Center in [location] to receive additional help with your writing!

Written Response Questions

While English teachers are very comfortable using literature to teach their content, other classes can also have students read books related to their content. Science teachers might supplement with *The Radioactive Boy Scout*, health teachers might discuss *Staying Fat for Sarah Byrnes*, and history teachers might include *Hiroshima*. The writing center can help create resources for those novels, especially in the area of writing. The following resource was created for a special education teacher who wanted students to connect with the story while also starting to have discussions about what makes good writing.

The Glass Castle by Jeannette Walls

Section: II - The Desert   Pages: 29-31

Connection Questions:
1. Jeannette and her sister count at least 11 places they've lived. Where have you lived? If you've moved, when and why did you move? What was your favorite place you've lived?
2. Jeannette and her siblings wait around talking and reading for several hours while their parents are in the bar. What do you do when you have to wait for hours? How do you keep yourself busy?
3. When Jeannette falls out of the car, she finds herself alone and in a sticky situation. What would you do in this situation?
4. Jeannette's dad calls her nose a 'snot-locker,' and it makes her laugh. When you feel bad, how do people try to cheer you up?

Writing Style Questions:
1. One writing technique is to use both long and short sentences to provide variety. You can tell readers the same information both ways. Consider the first sentences of this passage: "It was late afternoon, and we were parked outside of a bar in the Nevada desert. It was called the Bar None Bar. I was four and Lori was seven. We were on our way to Las Vegas" (Walls 29).Try re-writing these sentences to make two sentences instead of four. Include all of the information, but it does not have to be in the same order. What do you think is better for this paragraph: having four sentences or two? Why do you think this?
2. During this section, the story goes from Lori and Jeannette talking about where they've lived to the family eating at the Bar None Bar. The author ends the section with Lori saying "We'd get caught". Think about why the author used this as a transition. Did it make you want to keep reading? Why? How and where might you use transitions in your own writing?
3. Narrative and academic writing contain many key differences. Consider the following sentence: "I got up and began to walk back toward the houses, and then I decided that if Mom and Dad did come for me, they wouldn't be able to find me, so I returned to the railroad tracks and sat down again" (Walls 30).This sentence combines multiple complete thoughts into one, while in most other forms of writing these thoughts would be separated into multiple sentences. Why did the author make this decision? What kind of effect did it create? Why wouldn't you use this in academic writing?

Involving Writing in Athletics

Partnerships can go beyond traditional classrooms and learning spaces. In this entry, resource material focused on writing to learn in athletics is presented to help educate your writing center staffers about the place of writing in sports. Once your staff members familiarize themselves with the resources, they could present the material to your school's athletic administrator or interested athletic coaches. Staffers might also create a resource page on your writing center website for coaches and athletes both in your school and throughout the community. For more resources like the one below, visit www.writingathletes.com.

What's Being Said About Athletes and Writing?

Athletes

"Writing for me is a way to process what is buzzing around in my head. When I put my thoughts on paper, I begin to see things more clearly."
—Sam Morse, U.S. Ski Team

"Writing in a journal can help clear out negative thoughts and emotions that keep you feeling stuck."
—Serena Williams, U.S. Tennis Champion

"Athletes should write down anything that they think is important... thoughts about their technique, goals, favorite foods... keep track of their aspirations and their passion."
—Mikaela Shiffrin, U.S. Olympic Gold Medal Ski Racer

"I enjoy writing in my journal when I'm sitting on the plane. I'm sure I'll go through a couple of pages and write down all the moments and experiences that I've had here in London."
—Michael Phelps, U.S. Olympic Gold Medal Swimmer

Athletic Coaches

"Team notebooks create a different way for players to learn."
—Mike Keller, Head Coach
University of Southern Maine Men's Soccer

"With the use of the Game Analysis in the team notebook, we were able to address issues individually that we would not be aware of otherwise. It was also such a great learning tool for the players."
—Amy Edwards, Head Coach
Gonzaga University

"Writing provides another avenue for strengthening the player/coach relationship."
—Brian Bold, Head Coach
Burnt Hills-Ballston Lake Soccer (NY)

"I like to have my student-athletes write about their experiences, be it about practice, a game, or even an injury. Writing helps them to analyze their play, thought processes, and feelings. It brings more meaning to what they are experiencing. Writing ... is a reminder of what we all are playing for and working towards."
—Nicole Moore, Head Coach
Stetson University (FL)

Writing Experts

"Writing organizes and clarifies our thoughts. Writing is how we think our way into a subject and make it our own. Writing enables us to find out what we know—and what we don't know—about whatever we're trying to learn."
—William Zinsser (*Writing to Learn,* 1988)

"We write not to say what we know, but to learn, to discover, to know. Writing is thinking, exploring, finding out..."
—Donald Murray, writing teacher

Sports Psychologists

"Keep a journal... This type of daily 'mental muscle' work will gradually improve your focus in practice and games."
—Leif H. Smith and Todd M. Kays, sport psychologists

What Resources are Available for Coaches, Athletes, and Others?

Website Resource

WritingAthletes.com is the comprehensive online resource for coaches, athletes, athletic administrators, and researchers. The website includes models of team notebooks, athletes' journals, articles, videos, and contact information.

Foundational Book in the Field
Writing on the Bus: Using Athletic Team Notebooks and Journals to Advance Learning and Performance in Sports, Richard Kent (2012, Peter Lang Publishing & National Writing Project). A sample chapter titled "David's Story: Writing Toward the Podium" is available online: http://www.writingathletes.com/davids-story-writing-toward-the-podium.html

Television Interview of Athlete
In "McNealy Seeks Constant Improvement," Steve Burkowski of The Golf Channel interviews then-Stanford junior, now-PGA professional, Maverick McNealy about how writing in this notebook transformed his game and helped him to become the 2015 NCAA College Player of the Year. https://www.golfchannel.com/video/stanfords-mcnealy-seeks-constant-improvement/

Radio Interviews of Coaches and Athletes
A 5-minute radio program from the Public Broadcasting Network, Writing Boosts Performance of Student-Athletes, that features coaches and athletes talking about the use of writing to enhance athletic performance. http://www.mainepublic.org/post/umaine-professor-writing-boosts-performance-maine-s-student-athletes

A one-hour radio show from the National Writing Project, Writing on the Bus that features coaches and athletes discussing writing. https://www.nwp.org/cs/public/print/resource/3900

What Can Teachers Learn from Athletes' Writing?
Activity Journals are a byproduct of athletes' writing. A copy of this *English Journal* article, "Learning From Athletes' Writing: Creating Activity Journals," is available through the National Writing Project: https://www.nwp.org/cs/public/print/resource/4549

References

Crutcher, C. (1993). *Staying fat for Sarah Byrnes*. New York, NY: HarperTempest.

Hersey, J. (1989). *Hiroshima*. New York, NY: Random House.

Kent, R. (n.d.) *Writingathletes.com*. Retrieved from http://www.writingathletes.com/

Silverstein, K. (2004). *The radioactive boy scout: The frightening true story of a whiz kid and his homemade nuclear reactor*. New York, NY: Villard.

Walls, J. (2005). *The glass castle: A memoir*. New York, NY: Scribner.

Chapter 8
Middle School Writing Centers
By Susan Frenck

Guiding Questions

- Why have a writing center in a middle school?
- In what ways can/should middle school writing centers be like high school writing centers?
- How can middle school writing center directors make use of the wealth of materials that are already available but were created for high school writing centers?
- What adjustments and modifications need to be made in the selection process, training process, and logistics of a middle school writing center because of the age of students?

Resources

- Writing Tutor Job Description
- Client Description and Needs
- Tutoring Session Outline
- The Five Coach-Mandments
- "What if..." Troubleshooting
- Role Play

Resource Contributors

- Renee Brown, PTMS Writing Lab at Peters Township Middle School, PA

Discussion

That a middle school writing center chapter has been included in this toolkit says a lot about the success of writing center work in secondary schools. What started as an idea in colleges and universities, that students can improve their writing skills with the support of a writing center, made its way to high schools and worked so well there that now more and more middle schools are getting involved. In 2017 for example, the SSWCA annual conference included middle school presenters for the first time, and middle school writing center directors held a roundtable at the conference to share experiences and resources.

And it makes perfect sense, although it may not yet be the norm, for middle schools to have writing centers. The benefits of a peer-based writing center make just as much sense for seventh and eighth graders as they do for high schoolers and college students. We have seen that writing centers in high schools empower students, encourage academic agency, and send a message about the importance of writing to the entire school. Why not bring all of that to a middle school too?

In addition, by introducing the ideas of writing center work to students at an earlier age, students come to high school already understanding the value of writing centers in their learning. They know upon arrival that when they want writing support, a writing center is where they can get it. That already happens when high school students move on to college. Now, with middle school writing centers, students can develop an educational mindset that "gets" why writing centers are so important to them as learners that much earlier.

Similarities Despite Our Differences

Including middle school writing centers in this toolkit shows the rightful inclusion of seventh and eighth graders in the writing center world. At the same time, it's also important that middle school centers are given a consideration that is separate from high school centers. Sure, there is a lot that is shared between high school and middle school writing centers, especially in the larger purposes and general operations. Middle school writing centers can be peer-collaboration based, have trained peer tutors, and focus on developing students as more empowered and capable writers through their work. What differentiates middle school from high school writing centers is more a matter of the specifics and degree. Writing center directors in middle schools can certainly use high school writing centers as a starting point for their own centers, and they will find all the resources in the other chapters of this toolkit very helpful in that sense. At the same time, the resources and models will likely also need to be modified so they will work in a middle school setting and with slightly younger students. Still, once they are adjusted, many of the materials you saw in previous chapters of this publication work well. In other cases, materials need to be created from scratch.

My own experience directing writing centers is relevant here. Two years ago I started a new teaching position at a middle school (grades 7 and 8) after having taught for over a decade at the high school level. I founded and directed a high school writing center where I previously taught, and that experience fully convinced me of the importance of having a writing center at every school. I had worked with motivated, enthusiastic student tutors, had become involved with SSWCA (at the time called CAPTA) and other writing center organizations, and had seen first-hand the impact the center had on my students. I was also aware that a few middle schools in the area had started successful centers, although I didn't know much about them at the time.

Shortly after the school year began at my new middle school, I spoke with the administration about starting a writing center (See chapter 2 for information on proposing a writing center). I was excited to find they were fully supportive of the idea, and they gave me the flexibility to set it up as I saw fit. I decided the best way to start was by using the tools I already had at hand. Rather than starting with a blank slate, it seemed easier to just transfer as much as possible from my high school experience to the middle school. And I was happy to discover that in lots of ways, taking that approach worked well.

School-wide support for the writing center was enthusiastic. The staff was happy I was creating a writing center, and just like my experience at the high school, some staff members were already familiar with writing center work. A few teachers had even worked as peer tutors when they were college students. Others were unfamiliar with the peer-based tutoring model of writing centers and saw them as "fix-it shops." So, the same need was there, just as there can be in a high school, to make sure it is made clear to other teachers what writing centers do (and do not do) (For resources on outreach, see chapter 5).

I also discovered that I could use the same main steps for setting up the writing center, those included in this toolkit, that I had used at the high school. Planning, informing the school community, and setting up the infrastructure of the center was, at least in the larger sense, all familiar and much like my high school experience (For more detail on planning, see chapter 2).

Making Adjustments

Where I started to see differences was, as I mentioned above, more a matter of degree than absolutes. For example, middle school students, not surprisingly, have less experience with academic writing, peer collaboration, and their own sense of themselves as writers than do high school students. Prospective middle school tutors are less accustomed to acting as writing tutors to other students, and they are generally more tentative about stepping into that role. So, I adjusted.

One of most substantial adjustments I made was in the recruitment process (See chapter 3). Because middle school students have little experience with nominations or applications, I found that simplifying the process and providing a lot of information at each stage was crucial to its success. For example, after students have been nominated by their English teachers to become tutors, I hold a general interest meeting. During the meeting I give information about what writing centers are and what being a peer tutor would entail. I explain the process for completing the application and emphasize that the nominees are expected to complete the application in full by the deadline. I send that information home in a letter for the nominees' parents and encourage them to talk about the expectations and the how to complete the application. (Note: I recommend including parents in middle school writing centers as much as possible!) I then hold a brief second meeting, during which the students who plan to apply can ask questions and review the application process and expectations. In the end the process is effective, but I have discovered that it requires that I provide a lot of information and put some scaffolds in place. That kind of step-by-step approach wasn't necessary when I was a director at the high school level.

Once tutors apply and are selected, I continue to modify and adjust. I provide more practice and more step-by-step guidance than is usually necessary with the high school tutors. I make sure tutors always have "cheat sheets" handy to remind them about our procedures and writing center best practices. And where tutoring sessions at the high school are often about 25 minutes long, which makes sense when working on an essay or multi-page report, the sessions at the middle school center, which more often focus on a single paragraph or multi-sentence short essay responses, work better when they are only 10-15 minutes long.

Adapting and modifying in this way has helped make the writing center a success at my middle school. We now have a strong team of 17 returning tutors, we have effective procedures in place for recruiting and training our new tutors, the writing center is becoming increasingly counted on to support writing across the curriculum (See chapter 7 for information about WAC), and we are continuing to add our middle school voices to the writing center community. The students who are involved with the writing center are taking more control of their education and are improving as writers.

Resource Note

The resources provided here are currently used by middle school writing center directors. They are designed to reach students of that age group, but they could potentially be adjusted to be used in a high school or other settings. The language is clear and "kid friendly"; the guidance is direct and positive. These documents also assume tutors have less experience with peer work, academic writing, or taking on a leadership role. Bulleted lists, steps, mnemonics, and accessible examples also help reach middle schoolers best. Jeff Brooks' "Minimalist Tutoring" (1991) approach is drawn upon in the training materials, as it is accessible and straightforward in its delivery. It also really works; the steps make sense and are easy to put into practice immediately.

As is the case with all writing centers, guidance on how to interact on a personal level with clients is crucial for tutor training. At the middle school level, the interpersonal is a big deal, to say the least. You will see that the materials here reflect that priority and focus on how to interact as a tutor in ways that help the tutor and client feel good about their interaction (See chapter 4 for more about tutor training).

Heading in the Right Direction

Middle school writing centers may not, even when they are well established, be just like high school centers, and that's perfectly okay. Our students are younger, the bell schedule is more restrictive, the students are only with us in the school for a couple of years, and the writing tasks are different. But middle school writing centers, however they are configured, provide an opportunity to introduce students to the value of writing centers and their own ability to participate in them. They are a means for students to start seeing themselves as lifelong writers and empowered learners who are capable of contributing to the learning community that is their school. The work they do can shape how they see themselves, education, and the school, as go through middle school, high school, and beyond.

Resources

Note: In the interest of being consistent, I use "tutor," and "writing center" in the descriptions below for "coach" and "writing lab," terms you will see in the documents themselves.

Writing Tutor Job Description

This document explains why the role of a writing center tutor is really that of a writing coach. The metaphor is effective because it is familiar to middle school students and helps emphasize to them that the peer's job in a session is to guide student writers, not to do the work. An activity is included to reinforce the ideas presented in the job description. Consider what term you will use to refer to the students working in your middle school writing center.

Coaches are people who know their sport well enough to guide others. The coach does not run onto the field to play *for* the team, but he or she will make a plan of attack, shout encouragement, and point out areas in which individual players can improve. A writing coach is similar to a sports coach because you cannot write the paper *for* another student, just like a coach cannot play *for* the team. A writing coach will create a plan for how to improve the paper based on the needs of each individual student. A writing coach will encourage students who visit the Writing Lab by complimenting the strengths of each paper. A writing coach will make suggestions for how students can improve their writing. And while one game is important to a coach, the coach's real aim is to make the entire season the best it can be. Similarly, a writing coach wants to help the student improve on the paper brought to the Writing Lab, but the writing coach also wants to help the student learn how to write better on future papers as well.

A writing coach will not "fix" or rewrite papers for any student. A writing coach is not expected to make a paper perfect. We are teaching and guiding other [School] students. It should be *their* best work, not *the* best.

"What Would a Coach Do?"
- A player is confused and doesn't understand the play:
- A player thinks she/he is the best on the team and doesn't need practice:
- A player is depressed because she/he never scores:
- A player did the wrong thing on the field:
- A player made a great play:
- A player is nervous because they are new to the team/sport:
- A player isn't the best on the team, but is improving:

Client Description and Needs

Here's a great example of a resource that helps middle school tutors gain a sense of empathy for the students who visit the writing center. The list of various perspectives a student can bring to a writing center session is particularly useful, as the tutors may not have considered that their view of writing isn't necessarily shared by everyone. A bulleted list of tutor and student responsibilities is also included to make clear how tutors can best serve clients. The language is accessible and direct--perfect for middle schoolers.

You will be working with both seventh and eighth grade students at [School] from every subject area. Every student will be different and will have different needs. We must be respectful of all students who come to us for coaching.

Some students will be very nervous to come to the Writing Lab for help. They might be afraid that you will judge them for making a mistake; they might be very busy with other assignments or be distracted; they might hate writing; they might be shy; they may not want to do any work and want you to fix everything. You will see people who are poor spellers, people who don't know their comma rules, people who have trouble getting started, but also students who are better writers than you.

Remember that even A+ papers can be improved, and spelling and commas are only a tiny part of the writing process. Coaches encourage and help the player improve the game. We respect all writers who come to the Writing Lab; if students aren't comfortable enough to come to us for help, then there will be no Writing Lab.

Duties and Responsibilities:

Writing Coach Responsibilities	Student Writer Responsibilities
<ul><li>Be respectful and honest</li><li>Be flexible and patient</li><li>Find something positive</li><li>Give ownership to the author</li><li>Listen well</li><li>Understand the assignment</li><li>Suggest how the writer can improve his/her writing</li></ul>	<ul><li>Be respectful and honest</li><li>Bring assignment sheet/rubric</li><li>Be open to suggestions</li><li>Take ownership of his/her own writing</li><li>Ask questions</li><li>Take coach's suggestions with an open mind and revise appropriately</li></ul>

Writing Center Session Outline

The next document provides clear and comprehensive instructions for how to conduct a writing center session by breaking the session into three main parts. Included in the description are activities and examples that provide additional guidance for the tutors. The writing samples are grade-level appropriate for middle school.

1. Greet and Gather Information
    a. When a student arrives, he or she should be greeted immediately with a *smile and a friendly hello.* If you are busy, acknowledge the student and say you will be with him or her in a minute. Help the student get logged into the computer so we have a record of who we helped.

    b. *Sit side-by-side* and not across the table from each other. This makes you a friendly peer and not an intimidating boss.

    c. You need to gather information about the writer and the paper before you can help. Also, the student will be more comfortable and will learn more if he or she sees you as a friend and not as a critic. Take a minute or two to *connect with the writer.*

    d. You will need to ask some of the following *questions* to figure out how you can help the student:
        i. Describe the assignment and what you were supposed to do.
        ii. Can I see the assignment sheet? (Then read over the assignment.)
        iii. Where are you in the writing process?
        iv. What are you trying to say/argue/do in this paper? Summarize what you are writing about.
        v. How is the paper going? What are you concerned about?

    e. *Don't judge.* You should NEVER talk poorly about teachers or assignments. Comments like, "Oh, I hated that last year," or "I know, he grades too hard," will get you in trouble. Likewise, you should not judge the paper by giving it a letter grade. If the teacher assesses the paper as a lower grade, the student may blame you for misleading them.

2. Coach, Don't Correct
    a. This is not your paper, so you should not take over control. Keep scratch paper and a pen or pencil nearby, but *avoid writing on the student's paper.* If the student doesn't have a pen or pencil, offer him or her one so that the student can make marks on his or her own work. People learn more by doing and are more likely to remember if they do it themselves.

    b. Many common mistakes, especially typos, can be found when the paper is read out loud. *Ask the student to read the paper out loud to you.* You will notice that they trip over certain sections because there is an error there. This is an easy way to help students learn to find their own mistakes. Point out that the reason it is difficult to read is because something needs to be revised. If the student is truly upset about reading out loud, you can read the paper out loud to them.

    c. *Stop after each paragraph* to see if the student has concerns about that small piece of writing. Ask if they noticed anything or are worried about anything in that paragraph. You can ask, "How do you feel about that paragraph?" If they have problems that they didn't see, this is a good time to make suggestions. You can take notes on your scratch paper and summarize each paragraph to give the student an outline by the end of the session.

    d. I'll take a *sandwich*. Before you say something that sounds critical, start with a compliment. After you offer a suggestion, some students will feel insecure or disheartened. Adding another compliment will help them keep an open mind. We call this a sandwich: positive comment, critical comment, positive comment. Your compliments must be genuine; no one likes a phony:
        i. What an interesting/original topic!
        ii. I can tell you've put a lot of work into this!
        iii. This sentence/phrase/word/character/setting/example is very powerful/original.

e. *Suggestions are not requirements.* Ask the student why they did something rather than simply correcting. For example, why did you put this example first; or why did you use only one example here? Use one of the following phrases to encourage the student to make revisions, but remember that you are not the author and you are not the teacher, so the student may choose to ignore your suggestions.
    i. You might want to think about…
    ii. I wonder if…
    iii. I'm confused by…
    iv. What I'm hearing you say is…
    v. Tell me more about…

f. *Focus on the big problems* rather than sentence problems. While commas are important, if the paper doesn't have a thesis and is one big paragraph, those bigger problems need to be revised first. Sometimes the writer doesn't realize these problems exist. Don't worry about punctuation unless the paper appears to have no other issues. Big problems include:
    i. Did they do what the teacher assigned? Did they meet the requirements?
    ii. Is there a thesis or main idea that is focused?
    iii. Is there enough support, evidence, or detail?
    iv. Do you understand everything? Are there any confusing parts?
    v. Is the info organized well? Should anything be moved to another place?

g. It's ok to explain something and then *ask the student to fix the next paragraph on their own*. For example, if you explain how to format dialogue, give the student five minutes to fix the rest of the story. You can then go back to check to see if the student was successful. This can work for spelling, commas, vocabulary, sentence structure, adding details or examples, and much more. Be sure to WAIT at least a minute between each question or suggestion to allow the student to think. Don't just throw answers at the student.

h. Finally, *don't overwhelm* the student by trying to make the paper perfect. If you realize there are tons of problems, decide what is the biggest problem and focus on just that. If you try to fix everything, then it's not *their* best but *your* best, they probably didn't learn anything.

"What Would a Coach Do?"
Read this student's paragraph:
Queen Mary I of England was a well-known queen to the Elizabethan Era. She was famous for having the nickname of "Bloody Mary." Mary was born into a family of many kings and queens. Queen Mary Tudor of England was a strong-minded ruler of the Elizabethan Era because of her background, religious faith, and ways of ruling.
- What is something you would say to the writer to compliment this writing?
- How would you suggest that the student stop using the word "Mary" so much?
- How would you suggest that the student start with something broader?
- What is one other suggestion you could make about this introduction paragraph?

Example Student Papers:
Aerial warfare caused a revolution. Orville and Wilbur Wright flew the first plane in Kitty Hawk, North Carolina before war started Bombers were an important part of World War II. Air power in WWII played a vital role in the war. It was so vital because many countries began to use airplanes in warfare. The first use of powered aircraft was by the Italian Army. Italians using the first powered aircraft is important because it was one of the first times that airplanes were used in war. That is why aerial warfare is a vital part of war.

When getting The Black Death, the victim usually coughed up a bunch of blood, an immediate sign of being near death. Victims would also get flu-like symptoms such as, chills and a fever. Victims of the disease would not be able to move due to extremely weak limbs. When very close to death, large amounts of blood would gush from the nose. Also, the victims' lymph glands would swell severely. There wasn't much food available to the poor, so many people went hungry. If you were wealthy, this wasn't a problem. The worst part of the plague was Europe's population decrease. The Black Death killed countless people in Europe. The worst part was they ran out of graves so they floated bodies down rivers. They also dug large trenches and filled them with infected bodies. Non-infected plague survivors were not allowed near trenches.

3. So Long and Survey
   a. Watch the clock to make sure you don't spend too much time with one issue. Sessions should last only 20 minutes, so with approximately five minutes remaining, warn the student and find a good place to end.

   b. *Summarize* your suggestions for how the student can revise the paper, smile and *invite the student to return* if he or she has more questions.

   c. Check that the student was logged in when they arrived. Complete the survey in your journal so that we can keep track of who you are helping. Do this before you help anyone else so that you don't confuse two students.

Guidance for Writing Center Sessions

Based on the analogy of a writing center tutor as a coach, the following acronym is a way to remind tutors of what their role includes. An enlarged version of this could be displayed in the writing center.

The Five Coach-mandments
1. C – Connect with the client
2. O – Only the client will write on the paper because it's their work, not ours
3. A – Ask questions to see how best to help and what the client wants
4. C – "Cheer" on clients to make them feel welcome and see what they are doing well
5. H – Help the client see other ways to improve the paper they may have overlooked, but let them make their own changes

Troubleshooting FAQs

What follows here is a troubleshooting document with questions and answers about common issues tutors face. The questions and answers are presented in middle school-friendly language, and the scenarios and solutions are geared to middle schoolers.

How do I know what to tell them to fix?
- Use your common sense. After the student reads his or her first paragraph, you should be able to tell if this is a very rough draft that needs help with the ideas or if it is a polished piece of writing that will only need a few changes. Here are some questions you should ask yourself as you respond to a piece of writing:
- Did the writer do what the teacher assigned? If not, that is the first thing that you should point out. Be kind and specific. Point to the assignment sheet and ask where the author included that piece. Have the writer verbally tell you an answer, then say, "Write that down," and help the author find an appropriate place to include that idea.
- Is the writing focused on one idea? It's easy to get distracted while writing. If you summarize each paragraph as it is read to create an outline, you can help the author see which paragraphs are not focused.
- Does the piece have a beginning, middle, and end? Are they developed?
- Is each paragraph complete? If not, what needs to be added?
- Does anything not make sense? If it doesn't make sense, it might be off topic, it might be worded poorly, more information may need to be added, or it may need to be deleted. Ask the writer what he or she is trying to say and then have him or her write down those words in place of the confusing parts.
- Are there other examples or better examples that would help make the argument stronger? Don't give people your examples, but ask them questions to help them come up with their own examples. Point out weaker parts and ask students to describe them further or expand them.

What if the student's work sounds plagiarized?
- Never accuse a student of plagiarism. You don't know who else has been helping the student, and perhaps their teacher told them to include something that you believe is plagiarized, but that may not be the case.
- Use a phrase such as, "This sounds different," or "This sounds funny." Ask the student how they came up with that sentence or section. They may say it is a direct quote, and then you can show them how to cite it properly. They may say they read it in a book, and then you can show them how to paraphrase it properly.
- To paraphrase, pull the paper towards you so that the student can't see it clearly. Read the sentence out loud and turn the paper upside-down. Ask the student what the sentence is talking about or what it means. Have the student write his or her new words on the back of the paper. Show them how that is a paraphrase – the same idea in different words.
- If the student claims the sentence is their work, but you suspect plagiarism, you can suggest that they should check with a teacher, either their teacher or [Teacher Name]. When you aren't sure, it is best to ask the adult who will be the final judge.

What if the student says all he or she wants help with is commas?
- Most students will say they want you to proofread their paper because they don't know what else you can do. While you are probably very good with conventions, there are usually more important problems that the student doesn't realize he or she needs to address.
- Don't snap at the student, "We don't proofread," because that will make the student insecure and will lead to a less productive session.
- Tell the student that you can give them some help with conventions, but you will have a better idea about their topic once you start reading. As you look at each paragraph, politely point out that other changes can also improve their writing.
- At the end of the session, if there is time, go back to address ONE convention issue. No one is going to learn all the comma rules in 20 minutes, so pick one type of error that you saw. If they don't have compound sentence commas, point it out, explain it, and ask the student to find another place where they made that error.

What if I read something that makes me uncomfortable or that is inappropriate?
- You should never be asked to stay in a situation that makes you uncomfortable. If you are reading a paper that uses inappropriate language, you can suggest to the student that the audience of their teacher and classmates won't appreciate that language. If saying that makes you uncomfortable, then politely tell the student that while the paper has strengths, right now it isn't ready to be looked at by a writing coach. Ask them to talk to their

teacher about the assignment and come back to the Writing Lab once they have a stronger idea for the assignment. Always tell [Director] when you get a paper that makes you uncomfortable.

What if the paper is wrong?
- Sometimes people do research that leads to incorrect information. Some things are factual, and if you know they are wrong, you can politely point out the misunderstanding. For example, the Germans did not bomb Pearl Harbor with the atomic bomb. If you see a fact that you know is incorrect, you need to find a way to inform the student without putting the student down. You should say something like, "I thought I saw in our social studies book that the Japanese bombed Pearl Harbor. Maybe that's a typo, but you should double check that fact to make sure things didn't get mixed up."
- If you believe something is incorrect but you are not certain, inform the student to double check their research. It is ok to say to a student, "I'm not sure that date is correct. You may want to ask [Teacher] just to make sure."
- Sometimes people write about things that are neither wrong nor right. These are opinion pieces, such as who will make a better president of the USA. If you disagree with the author, you should not raise your opinion in the coaching session. Be polite and respectful. Check the paper and help the student as you would with any other paper.

What if there is too much wrong with the paper?
- You can't fix everything in twenty minutes. You need to prioritize. When you see the first paragraph, decide what is the biggest problem and start with that. Go back to "Focus on the big problems." Remember, the student can always come back to get more help once they have revised.

What if the student asks a question that I can't answer?
- You are not expected to be perfect. If the student genuinely needs help with punctuation, first, try your best to help. Explain why certain spots need punctuation. If you feel you cannot help, ask another writing coach if they are available to work with that student. If there are one or two specific questions that you are unsure about, ask [Directors]. You know more than you think you do, so do your best to help in any way you can, but it is ok to tell the student that you don't know something. You're a writing coach, not a professional editor.

Role Play Scenarios

This document includes a series of scenarios that can be used to role play how tutors can effectively approach various writing center situations. These were inspired by *The Bedford Guide for Writing Tutors* (2016) but were adapted to be more accessible and relatable to middle school students. Note that the students are asked to take the perspective of a student who is seeking help, which helps middle school tutors consider their clients' points of view about writing and the writing center. The details in each scenario make them realistic and allow for a rich conversation of the tutor's approach.

1. Teacher's Assignment: Your art teacher tells you to describe your room is great detail using all five senses. She tells you it can be one big paragraph, but it needs an intro and conclusion.
   - Your Role: You didn't have a lot of time because the teacher assigned this on Monday and it's due tomorrow (Wednesday), plus, you have tests in your core classes that you have been studying for. You haven't really checked this paper yet. The paper is for art class, so you don't think the teacher will really care about conventions.
   - One Real Problem in Your Paper: Use the word "you" too much and don't put any commas in the paper at all. If the coach comments on this, say that you don't think the teacher will care because it's for art class.
   - What You Ask for Help With: Tell the coach you want to make sure you got all five senses and enough description to make your art teacher give you an A. If the coach offers other advice, you can say you're only interested in the details, but if the coach continues, allow the coach to offer you other advice as well. Don't be too closed-minded.

2. Teacher's Assignment: Your Social Studies teacher asked you to write a three-paragraph essay about the most important invention in history. You need an intro, body, and conclusion. (You can choose your own invention or you can borrow one of these if you are stuck: light bulb, airplane, internet)
   - Your Role: You are a terrible speller and don't have any idea how to use commas. Your ideas are solid, but spell everything wrong you can and put commas in completely random places. Make your sentences all very long run-on sentences. Capitalize random words and lowercase the first word on most sentences.
   - One Real Problem in Your Paper: Conventions!
   - What You Ask for Help With: Tell the coach you are a really bad speller and need help to make sure everything is "right."

3. Teacher's Assignment: Your homeroom teacher is making you write a paragraph about your ideal friend as part of our character-building activities. You will have to share your paragraph out loud with the class.
   - Your Role: You have no organization or transitions. Include characteristics of a good friend, but put no intro or conclusion. Don't use words like *also, first*, etc. Start most sentence with the words "A Good friend…" Your ideas are ok and your conventions are ok, but your ideas are very scattered. Talk about a quality like being honest in the first sentence then not again until much later in the paragraph.
   - One Real Problem in Your Paper: In your paper you need help connecting and combining ideas to help your paragraph "flow." You need transitions like "First…" "In addition…" "Finally…"
   - What You Ask for Help With: Tell the coach that when you read it to your homeroom you don't want to sound stupid. Point out that because you are reading it out loud, spelling and commas won't count.

4. Teacher's Assignment: Your teacher wants a paragraph about the biography of a famous person. It's only a paragraph but you need lots of specific information like when and where they were born, all their accomplishments, etc. (I've attached an article on Shakespeare for you to use in case you forgot what you learned last year in ELA.)
   - Your Role: You forgot about this paper until last night. It is due by the end of the day. You went online and copied word for word some sentences about Shakespeare because you don't have a lot of time. Start the paragraph with your own words, then copy word for word two or three sentences from the attached paper. Then end with your own sentence again.
   - One Real Problem in Your Paper: Your paper is plagiarized. See if the coach can spot the copied parts and if so, what the coach says.
   - What You Ask for Help With: Tell the coach it's due at the end of the period so just make sure it "sounds ok." Don't tell the coach you copied. If the coach asks you if you copied, say that you didn't have a lot of time so you "used the internet to help you." Don't ever admit that you "copied" or "plagiarized," just say you needed some extra "help."

References

Brooks, J. (1991). Minimalist tutoring: Making the student do all the work. *The Writing Lab Newsletter*, 15 (6), 1-4.

Ryan, L., & Zimmerelli, L. (2016). *The Bedford guide for writing tutors* (6th ed.). Boston, MA: Bedford/St. Martin's.

Chapter 9
University Partnerships
By Jeffrey Austin and Christine Modey

Guiding Questions

- How can a secondary school writing center director start a partnership with a university?
- How can a cross-level partnership be beneficial to both collaborators?
- What should be the goals of such a partnership, jointly and separately, for students and directors?
- What practical and logistical considerations need to be considered when forming such a partnership?

Resources

- Email of Introduction
- Planning Timeline and Field Trip Communication
- Student Visit Worksheet
- Agenda for a University Visit
- Conference Proposal
- Professional Learning Network Expansion

Resource Contributors

- Jeffrey Austin, Skyline Writing Center at Skyline High School, MI
- Renee Brown, PTMS Writing Lab at Peters Township Middle School, PA
- Amber Jensen, George Mason University, VA; formerly of Edison Writing Center at Edison High School, VA
- Christine Modey, Sweetland Center for Writing at University of Michigan, MI
- Stacey Waldrup, Raider Writing Center at Crescent Valley High School, OR

Discussion

A working relationship with a college or university partner can open doors and break barriers for secondary school directors and tutors, while benefiting tutors and directors at postsecondary institutions as well. The partnership between the Skyline High School Writing Center and the Sweetland Center for Writing at the University of Michigan, formed in 2014, features a framework rooted in co-learning among equals – each of us has something to contribute, each of us has something to gain.

Our egalitarian model is only one possible framework that you could select for your partnership, a choice which is ultimately contextual. Jeff was trained as a Sweetland consultant and had an operational center when Christine extended invitations to local high school faculty and students to visit Michigan's campus to explore the possibility of starting high school writing centers in their buildings. After the open house, Jeff reached out to Sweetland to explore a partnership. After discussing our institutional contexts, we decided that the most mutually beneficial framework was one that would build capacity for tutors at both institutions through shared professional development. However, a secondary school center's need for additional training, more resources, or more intensive mentorship might require a different partnership style, one in which the university center, using a service-learning model, provides expertise to the secondary school writing center director and tutors. Yet another framework might be necessary to reach a different goal. For instance, Skyline also maintains a partnership with the Eastern Michigan University Office of Campus and Community Writing (C2W) focused on amplifying literacy skills for K-8 students in our surrounding communities. Here, C2W provides training around community literacy to Skyline students before partnering them with a community or school organization who needs volunteers. This is a third model for a secondary school-university partnership, where the two writing centers work together to extend their reach into the broader community. In such a case, the secondary school writing center can often provide deeper access to community members while the university provides connections between agencies and writing center personnel.

Regardless of the framework you select for your partnership, there are a range of issues that need to be carefully considered to help ensure the lasting success of your collaboration.

Mission

For both the secondary school writing center and for the college writing center, finding energy and support for the collaboration will be easier if the purpose of the collaboration dovetails with the missions of both organizations (See chapter 2). This consideration is perhaps even more crucial for the college writing center, whose "mission" is typically to provide academic support to enrolled students. This consideration may be driven strongly by the funding model of the writing center, as well as by the mission of the college or university. For instance, at the Sweetland Center for Writing, the role of the writing center is clearly articulated in our mission statement: "to support student writing at all levels and in all forms and modes." The center has neither funding for community outreach, nor an institutional mandate for it. Nevertheless, by tailoring the purpose of the collaboration to goals of the program (i.e. the practitioner development of undergraduate writing consultants), we've received modest funding to support our work and an acknowledgment of its value in helping our writing consultants to continue to develop their skills to support student writing. In another context, the writing center at Michigan State University; broader institutional support for community outreach and missional commitment to "the community;" and work "beyond traditional modes and geographic boundaries" enables an ongoing program, Beyond Insights, staffed and administered by the writing center, to take place in the Lansing public schools. To effectively leverage resources, each partnership will need to negotiate a collaboration that is appropriate within its local context.

Labor Involved

Both secondary school and college partners need to be aware of the labor entailed in developing and sustaining a partnership. For both partners, the labor will include joint meetings to get acquainted, discuss shared and divergent interests, and design and develop the collaboration. For the college partner, additional meetings may be required with other stakeholders, for example, the university community outreach office or service learning office. Depending upon the program, some training for the college partner faculty and peer tutors may also be involved, to understand the nature of service learning, to train for their role, to develop cultural competence, and to understand how to enter and exit a community appropriately. The college partner will likely also be responsible for ensuring that participating peer tutors have the required background checks to work with minors. The secondary school partner will have to complete the required paperwork for taking students off campus and perhaps work to ensure adequate chaperones. They will need to prepare their students for the activities of the partnership, either by preparing them to welcome their partners for training and coaching them for their presenting roles or by ensuring that they are prepared for whatever intervention the college writing tutors have been enlisted for. Other labor might involve applying for funding to support the partnership or reporting back to stakeholders about the activities. Some evaluation of the program, to ensure it is meeting its goals, is also appropriate and possibly expected, depending upon the nature of the program, its stakeholders, and its funding source.

Mutual Benefit

In our view, it is essential that both partners in the collaboration – the secondary school and the college or university writing center – benefit from the program. In some models, the secondary school is positioned as the primary beneficiary: because its tutors get free training, because its students get additional, free help with writing-related tasks, or because its faculty leader gets professional development and access to a professional learning network. In such models, based on service learning principles, the benefits to each party are different. In more collaborative models, however, benefits can be more similar. By designing a program that requires parallel contributions from both the secondary school and the college writing center, tutors learn a variety of collaborative skills. Among the collaborative skills they learn are negotiating interests, goals, and agendas; working across grade level; presenting content and facilitating discussion; and expanding their tutoring strategies. Discussing the differences between writing centers at the college and the secondary school levels also provides insight into the different conditions of our work, as well as into the differences between secondary school and college writing. Considering our commonalities, however, allows tutors to learn tutoring strategies from those older and younger than they and for the collaborating faculty to consider how they might learn from each other's programs. In such a collaborative model, not only are the benefits mutual, they are reciprocal.

Program Goals

Clarity around the goals of the collaboration will aid in choosing among various possible activities, focusing time and energy among collaborators, and evaluating success. The goals may require some negotiation, as each party may have a different interest in the partnership. Clarity around goals allows the partners to identify activities that will provide benefits to both parties and both programs. For instance, the Sweetline partnership has chosen additional professional development as our main goal, which means that our programming focuses on various peer tutoring topics. This addresses Skyline's interest in supplementing its brief weekly professional development opportunities with an extended half-day workshop once in the fall and once in the winter, alternating between Sweetland and Skyline locations. It also addresses Sweetland's goal of providing alternative professional development for tutors who cannot attend regular weekly staff meetings or who wish to have exposure to a secondary school setting. Increasing ties between Skyline and Sweetland also achieves the program goal of enlarging the tutors' writing center community of practice, showing high school writers possibilities for writing center work at the college level. We agree that another shared goal is the development of a writing center partnership with a close colleague with whom one can discuss topics of writing center practice and administration. The clarity around these shared goals has allowed us to spend our time together in productive ways. When we evaluate our program, we are able to consider whether our tutors' thinking about writing center work changes, whether they implement or discuss the topics presented in our semi-annual workshops, and whether our partnership, as directors, changes practice in our own writing centers or bears fruit for the broader writing center community.

Benefits

Directors can find local professional partners in a field where nearby support can sometimes prove difficult, while tutors are able to connect with post-secondary colleagues who can serve as mentors, guides, and co-learners. These relationships can help those in secondary school centers work against the sense of isolation and the fear of misunderstanding that account for much of their expended emotional labor (See chapter 1 for more on directors' emotional labor). Connecting with members of a local community expands the circle of people who care about your program's well-being and success. In addition, inviting post-secondary partners into secondary school directors' professional learning networks (PLNs) can have the effect of helping secondary directors, tutors, and programs develop a writing center "ethos." In 2017, Jeff worked with a team of people to develop and administer a census of secondary school writing centers detailed in chapter 1. It showed, among other things, that most people in a directorial position were self-trained by reading about writing center pedagogy and doing online research. While SSWCA and IWCA have growing mentorship programs, many folks lack direct access to local mentorship, which can be a vital part of any substantive PLN. New entrants to our community require support and mentorship from multiple sources to reflect, learn, and grow to prevent burnout and aid in retention. A university partnership is one tool to consider in order to address this issue.

Post-secondary partners can also find valuable professional relationships from which they and their tutors can directly benefit. The insight and expertise gained through these partnerships can help incubate and support new initiatives at the post-secondary writing center. Last year, we used our cross-level partnership to bring secondary and postsecondary writing center directors together at Sweetland for a "meet up" in an effort to strengthen the exceptional programs we have in the region. In addition, we have presented at national and regional conferences about cross-level issues as part of our partnership. On the consultant side, college and university students working alongside high school and middle school students may not only receive valuable professional development, but they may also find a kind of "vocational clarity," particularly if they are inclined toward careers in education. Two of Christine's former tutors have gone on to student teach with Jeff and several of Jeff's former tutors have become Sweetland consultants.

Moving Forward

Any successful partnership must begin with an understanding of the often marginalized place of secondary schools in the broader writing center community. The histories of secondary school writing centers deserve a prominent place in the histories of writing centers. Such revision is encouraged by substantive partnership and responsible allyship from those in privileged spaces within our community. Support doesn't mean saving; secondary school writing centers aren't broken and don't require fixing. Indeed, honoring the funds of knowledge of secondary school writing centers is imperative for an equitable relationship. This means that the voices of secondary school directors and tutors are included at any level of the partnership from program design to social media marketing to conference presentations and articles. Joining together allows secondary school writing center directors to contribute to a conversation that they may not have previously been able to access, expanding their PLNs and making original contributions to writing center scholarship. Partnerships between secondary school and university writing centers can help secondary school writing centers move from the periphery to the center of the writing center universe.

Resources

Email of Introduction

This is the email a SSWC director sent to a university to establish a partnership. It is an example of how a director may "cold-call" directors at the collegiate level to open lines of communication.

Hello, [director's name],

[Introduce who you are and where you teach]. I am also the director of the writing center in our building where I work with a group of [age or number] students who work within the writing center model to give one-on-one tutoring and writing feedback to their peers.

I'm emailing you because I'm looking for a way to enrich their experiences here in our WC, and I wondered if you might be open to having my tutors visit the [name of university WC] for an afternoon.

I have [number] students, all of whom have been trained in the basic theories of writing center practices. I built this program based on [list your own training or books you use]. This is my [number] year running a secondary level WC, and while I am extremely pleased with my students and the work they do, I am always looking for opportunities to enrich their experiences and to improve the help they offer.

I'd love to bring my students to [university] in order to spend a few hours with some of your consultants if you believe that is possible. I've listed my contact information below.

Thank you so much for your time and consideration. I look forward to hearing from you.

Planning Timeline and Field Trip Communication

For secondary school directors, navigating the logistics of taking students off-site can be one of the most challenging parts of a postsecondary partnership. The administrative and emotional labor of seeking approval for field trips can sometimes be overwhelming, but tensions can be reduced with excellent planning and clear, consistent communications with all pertinent stakeholders, such as tutors, their parents, and your school and district administrative team. The first resource is a sample timeline one director uses when her tutors visit their local university partner. The second is a sample letter used to communicate logistics and goals of the trip to the parents and guardians.

Sample 1

- Contact college WC director with a clear statement of goals and vision for the trip (first weeks of the school year)
- Communicate with district administration to organize transportation and other logistics (as soon as logistics are confirmed with university director)
- Communicate with parents via letter and permission slip (6-8 weeks prior to visit)
- Prepare students by asking each to choose a piece of writing to take to the university WC and complete associated handouts (2-3 weeks prior to visit)
- Provide students with time to prepare a short presentation about the SSWC (2-4 students) (2 weeks before visit)
- Discuss schedule for the day (i.e. dress, time to leave, lunch/snacks, what to bring, time returning) (the week prior to visit)
- Provide students with time to reflect on and discuss their observations and experience as well as how to implement new techniques into the SSWC (immediately after the visit)

Sample 2

Dear Parents and Guardians,

I am so very pleased with the work that your child is doing as part of our writing center. In an effort to further enrich the experience your child is receiving from his/her participation as a tutor, I have arranged a field trip.

The students who work in our writing center will be traveling to [University] to visit with the college writing center on their campus. We will tour their facility to see what a college level writing center is like and have time to share our experiences with them. In addition, students will work one-on-one with the college-student-consultants to improve a piece of writing. Our students will observe these sessions offered to see similarities between our two centers and how we can improve our own practice.

We will leave the school at [time and date]. [Add information about cost, lunch, dress code, mode of transportation, or other logistical concerns parents may have.] We will return to the school at [time].

This trip is an amazing opportunity for our students to see how the work they do is on par with much of what is done at the collegiate level, and the knowledge we gain from going to [University] will certainly improve our writing center further.

Please let me know if you have any questions.

Student Visit Worksheet

If you have a chance to visit a college writing center in your area for an observation, this form provides a structure for tutors to record what they notice for later discussion. It's a great way to help them see the connections between what tutors at a secondary school are doing and what tutors in other schools' centers are doing as well. (Note: They'll be surprised tutoring approaches are so universal!) The following two forms are ways to direct students' observations, organize future discussions about their observations, and make connections to their home writing center.

Sample 1

What school did you visit?	
With who did you speak? (Names and positions)	
Overview of the Writing Center	
When is the writing center open?	
What kinds of students come into the writing center? Are students required to come or do they come on their own?	
What is the process of signing up for an appointment?	
How long does each appointment last?	
Writing Center Tutors	
What are the tutors called?	
How are student tutors selected? (Application/interview process? Prerequisites? Undergrad/Grad students? Areas of study?)	
What does tutor training entail? (Course work, tutor training sessions, observations, tutor portfolios?)	
How are tutors compensated? (scholarship, hourly pay, yearly stipend?)	
What are the expectations of tutors?	
Reflection on Visit	
What did you notice that was similar to our writing center?	
What was different?	
Did you see evidence of Writing Across the Curriculum? Explain.	
What good ideas can you bring back to contribute to our Writing Center?	

Sample 2

Pre-Field Trip Anticipatory Questions

1. What is the title of the piece you brought to the writing center?
2. What type of writing is it (creative, essay, etc.)?
3. Summarize the piece.
4. What are your concerns about your writing (content, style, organization, conventions, etc.)?
5. What are your concerns about working with a college writer?

Post-Field Trip Reflection Questions

1. Describe the feeling of working one-on-one with someone that you know is a better writer than you are.
2. What was something positive that resulted from this session?
3. Was there anything uncomfortable during this time or something you wish the consultant had done to make your time together better?
4. What is something that you learned today about writing that you can include when you write in the future?
5. What is something you will do differently when you work in our writing center since you had this experience?

Agenda for a University Visit

The form and function of the agendas you set for your visit will depend largely on the goals and outcomes you have established for your partnership. Below are two agendas used in professional development workshops for tutors. Directors should work with their tutors to create interactive, multimodal workshops that feature short bursts of direct instruction, time for guided and independent practice, and ample time for self and whole-group reflection.

Sample 1

Play + Funds of Knowledge in the Writing Center

	8:00-8:15 AM	Welcome: Breakfast - (Re)introductions - Mingling
Time	**Description of Activities**
8:15 am – 8:50 am	What Is Education for?
	In small groups at your tables, identify what others (teachers, parents, counselors, etc.) say education is for. What do YOU say it's for? Distribute copies of Whitman's poem and Gutting's article. Read these two pieces silently. Discuss the following questions in your table groups: 1. What do these two pieces have to say about knowledge and education? 2. Where do you find yourself agreeing and disagreeing with the writers? 3. To what extent has your education mirrored the education(s) described here? Collect responses. ---- Materials: index cards, pens, copies of Whitman's poem and Gutting's article
8:50 am – 9:25 am	Our Funds of Knowledge
	Writing: What do you know, or are able to do, that is given little value in school? (5 min.) Link icebreaker: everyone stands in a circle. One person starts in the middle and names something they know or can do that is given little value in school. Someone in the circle who shares that same piece of knowledge then takes their place and names something else. Game continues until everyone has been in the circle. (10 min.) Collect the responses on paper and then look at them together. Are there patterns? ---- Materials: Google Slides
	9:25 am – 9:35 am BREAK

9:35 am – 9:45 am	**Defining Funds of Knowledge**
	Watch video about funds of knowledge.

Share David Sheridan's anti-curriculum schemata.

Why does understanding funds of knowledge matter for peer tutors? How can we help students who might not have access to the normative funds of knowledge a) access their own funds of knowledge and b) use them to complete work within the context of the institution that privileges different kinds of knowledge and learning?

Materials: Google Slides |
| 9:45 am – 10:30 am | **Play** |
| | Think/pair/share: How do you play?

Characteristics of play: self-chosen and self-directed; means are valued more than ends; guided by mental rules; non-literal, imaginative, marked off in some way from reality; active, alert non-stressed state of mind

Types of play: Creative; Games with Rules; Language play; Physical play (physical play; exploratory play; manipulative play; constructive play); Pretend (pretend, role playing; small world; socio-dramatic play)

Goals (to be drawn from a bowl): risk; structure; expand & explore; engage; complicate

Activity: play stations

Debrief: How did you and your group members draw on funds of knowledge in your play?

Materials: blocks, Legos, pattern blocks, art supplies, dress up, Fraggles, list of goals |
| 10:35 am – 11:00 am | **Playing with Funds of Knowledge in Academic Writing** |
| | Focused freewrite:

How can we use play to help writers draw on their funds of knowledge as they approach academic writing tasks?

Debrief.

Photos.

Materials: sample writing assignment |
| | 11:15 am-11:30 am \| Room Clean-Up - Material Return - Adjournment |

Sample 2

The Growth Mindset: Writers, Tutors, and Programs

One of the important things that peer writing tutors do is to help others learn. In that process, we draw on our own learning experiences. The work of Carol Dweck suggests that those who cultivate a positive attitude toward difficult learning tasks (what she calls a "growth mindset") often outpace those who believe their intelligence is fixed and that lack of skill means lack of ability. Cultivating a growth mindset in the writers who visit us can help them to see writing as a set of learnable skills they can improve through practice. For peer tutors, cultivating a growth mindset can help them overcome the inevitable challenges and frustrations of their work to grow and thrive in their role. In this workshop, we will learn about growth mindset and also about how well-designed feedback can help us to grow as tutors.

Time	Description of Activities
8:00 am–8:30 am	Breakfast and Mingling
	After everyone gathers some breakfast snacks, the table facilitators will facilitate a discussion in response to the following prompt: Describe a time when you struggled to learn something. What factors contributed to your success or failure in learning? Debrief this discussion and make a list of the factors we identify. --- Materials: paper, markers
8:30 am–9:30 am	Growth Mindset Video
	Introduce and watch Carol Dweck's TED Talk about growth mindset. Then, in NEW small groups, discuss the following questions: 1. How might what we know about learning (our own experiences and Dweck's research) help us to work more effectively with writers in the writing center? 2. What concrete strategies might we use to work more effectively? 3. How will we know when we're working effectively? ---- Materials: paper, markers
	9:30 am - 9:40 am Break
9:40 am–10:00 am	Data in the Writing Center
	How and what can we learn from the data we collect? [Directors] will describe the data their writing centers collect, why they collect it, and for whom. Compiled data will be distributed and reviewed. What does it reveal? What does it conceal? ---- Materials: PowerPoint slides, copies of compiled writing center data

10:00 am - 10:30 am	**Design Your Ideal Feedback Form**
	Taking into account what we've learned about ourselves as learners, about growth mindset, and about our centers, working with your small group, design your ideal feedback form. Be prepared to explain what you'll collect, why you'll collect it, and for whom. ---- Materials: paper, markers
10:30 am- 11:00 am	**Gallery Walk**
	With your small group, walk around and view the other ideal feedback forms that have been created. • What do they have in common with your ideal form? • What is different? • What might your writing center take away from this exercise? Observations/reflections/next steps
	11:00 am-11:25 am | Room Clean-Up - Material Return - Adjournment

Conference Proposal

As a partnership between secondary and postsecondary school writing centers grows, the professional relationship between their directors often grows as they find shared interests, ideas, and values. As the Professional Learning Network becomes increasingly sophisticated, there may be a desire by both parties to share their work with an external audience, potentially at a local, regional, or national meeting or conference. The topics of the presentations and collaborations aren't necessarily limited to just the partnership itself, as there are many issues that impact the work of writing centers and tutors at both levels. Below is an example of what was submitted for presentation at our regional WC conference. On the left is a breakdown of what each part of the proposal is.

> **Literature review, theory on which the presentation is based**

In *The Working Lives of New Writing Center Directors* (2016), a case-study of nine first- and second-year writing center directors in a variety of different contexts, Grutsch McKinney, Caswell, and Jackson offer a tripartite construction for classifying directors' labor: "everyday" (i.e., administrative tasks), "disciplinary" (e.g., academic engagement), and "emotional" (i.e., building and maintaining community). The everyday and disciplinary elements of writing center labor are the most intellectually tangible to external stakeholders as both seem to speak starkly to the success of a program and its director, but the "emotional" work of writing centers, which is often the driving determinant of success, often remains invisible precisely because of non-quantifiability. As Grutsch McKinney et al. write, emotional labor, especially building functional communities, "must be done, but it doesn't 'count'" (p. 187), at least not in the sense that one could use it on a review or to present to stakeholders or evaluators as a metric of success. Here, the emotional work--building and sustaining internal and external relationships--becomes "invisible institutionally" (Grutsch McKinney et al. p. 195), perpetuating narratives of writing center leadership as a difficult, solitary endeavor.

> **Literature discussion, conclusions drawn from research, statement of a problem the conference presentation will address**

The case studies in *The Working Lives of New Writing Center Directors* reveal that while emotional work is perhaps the most invisible of the labor classifications, it is also the work that provided a high level of personal and professional satisfaction to directors. This echoes the point that Anne Geller and her co-authors make in *The Everyday Writing Center* (2007): writing centers are not so much about a place but about attachments, connections, meaning and experience. Indeed, they argue: "we can discern that at the heart of meaningful writing center administration lies not efficiency, marketing or recordkeeping (these are peripheral matters in fact), but the leaderful, learningful stewardship of a dynamic learning and writing culture and community" (p. 14). While these emotional components of writing center work, namely community building, are seen as having vital importance to a center's success and a director's happiness and longevity, Grutsch McKinney and her co-authors found no scholarship on how to actually do the emotional labor that, as previously noted, is absolutely central to directing a writing center: "there are no other writing center studies addressing emotional labor and only a few mentions of emotional labor elsewhere in writing studies" (p. 186). While writing center directors are often prepared for many tasks of administration inherent in their work, they are perhaps the least prepared for the toil of building and sustaining community within the writing center and with the institution because it is ethereal, intangible, densely qualitative, and, in general, involves work that cannot be prepared for in advance. Without community and a recognition of emotional labor, writing center directors problematically become strangers because, as Sara Ahmed argues in *Strange Encounters* (2000), they are unable to participate in important exchanges of social capital within their institution that legitimize their existence.

> **Proposal for presentation, what the presentation will do and offer**

Given the importance of community building to writing center directors and the relative lack of supportive scholarship on the issue, our presentation will look at intentional, visible community building efforts in two different institutional contexts--a secondary school writing center at Skyline High School in Ann Arbor, Michigan and the Sweetland Center for Writing at the University of Michigan--as the urgent issue of how to make emotional labor "count" cuts across centers at all levels. In *Working Lives*, Grutsch McKinney, et al. echo this idea: "Although we buy the notion that context matters...we noticed our case-study participants had commonalities in their labor despite very different local contexts" (p. 168). Using Wenger's notion of a community of practice and Grutsch McKinney's reflections on the writing center "grand narrative" from *Peripheral Visions for Writing Centers* ("a writing center is place all students go to get one-on-one tutoring on their writing"), our presentation will offer attendees opportunities to consider how changing the narrative of their center can provide more time to do the satisfying work of building community within and beyond the writing center. Indeed, by shifting writing center narratives away from an all-consuming focus on one-to-one tutoring as a "raison d'etre," directors can involve themselves less in the administrative minutiae of contact numbers and session hours--what Grutsch McKinney and co-authors refer to as "everyday" labor--and more on the deliberate construction of local and global communities through processes like consultant recruitment and training and campus-wide service and engagement. These processes allow writing centers and their directors to participate more fully in the social exchange of capital within their institutional ecologies, making them more visible to the community at large.

(Note: See chapter 1 for more information about director's labor.)

Professional Learning Network (PLN) Expansion

As cross-level discourse and partnerships expand, it might be natural to expand your local PLN with directors, tutors, and interested parties from other institutions. This can be accomplished by having cross-level "meet-ups" about cross-cutting issues impacting writing centers. This can build even more robust local and regional partnerships giving directors and tutors at all levels even more professional support and resources. Below is an invitation to directors at both levels to meet face-to-face to network.

Sample 1

Directors' Day Out Invitation

The writing centers at [university and high school] are hosting a Directors' Day Out (DDO) at [location]. This DDO is centered around studio pedagogy and Nordlof's 2014 article "Vygotsky, Scaffolding, and the Role of Theory in Writing Center Work." After a tour and discussion of the [Name] Writing Center (where studio pedagogy is put into action), we will have a working lunch discussing Nordlof's article. Following, directors from both centers will facilitate discussion on implications from secondary and collegiate perspectives, respectively. There will be dedicated time to talk about these concepts in participant's centers with the goal of working from the theoretical to the practical. Our day will conclude with a debrief and open conversation about other matters arising.

The following is an example of what the coordinators for the DDO used to communicate with participants:

Hi [Name],

We're excited to have you join us for the Directors' Day Out at [location] on [date] from [time].

- You'll find parking information here. (We can validate parking.)

- Attached is a copy of Nordlof's 2014 article "Vygotsky, Scaffolding, and the Role of Theory in Writing Center Work."

- We will be using Google Hangouts for virtual attendance and will be in contact as the date approaches regarding connection. Please let us know if you plan on attending the entire DDO or only a part. Following is our breakdown to give you a better idea:
    - 10:00-11:00 a.m.: Tour of writing center / Review of studio pedagogy
    - 11:00-11:45 a.m.: Discussion of Nordlof
    - 11:45 a.m.-12:00 p.m.: Break
    - 12:00-1:00 p.m.: Secondary take
    - 1:00-2:00 p.m.: 2-year, 4-year take
    - 2:05-3:00 p.m.: Creation of a personal action plan
    - 3:10-4:00 p.m.: Debrief and matters arising

Sample 2
Southeast Michigan Director Meet-Up Agenda

The intent of this director meet-up was to use the SSWC/univeristy partnership to establish more collaborative relationships between regional writing centers and their directors.

9:00 a.m.	Welcome & coffee
9:10 a.m.	Directors' carnival
	Please bring an example from your work over the past year and be prepared to share about it for 1-1.5 minutes. (*If you'd like to show a slide or an extremely short video, please send it to [email address] by [date].)
9:50 a.m.	Break
10:00 a.m.	Wellness for writing center directors
10:45 a.m.	Break
11:00 a.m.	Hosted conversation about writing centers and citizenship
	Some questions to think about in advance, based on the IWCA call for proposals:
	1. What does active directorship and centership mean or look like?
	2. What is the scope of a WC director's responsibility to social justice work?
	3. What are some of the ways our centers are already working with our campus and surrounding communities?
	4. How is active centership present in or absent from the missions and visions of our centers?
12:00 p.m.	Lunch with Table Topics Discussions
12:45 pm	Wrap up and next steps: What do we hope/want/need from this group?

References

Ahmed, S. (2000). *Strange encounters: Embodied others in post-coloniality*. London: Routledge.

Dweck, C. (2014, November). *The power of believing you can improve*. Retrieved from:
https://www.ted.com/talks/carol_dweck_the_power_of_believing_that_you_can_improve

Geller, A.E., Eodice, M., Condon, Carroll, M., & Boquet, E.H. (2007). *The everyday writing center*. Logan, UT: Utah State University Press.

Gutting, G. (2011, December 14). What is college for? *New York Times*. Retrieved from
https://opinionator.blogs.nytimes.com/2011/12/14/what-is-college-for/

Grutsch McKinney, J. (2013). *Peripheral visions for writing centers*. Logan, UT: Utah State University Press.

Grutsch McKinney, J., Caswell, N.I., & Jackson, R. (2016). *The working lives of new writing center directors*. Logan, UT: Utah State University Press.

Nordlof, J. (2014). Vygotsky, scaffolding, and the role of theory in writing center work. *Writing Center Journal*, (34)1, 45-64.

Sheridan, D. (2014, March). *Multiple modes, multiple mediums, multiple literacies: Writing center work today*. Presented at the East Central Writing Centers Association Conference, Mount Union, OH.

Whitman, W. (1865). When I heard the learn'd astronmer. Retrieved, September 9, 2018, from
https://www.poetryfoundation.org/poems/45479/when-i-heard-the-learnd-astronomer

Appendix A
All-Subject Peer Tutoring Centers
By Heather Barton

Appendix Note

We, the SSWCA board and the editors of this publication, have noticed over the last few years through the attendees at our annual conference and conversations between directors that many schools are opening or expanding their writing centers into "peer tutoring centers." In this model, students are trained to tutor in any subject a client needs help in, be it English, math, health, science, etc. With this model growing in popularity, we wanted this publication to add to the conversation about peer tutoring centers and to help support those directors as well. We will continue to seek out resources specific to that configuration, and future editions of this toolkit will provide more tangible examples. At this time, we would like to acknowledge the work our fellow directors are doing and provide a brief discussion to help you consider an all-subject center in light of your school's situation and ambition.

Guiding Questions

- How can a writing center peer tutoring model be used to support an all-subject peer tutoring center?
- How can a shift to all-subject tutoring benefit student learning?
- In what ways are tutor selection and training the same and different for all-subject centers?

Discussion

English teachers often lament the multitasking that occurs within a writing-centric classroom, and for me, the juggling of activities, curriculum, and feedback left me feeling as if I was shortchanging my students and their education. I knew that students needed time to write often, but I struggled to give away precious instructional time to allow students to write; I knew that students thrived when writing in a classroom that embraces the writing process, but I struggled to move beyond a one-draft approach to writing. In fact, I found that I spent hours upon hours poring over student drafts, providing what I thought was useful feedback that students would incorporate into their writing without any involvement of the student within the revision cycle and without any connection between my feedback and the student's growth. The less than compelling experience of process writing in my classroom led me to search for a way to empower my students as the owners of their writing process all while creating a writing-centric classroom environment that cultivated a feedback-rich writing culture. The outcome of my search led to the opening of my school's Writing Across the Curriculum Center (WACC) in August 2015 (See chapter 7 for more about school-wide writing initiatives like WAC).

In year one, the writing center opened with much fanfare and enthusiasm and served 1,000 students (out of a student body of 2,500). With the support of administration, ELA faculty, and the student leaders, the WACC continued to thrive and grow. During year two, I added a class dedicated to teaching tutors soft skills and writing center scholarship. The course allowed for an increase in visibility in various clubs and organizations as a way to earn service hours. Furthermore, tutors worked with the ELA department as a support for what was happening in the classroom, and they ran workshops, which supported a wider group of writers across the curriculum. As a result, the number of sessions grew to 1,300, but then stagnated. In year three, the goal was to increase the number of students who used the center. During the first three months, the numbers were the same as or lower than the previous years. Students were seeking help for writing, but only when assigned by a teacher. The tutor leaders of 2017-2018 began to look at new ways to keep growing the WACC. This included a campaign to find a solution by talking with teachers in subjects other than ELA and by communicating with friends and other members of the student body. Quickly, it became obvious that many students who were hesitant about getting help in writing wanted help in chemistry, math, and organizational areas.

With the evidence of needs and wants of the various stakeholders, the student leaders prepared to meet with administration in order to pitch a change in structure. In their preparation, they gathered statistical data from years past (See chapter 6), they interviewed science teachers and math teachers for quotes that could be used, and they began a marketing campaign to transition to a new name for the new brand. No longer would the Writing Across the Curriculum Center name fit the new vision and focus. After many brainstorming meetings, the leaders settled on a name that embraces our school culture. We are located on the East Campus of our school and our mascot is an Eagle - thus, the proposed name became The East WING (it's "Where I Need to Go"). By incorporating school culture into our name, the student leaders hoped that the student body would internalize that the center is a place of support and guidance for all subjects. With a new name, data, and research, the student leaders sat down with administration and pitched their plan to evolve from the WACC to the East WING. The pitch was a success due in part because administrators are always thrilled when students genuinely lead a charge for change and progress. With the green light, the WACC became the East WING midyear.

Things to consider:
- How can current writing across the curriculum endeavors be a first step to an all-subjects model?
- How can you cohesively meet the needs of current tutoring services in your school (writing center, math lab, science study tables, after-school tutoring, etc.)?
- How can you assist with the writing process in other languages?
- What new mission and branding are needed to transition to a new center?
- What will a full-time director position of an all-subject center look like?

The student leaders and I thought that the shift would flood our center with new students and new tutoring styles. What we found was that we still had a lot to do to convince content teachers outside of ELA to trust the services we provide. Teachers in the area of chemistry and math were the first to embrace the new model, with a little coaxing and research. Within the all-subject peer tutoring center, the sessions, although designed to be brief and focused, increase the collaborative nature of learning beyond the classroom walls. As an instructional strategy, educational research supports that the key to learner success resides in the peer form of tutoring (Harris, 1988; Turner, 2006). Regardless of the tutoring structure or faculty advisor's discipline, "the ideal situation for teaching and learning . . . is the tutorial, the one-on-one, face-to-face interaction between a [client] and a trained experienced tutor" (North, 1984, p. 28). Our Professional Learning Communities began working with John Hattie's (2012) research of visible learning. Hattie stated that peer tutoring leads to a learner's growth in skills. As a faculty, we grew in our understanding that peers often achieve success through the dialogue during a peer tutoring session. Thus, the teachers in the STEM fields quickly understood the power of an all-subject tutoring model for our shared students and their learning growth. With faculty support, we saw a significant increase in clients to nearly 1,900 students in our remaining six months. Writing sessions still were the primary sessions, but close seconds were chemistry and geometry sessions (See chapter 5 for more outreach strategies).

At my school, we make it a priority to relay information about each tutoring session back to the content-area teacher. This helps to build trust among the faculty so they will continue to recommend the East WING's services. After each appointment, the tutor crafts and sends a report to the classroom teacher. In order to prioritize and streamline the communication, the tutors use the following formula: ASAP. While the acronym is the same for all subjects, what it stands for differs. For English, career tech, social studies, and world language subjects, the report focuses on the aspects of writing. Regardless of genre (essay, presentations, resumes, etc.), writing tutors always include the following information: A: Attitude of the student; S: Strengths in the student's writing; A: Advice given to the student; P: Pointers for what the student could work on next in their writing. For math and science reports, the focus is on the skills of the client, the progress made, and gaps in understanding using this ASAP formula: A: Attitude of the student; S: Skills known prior; A: Applied concepts (strategies) used during the session to help the student understand; P: Progress shown during session and next steps for the student. Having a consistent and easy report has helped in the tutor training process and in building relationships with the faculty.

As we enter into year four (and only six months into operating an all-subjects center), I find myself in the position of the new director again navigating the role of support and instruction of tutoring basics balanced against my lack of knowledge in other subjects (See chapter 1 for more about directors' roles). When I first perceived this, it caused me to return to the basics of writing center theory to prepare the tutors regardless of the subject of the session. Overall, tutors must be well-versed in the vast area of soft skills: how to create a welcoming environment; how to ask questions; and how to build a relationship of trust. Risks in being vulnerable are honored and are grounded in support of the client's desired goals for each session. Sessions must remain a non-threatening experience that flows based on the individual need expressed by the learner. Furthermore, the all-subjects tutoring model cannot work without a connection to each classroom teacher whose students use the center. For each student who applies to be a tutor, the content teacher must provide a letter of recommendation. Staffing the center with tutors who receive recommendations from previous teachers allows the center to retain credibility of the services offered for each specific area of focus (See chapter 3 for more information on recruiting).

Things to consider:
- How can you connect into your school's culture around student learning?
- How can you use the trained writing center tutors you already have to assist in this transition?
- What current resources can be modified to train tutors?
- How will you ensure tutors are knowledgeable in their content areas?
- Will you want to have tutors go beyond general tutor training and be trained as specialists in specific content areas?
- How can content-specific training involve other content teachers?
- What kinds of credit options can be created or modified to attract tutors?

The key to the improvement of writing beliefs includes the incorporation of a feedback-rich writing process focused community (Nystrand, 2006; Prior, 2006). Writing intertwines with all that we do on a daily basis and transcends a specific subject or area of study. Often, writing centers are perceived as places only for writers and are avoided by traditional math and science subjects. By using writing center theory research in an all-subjects peer tutoring center, the center provides support for students in all aspects of writing and in all disciplines through a strong connection with faculty, steeped in research-based best practices. Student leaders, trained in all aspects of feedback, provide a community approach to writing that perceives the craft as more than a function of the English classroom, translating student success beyond the classroom walls. This same approach is carried through in viewing all disciplines as more than just school-based. Through a staff trained in conversation, a culture forms in which students and teachers encourage a community of feedback and growth, and student leadership skills flourish.

References

Harris, M. (1988). Writing center concept [fact sheet]. *The National Council of Teachers of English.* Retrieved February 21, 2015 from writingcenters.org.

Hattie, J. (2012). *Visible learning for teachers: Maximizing impact on learning.* London: Routledge.

North, S. M. (1984). Writing center research: testing our assumptions. In G.A. Olson (Ed.) *Writing centers: Theory and administration.* Urbana, IL: National Council of Teachers of English, pp. 24-35.

Nystrand, M. (2006). The Social and Historical Context for Writing Research. In C. A. MacArthur, S. Graham, & J. Fitzgerald (Eds.), *Handbook of writing research.* New York, NY, US: Guilford Press.

Prior, P. (2006). A socio-cultural theory of writing. In C. S. MacArthur, S. Graham & J. Fitzgerald (Eds.), *Handbook of writing research.* New York, NY: Guilford.

Turner, M. (2006). Writing centers: Being proactive in the education crisis. *Clearing House, 80*(2), 45-47.

Appendix B
About the Contributors

Jeffrey Austin
Director of the Skyline Writing Center
Skyline High School, Ann Arbor, Michigan

> Jeffrey's work in writing centers began as an undergraduate peer tutor at the University of Michigan's Sweetland Center for Writing, and it continued when he founded the Skyline Writing Center in 2012 to help close persistent achievement gaps using an asset-based approach to learning. In addition to completing 1,500 tutoring sessions each year, Skyline tutors maintain a partnership for tutor training with Sweetland and a collaboration with the Eastern Michigan University Office of Campus and Community Writing that helps provide literacy services to K-8 students and their families. Jeffrey and his tutors also produce *Teen Spirit*, an award-winning literary magazine. Jeffrey currently serves as the Secondary School Representative for IWCA and the Midwest Regional Representative for SSWCA.

Hannah Baran
Director of the Peer Tutoring Center
Albemarle High School, Charlottesville, Virginia

> Hannah Baran was first exposed to peer tutoring via her work as a founding tutor at Lake Highland Prep's Rossman Writing Center. While studying Secondary English Education at the University of Virginia's Curry School of Education, she tutored for the athletic department's Cavalier Academic Support Team. Following graduation, she founded the Writing Center at Louisa County High School (2011) and the Peer Tutoring Center at Albemarle High School (2013). Administering the peer tutoring program (including teaching a credit-bearing class) is her full-time job; her staff of 80+ tutors conducts over 5,000 sessions annually. When not working with tutors, she enjoys reading, visiting farmers markets, and playing outside with her children, Eliza and Charlie.

Heather Barton
Director of The East WING
Etowah High School, Woodstock, Georgia

> Heather Barton is a high school teacher and writing center director working at Etowah High School in Woodstock, Georgia. In 2018, Heather earned her Ed.D. from Kennesaw State University. Barton's practice and research interests include writing instruction strategies and writing theory. Her scholarship led to the founding of The East WING Tutoring Center at Etowah. The center supports all subjects through a writing center theory focused facility. Heather is currently a Member At-Large of the SSWCA board.

Beth Blankenship
Director of the Center
Oakton High School, Oakton, Virginia

Lauren Brown
Former Director of the Herndon Writing Center
Herndon High School, Herndon, Virginia

Renee Brown
Director of the PTMS Writing Lab
Peters Township Middle School, McMurray, Pennsylvania

After working as an undergraduate tutor at Indiana University of Pennsylvania with Dr. Ben Rafoth, Renee took a position teaching eighth grade English at Peters Township Middle School south of Pittsburgh. She advocated for and eventually opened the Writing Lab there in 2011. Since then, her former middle school tutors have been published in the online journal *The Peer Review* and started a writing center at their high school, building on what Renee taught them. Her MS writing center trains approximately fifteen eighth grade tutors each year who then host over 200 one-on-one sessions in addition to classroom visits. In 2012, she earned a Master's degree in English from the University of Pittsburgh. Renee served as Middle School Representative of CAPTA and is currently the Vice-President of SSWCA and co-editor of this toolkit.

Trisha Callihan
Director of the Eagle Writing Center
Osbourn High School, Manassas, Virginia

Trisha Callihan is currently the director of the Eagle Writing Center as well as being an English teacher and department supervisor at Osbourn High School. Her exposure to writing center work started during her undergraduate studies at Clarion University of Pennsylvania as a tutor, and she immediately began to work to implement a high school center after moving from Pennsylvania to teach English. The Eagle Writing Center was established in 2015, and her interest and passion has only continued to grow. While completing her Master's thesis from Columbia's Teachers College on writing center work, she continued to serve in various positions on the SSWCA board. She wants to thank all of her past and present tutors and colleagues that have supported secondary writing center work.

Seth Czarnecki
Director of the Algonquin Writing Center
Algonquin Regional High School, Northborough, Massachusetts

Seth Czarnecki directs the Algonquin Writing Center, teaches English, and advises the Poetry Out Loud club at Algonquin Regional High School in Northborough, Massachusetts. He received his M.Ed. with a focus on composition from the University of Massachusetts-Boston. For the past several years, Seth has focused his studies and professional development around approaches to writing across the curriculum in secondary schools. He has served on his department's writing program development committee and continues to work with colleagues across the disciplines to create a framework for teaching writing at his school. Seth is currently serving as the Northeast Representative for SSWCA.

Susan Frenck
Director of the Irving Writing Center
Washington Irving Middle School, Springfield, Virginia

Susan Frenck first discovered the value of peer tutoring in college and graduate school, where she worked as a writing tutor. She became part of the secondary school writing center community in 2012, when she founded a high school writing center while working as an English teacher at Robinson Secondary School in Fairfax, Virginia. In 2016, she became a teacher of seventh grade English at Irving Middle School in Springfield, Virginia, and founded one of the few writing centers for middle school students in northern Virginia. Her students were among the first middle school students to present at the CAPTA/SSWCA annual conference. Susan has been a CAPTA/SSWCA board member since 2013 and is currently the SSWCA Treasurer.

Joseph Golimowski
Director of the Cougar Writing Center
Kettle Run High School, Nokesville, Virginia

After finishing a course at George Mason University in late spring 2017 on writing centers as part of his work toward a Masters in English, Joe presented his final project, a proposal to create a high school writing center, to the administration at Kettle Run High School in Northern Virginia. Joe won approval to open the Cougar Writing Center for the 2017-2018 school year as its first director. Midway through the school year, Kettle Run tutors visited the GMU writing center run by Dr. Susan Lawrence and brought back a wealth of knowledge and techniques to help their fellow Cougars. At Kettle Run, Joe also chairs the English Department, coaches the Scholastic Bowl team, and is the lead faculty advisor for the school's National English Honor Society Chapter. Joe is the Capital Area Representative for SSWCA.

Jenny Goransson
Director of the Peer Tutoring Center
West Springfield High School, Springfield, Virginia

Alison Hughes
Former Director of the Wildcat Writing Center
Centreville High School, Clifton, Virginia

Kate Hutton
Director of the Herndon Writing Center
Herndon High School, Herndon, Virginia

> Kate Hutton directs the Herndon Writing Center, teaches English, and serves as the English Curriculum Support Specialist at Herndon High School in Herndon, Virginia. Through a combination of her interests in literacy and social justice, and the good fortune of being in the right place at the right time, Kate found herself in the writing center world in 2012, when she began co-directing the Herndon Writing Center. Since then, she has co-founded the Capital Area Peer Tutoring Association (2014), earned her MA in English from George Mason University (2016), and transitioned CAPTA from a regional organization into the national organization that is now SSWCA. She extends the most heartfelt gratitude to all of her tutors, past and present, without whom any of this work would be possible. Kate currently serves as President of SSWCA.

Amber Jensen
Doctoral Candidate
George Mason University, Fairfax, Virginia
Former Director of the Edison Writing Center
Edison High School, Fairfax, Virginia

> As a high school English teacher at Edison High School in Alexandria, VA, Amber drew upon her experience as an undergraduate Writing Fellow at Brigham Young University to propose and found the Edison Writing Center in 2009. During her seven years as the EWC's director, she created the curriculum for Advanced Composition, a credit-bearing course for student tutors adopted by Fairfax County Public Schools. She mentored and collaborated with other English teachers in her school district and region to chair the annual tutor conference, becoming a co-founder and the first president of the Capital Area Peer Tutoring Association. She also served as the Secondary Schools Representative on the IWCA Executive Board from 2012 - 2016. Amber left teaching high school and directing a writing center to pursue a PhD in Writing and Rhetoric, but she remains actively involved with SSWCs in her research and leadership with the Secondary School Writing Centers Association as current Past President.

Richard Kent
Professor
University of Maine, Orono, Maine

> Professor Richard Kent serves in the School of Learning and Teaching at the University of Maine. He's director emeritus of Maine's National Writing Project site. Throughout his 43-year career, Rich has researched student-staffed writing centers, athletes' writing (WritingAthletes.com), and literacy portfolios. Since 2006, he has curated WCenters.com, a high school writing center resource. He is the author of 19 books, including *A Guide to Creating Student-Staffed Writing Centers, Revised*, the Book of the Year in 2006 for the International Writing Centers Association. As a high school teacher, writing center director, and athletic coach, Rich was named 1993 Maine Teacher of the Year and received the $25,000 National Educator Award. In 2014, he received the Research and Creative Achievement Award at UMaine. Rich currently serves as an advisor to the SSWCA board.

Kyle Krol
Director of the Lakeshore Writing Center
Lakeshore High School, Stevensville, Michigan

Kyle has had the privilege of directing a secondary writing center for ten years, founding three separate and successful high school writing centers in Southwest Michigan. Her experience with writing center work predates that, however; she was a tutor and assistant director of the Western Michigan University Writing Center during her undergraduate work at WMU. This experience served as a springboard into what would become her passion– the field of secondary school writing centers combined her high school calling with her love of composition. Kyle has been a teacher for ten years, but views her role as an educator to model lifelong learning to her students. She is currently enrolled in Indiana University of Pennsylvania's Composition and Applied Linguistics PhD program, where she is working on her dissertation. Currently, Kyle is the Social Media Manager on the SSWCA board.

Jim LaBate
Writing Specialist of the Writing and Research Center
Hudson Valley Community College, Troy, New York

Since January of 2000, Jim LaBate has worked as a writing specialist in the Writing Center at Hudson Valley Community College (HVCC) in Troy, New York. Originally from Amsterdam, New York, Jim earned his bachelor's degree in English from Siena College in Loudonville, New York, and his master's degree, also in English, from The College of Saint Rose in Albany, New York. Jim taught physical education as a Peace Corps Volunteer in Golfito, Costa Rica for two years; he taught high-school English for ten years; and he worked for ten years as a technical writer before moving to HVCC. Jim lives in Clifton Park, New York, with his wife, Barbara; they have two daughters: Maria and Katrina.

Christine Modey
Faculty Director of Peer Writing Consultant Program at the Sweetland Center for Writing
University of Michigan, Ann Arbor, Michigan

Christine Modey is a lecturer in the Sweetland Center for Writing, where she directs the Peer Writing Consultant Program and teaches courses in peer writing consulting and new media writing. As a teacher, she is interested in developing more inclusive writing classrooms and in helping writing consultants leverage their writing tutoring experience in professional contexts. Her past writing center research has concerned the effects of questions in writing workshop sessions. Her current research, conducted with colleagues from other Research I universities, considers what corpus analysis of writing center session reports reveals about the nature of writing center work.

Stephanie Passino
Director of the Hawk Writing Center
Hayfield Secondary School, Alexandria, Virginia

After student teaching at Centreville High School and learning about the success of their writing center from Alison Hughes, Stephanie knew serving as a director was something she wanted to do. She opened a center at Hayfield Secondary in 2013 and has been serving as the director ever since. Her center has grown in tutors and is open four days a week for students in grades 7-12. Stephanie has served as a Member At-Large for CAPTA since 2015 and has been the Secretary of SSWCA for two years.

Kimberly Sloan
Literacy Resource Teacher of the IAS Virtual Writing Lab
Interagency Alternative Schools, Fairfax, Virginia

Kim Sloan is the co-director along with Diane Hughart of the Interagency Alternative Schools Virtual Writing Lab. She works collaboratively with a group of tutors to provide feedback to students who submit their work from 28 different alternative sites and then videoconferences with tutors who share the feedback. Kim has been a member of CAPTA/SSWCA since the beginning, presenting to tutors at the first conference. She serves as the Literacy Resource teacher for IAS as well as teaches at George Washington University. She became involved with writing centers through her work as a teacher-consultant with the Northern Virginia Writing Project (NVWP) and was the Co-Director of the NVWP for a decade.

Liz Reilly and Eric Weiss
Supervisors of the Mariemont High School Writing Center
Mariemont High School, Cincinnati, Ohio

Liz and Eric first heard about student-run writing centers through their work with Ohio Writing Project (OWP), in particular, Betsy Woods of Milford High School. After taking a weekend workshop led by OWP and Betsy, they submitted a proposal and worked with student leaders to open their center the following fall semester. The writing center staffs anywhere from three to seven students per study hall period where student clients visit, and multiple teachers often take advantage of the ability to pull consultants into their classrooms for the period. With the beginning of the new school year and thus the second year of the writing center, student consultants have already approached Liz and Eric with ideas for marketing the center and increasing its usage across content areas.

Stacey Waldrup
English Teacher
Meridian High School, Meridian, Idaho
Former Director of the Raider Writing Center
Crescent Valley High School, Corvallis, Oregon

> Stacey's love of writing centers started when she first worked in the Central Michigan University Writing Center as an undergraduate consultant for two years. A session by high school tutors at the 2008 MiWCA conference inspired her to eventually direct a secondary school writing center, and after teaching high school English for five years, in 2016 she became the full-time director of the Raider Writing Center at Crescent Valley High School. In 2017, she completed her M.Ed. in Curriculum, Instruction, and Assessment, with a focus on a writing center tutor training curriculum. Stacey now teaches English at Meridian High School and continues to be excited about promoting secondary school writing centers. She currently serves as a Member At-Large for SSWCA and is the co-editor of this toolkit.

STUDY GUIDE for

The TRUTH About YOU

Overcoming *Seven Lies* You Believe About Yourself

Amy Keesee Freudiger

Study Guide for The Truth About You
Copyright © 2023 by Amy Keesee Freudiger.

Unless otherwise noted, all Scriptures are taken from the New International Version® (NIV)® of the Holy Bible. Copyright © 1973, 1978, 1984, 2011 by Biblica, Inc.™ All rights reserved worldwide.

Scripture quotations marked (TPT) are taken from The Passion Translation® of the Holy Bible. Copyright © 2017, 2018, 2020 by Passion & Fire Ministries, Inc. Used by permission. All rights reserved. ThePassionTranslation.com.

Scripture quotations marked (KJV) are taken from the King James Version of the Holy Bible. Public domain.

Scripture quotations marked (NKJV) are taken from the New King James Version® of the Holy Bible. Copyright © 1982 by Thomas Nelson. All rights reserved.

Scripture quotations marked (NLT) are taken from the New Living Translation of the Holy Bible. Copyright © 1996, 2004, 2015 by Tyndale House Foundation. Used by permission of Tyndale House Publishers, Carol Stream, Illinois 60188. All rights reserved.

Scripture quotations marked (NASB) are taken from the New American Standard Bible®. Copyright © 1960, 1971, 1977, 1995, 2020 by The Lockman Foundation. All rights reserved. www.lockman.org.

Scripture quotations marked (NASB 1995) are taken from the New American Standard Bible®. Copyright © 1960, 1971, 1977, 1995 by The Lockman Foundation. All rights reserved. www.lockman.org

Scripture quotations marked (AMP) are taken from the Amplified version of the Holy Bible. Copyright © 2015 by The Lockman Foundation. www.lockman.org.

Scripture quotations marked (AMPC) are taken from the classic edition of the Amplified version of the Holy Bible. Copyright © 1954, 1958, 1962, 1964, 1965, 1987 by The Lockman Foundation. Used by permission. www.lockman.org.

Scripture quotations marked (MSG) are taken from The Message version of the Holy Bible. Copyright © 1993, 1994, 1995, 1996, 2000, 2001, 2002. Used by permission of NavPress Publishing Group.

Scripture quotations marked (BSB) are taken from the Berean Study Bible. Copyright © 2016, 2020 by Bible Hub. Used by permission. All rights reserved worldwide.

Scripture quotations marked (TLB) are taken from The Living Bible. Copyright © 1971 by Tyndale House Foundation. Used by permission of Tyndale House Publishers, Carol Stream, Illinois 60188. All rights reserved.

Scripture quotations marked (ISV) are taken from the International Standard Version® Release 2.0 of the Holy Bible. Copyright © 1996-2013 by the ISV Foundation. Used by permission of Davidson Press, LLC. All rights reserved internationally.

Scripture quotations marked (CSB) are taken from the Christian Standard Bible®. Copyright © 2017 by Holman Bible Publishers. Used by permission. Christian Standard Bible® and CSB® are federally registered trademarks of Holman Bible Publishers.

Scripture quotations marked (GNT) are taken from the Good News Translation of Today's English Version of the Holy Bible, Second Edition. Copyright © 1992 by American Bible Society. Used by Permission.

Scripture quotations marked (NET) are taken from the NET Bible®. Copyright © 1996, 2019 by Biblical Studies Press, LLC., http://netbible.com. Quoted by permission. All rights reserved.

All rights reserved. No part of this book may be used or reproduced by any means, graphic, electronic, or mechanical, including photocopying, recording, taping, or by any information storage retrieval system without the written permission of the publisher, except in the case of brief quotations embodied in critical articles and reviews.

ISBN: 978-1-960387-01-1

Published by Honest Beauty Publishing.
Healedovernight@gmail.com

Cover design and graphic design: Establishr.co

TABLE OF CONTENTS

INTRODUCTION..05

PART I:

CHAPTER 1: CAN YOU RELATE?.....................................07

CHAPTER 2: WHO IS MY DADDY?..................................17

CHAPTER 3: LIE #1: "I CAN'T TRUST GOD."..................27

CHAPTER 4: LIE #2: "I AM NOT ENOUGH."....................37

CHAPTER 5: LIE #3: "SIN WON'T HURT ME."................47

CHAPTER 6: LIE #4: "I SHOULD BE ASHAMED OF MYSELF."..........59

CHAPTER 7: LIE #5: "I DESERVE THE BLAME."............69

CHAPTER 8: LIE #6: "I AM REJECTED."..........................81

CHAPTER 9: LIE #7: "I AM A FAILURE."..........................93

PART II:

CHAPTER 10: I AM BECOMING..103

CHAPTER 11: I'M A MONA LISA MASTERPIECE..............115

CHAPTER 12: I CAN BREAK FREE FROM DARKNESS......125

CHAPTER 13: I HAVE THE ANOINTING..............................133

CHAPTER 14: HELLO, MY NAME IS _____.....................143

CHAPTER 15: I AM RECLAIMING MY IDENTITY...............153

INTRODUCTION

First, I want to commend you. You've taken an important step just by opening this study guide and being willing to consider that you may have believed some lies about who you are. It takes courage to question what you believe about yourself, and whether or not it's really God's Truth.

In *The Truth About You: Overcoming Seven Lies You Believe About Yourself*, I talk about how my husband, Jason, and I renovated our main bathroom in our home. It was a messy process to gut the bathroom in the first place, and it continued to be messy as we built the beautiful end result.

If you've ever watched a renovation show, you know how chaotic, messy, and costly it can be. A homeowner wants to remove a wall to open up a space, but they tear down the drywall only to find it's been hiding a maze of plumbing, electrical, and ductwork that will all have to be rerouted through other walls or the ceiling. Or old flooring is removed to allow for a fresh, new replacement, but contractors discover that water has damaged and rotted the subfloor, which will have to be replaced before anything new can be laid. Termite damage, bad electrical wiring, rusted plumbing… the list of things you encounter when you take on a renovation can be endless, especially if you don't know what you're getting into.

STUDY GUIDE for *The* TRUTH *About* YOU

Since I compared *The Truth About You: Overcoming Seven Lies You Believe About Yourself* to a renovation for your soul, I want you to know exactly what you're getting into.

I love all of the definitions of the word "renovation." It means *cleaning, repairing, reclaiming, renewing, restoring, reinvigorating, and reviving*. To renovate means bringing life back to something or to make it an even better version of what it once was.

So, if *The Truth About You: Overcoming Seven Lies You Believe About Yourself* is like a renovation, this study guide is like your toolset. That means, that at times, it might feel like a sledgehammer, crashing through and breaking up long-held lies you've believed about yourself, or a pry bar, helping to disconnect you from rotten beliefs about your identity. At other times, though, I hope this study guide feels more like a voltage tester, helping you to measure areas of your life where you're not walking in full power, or like a stud finder and drill, helping you to know the security of God's Truth and how to anchor your identity to it.

There will be times that this process might feel chaotic and messy and maybe even spiritually and emotionally costly. But it will be worth it, because YOU are worth it. Learn from this study as if your life depends on it, because *it does*.

And, in the end, as you wrap up this study, I hope this study guide most feels like not another tool, but a key in your hand that you have used to unlock the door to the most breathtaking renovation project ever—the masterpiece God made you to be.

—*Amy Keesee Freudiger*

01

CAN YOU RELATE?

I praise you because I am fearfully and wonderfully made; your works are wonderful, I know that full well.
—Psalm 139:14

REMOVING THE MASK

Too often, there is a version of ourselves that we show to others that is different from the way we truly are.

It's time to get honest with ourselves.

Use this table and name some ways you show the world something different than you really are (masks) and what the Truth is about you. Examples from the book are included here to help you get started.

MASK	TRUTH
Smiling and happy	*Sad and fearful*
Confident	*Insecure and less than*

In Chapter One of The *Truth About You: Overcoming Seven Lies You Believe About Yourself*, I list the negative, intrusive, painful thoughts and beliefs that would run through my mind constantly years ago.

From that list, which thoughts or beliefs do you most relate to hearing in your own thought life?

_____

_____

_____

_____

> ### *Know This:*
> You don't have to live with those thoughts anymore. There's a way out of the cycle of self-hatred, insecurity, and identity crisis.

Why do people struggle with unworthiness?

1. No family is perfect.
2. The Bible says we have an adversary called the devil or satan, and he is looking for ways to _____

_____

_____

What are you most hoping to gain from this study? Circle all that apply.

To reclaim my lost identity

To get MYSELF back

To destroy the cage I've put myself in

To stop feeling suffocated under negative thoughts and labels

To feel happy and satisfied with who I am

To tear down the walls that have kept love from my life

To make peace with the things I see as weaknesses or flaws

To realize how amazing God is and how He made me to reflect Him

To understand the power and authority God has given me as His child

_____

(fill in the blank)

Know This:

No medical diagnosis, mental health disorder, psychiatric label, or soul sickness is greater than the Creator God of the universe.

List two things that encouraged you as you read this chapter:

1 _____

2 _____

TAKE ACTION!

Dale Carnegie said, "Knowledge is not power until it is applied."

You have more knowledge now, so it's time to apply it.
This week, pay attention to two things:

1. Any times or situations where you feel like you're "faking it" with people.
2. Any time negative thoughts come into your mind about yourself.

Jot down notes here in this study guide, on your phone, or in a journal. Recognizing the areas that need to change is the first step in your personal renovation project.

Be sure to also listen to "The Lost Family" audio presentation using the QR code at the end of the Introduction of *The Truth About You: Overcoming Seven Lies You Believe About Yourself,* and complete the Challenge at the end of Chapter One.

Prayer

This week, pray the prayer from Chapter One of the book. Also ask God to show you what masks you've been wearing and what negative thoughts you need to overcome through this study.

> God, as I start this journey to freedom and wholeness, I ask You to be with me. Help me to see myself the way You see me. I'm ready to reclaim my identity and make some changes for the better.
>
> I ask that You show me any masks I've been wearing and every negative thought I need to overcome.
>
> In Jesus' name, I pray. Amen.

NOTES FROM THIS CHAPTER

> *I have never called you "servants," because a master doesn't confide in his servants, and servants don't always understand what the master is doing. But I call you my most intimate and cherished friends, for I reveal to you everything that I've heard from my Father.*
>
> —John 15:15 TPT

> *You will be called priests of the Lord, ministers of our God. You will feed on the treasures of the nations and boast in their riches. Instead of shame and dishonor, you will enjoy a double share of honor. You will possess a double portion of prosperity in your land, and everlasting joy will be yours.*
>
> —Isaiah 61:6-7 NLT

> *Those who look to him for help will be radiant with joy; no shadow of shame will darken their faces.*
>
> —Psalms 34:5 NLT

02

WHO IS MY DADDY?

I praise you because I am fearfully and wonderfully made; your works are wonderful, I know that full well.
—Psalm 139:14

"There is a God-shaped vacuum in the heart of each man which cannot be satisfied by any created thing but only by God the Creator, made known through Jesus Christ." —Blaise Pascal

You can leave the fingerprint!

THE COMPARISON TRAP

God created each of us uniquely. But we spend way too much time comparing ourselves and our lives to others instead of looking at ourselves as made in His image and for a specific plan and purpose.

It's time to get honest, again.

Use this table to name some people you compare yourself to and how. A few examples are included here to help you get started.

PERSON	COMPARISON
Friend	*She's tall, thin, popular, outgoing, fun, better dressed*
Coworker	*More productive, better ideas, better dressed, favorite*

CHAPTER TWO: WHO IS MY DADDY?

When you look at the comparisons you filled in in the table, can you say you are listening to the correct voice? Why or why not?

NOTES

Write out 2 Corinthians 10:12:

Write out Philippians 4:11-12:

> ## "COMPARISON IS THE THIEF OF JOY."
> — Theodore Roosevelt

Know This: Getting to know our Creator, our "Dad," has to be our foundation for everything else we will learn about identity.

Of the list of characteristics and nature I listed in Chapter Two of *The Truth About You: Overcoming Seven Lies You Believe About Yourself*, which do you truly believe about Him? Circle all that apply.

The definition of love	Forgiving	Merciful
Loves me unconditionally	Believes the best in me	Patient
A close friend	Faithful	Accepting
Gentle yet firm	Kind and caring	Truthful / honest
Cares about my problems	Generous / giving	Keeps His word
Fair / doesn't play favorites	My biggest cheerleader	My greatest ally
A just judge	Proud of me for who I am, not what I do	Optimistic about my potential

CHAPTER TWO WHO IS MY DADDY?

We struggle with the love of God because we have been programmed to the _____, tainted, _____, _____ kind of love of this earth.

> **Know This:**
> God loves you, and He is ONLY good. He is better than the best things you can imagine in this life.

What are three things you think of when you think of "the best things in life?"

1 _____

2 _____

3 _____

GOD IS GOOD!

Of the earthy examples I listed in Chapter Two to paint a picture of God, which of them encourage you the most, and why? _____

_____

_____

Of the earthly examples I listed in Chapter Two to paint a picture of God, which of them do you have the most trouble believing? Why? _____

_____

_____

What is one thing that surprised you as you read this chapter? _____

_____

_____

TAKE ACTION!

It's time to do some more renovating.

When we compare ourselves to others, we are agreeing with the plans of the enemy for our lives. Comparison isn't just the thief of joy, it is the denier of Truth.

This week, read these two paraphrased and personalized Scripture declarations out loud in the morning and at night and every time you start to compare yourself to someone else. Consider writing them out and posting them on your bathroom mirror or somewhere else you will regularly see them.

> *I fill my mind and meditate ONLY on things that are true, noble, reputable, authentic, compelling, gracious—the best, not the worst; the beautiful, not the ugly; things to praise, not things to curse, in others and in MYSELF.*
>
> — Philippians 4:8 The Message

> *We are like the various parts of a human body. Each part of the body gets its meaning from the body as a whole, not the other way around. The body we're talking about is Christ's body of chosen people. Each of us finds our meaning and function as a PART of his body. But as a chopped-off finger or cut-off toe we wouldn't amount to much, would we? So since we find ourselves fashioned into all these excellently formed and marvelously functioning PARTS in Christ's body, I will go ahead and be what I was made to be, without enviously or pridefully comparing myself with others, or trying to be something I am not.*
>
> — Romans 12:4-8 The Message

Be sure to also complete the Challenge at the end of Chapter Two, noting your responses here in this study guide, on your phone, or in a journal.

Prayer

This week, pray the prayer from Chapter Two of the book. Also ask God to show you any ways that you have believed something incorrectly about His character or about yourself as you've compared yourself to others.

> Father God, I want to know You; really know who You are and have a relationship with You. What do You want to say to me today? Help me hear.
>
> Thank You for being pure, always thinking good thoughts toward me, and for loving me unconditionally. Help me through this study to discover my true identity and get the real me back.
> I ask that You show me any lies I have believed about who You are or how much You love me. I also ask that You show me any lies I have believed about myself and who You have made me to be. Help me to stop comparing myself to others and only see myself as You see me.
>
> Let it be done in Your Son's name, Jesus. Amen.

> Let perseverance finish its work so that you may be mature and complete, not lacking anything. If any of you lacks wisdom, you should ask God, who gives generously to all without finding fault, and it will be given to you.
>
> —James 1:4-5 NIV

CHAPTER TWO **WHO IS MY DADDY?**

> *No, in all these things we are more than conquerors through him who loved us. For I am convinced that neither death nor life, neither angels nor demons, neither the present nor the future, nor any powers, neither height nor depth, nor anything else in all creation, will be able to separate us from the love of God that is in Christ Jesus our Lord.*
>
> —Romans 8:37-39 NIV

> But he answered me, "My grace is always more than enough for you, and my power finds its full expression through your weakness." So I will celebrate my weaknesses, for when I'm weak I sense more deeply the mighty power of Christ living in me.
> —2 Corinthians 12:9 TPT

03

Lie #1
"I CAN'T TRUST GOD"

I praise you because I am fearfully and wonderfully made; your works are wonderful, I know that full well.
—Psalm 139:14

"Never be afraid to trust an unknown future to a known God." —Corrie Ten Boom

BACK TO THE BEGINNING

The greatest gift that Father gave His children wasn't authority; it was _____.

Chapter Three of The Truth About You: Overcoming Seven Lies You Believe About Yourself covers the very beginning—God's plan for mankind and how the enemy deceived Adam and Eve. As you read through this chapter, did it change how you think about God, His plan for mankind, or the fall of Adam and Eve? Why or why not?

Know This:

To get Adam and Eve to disobey God, satan first had to twist God's character so they would question His goodness.

Write out John 10:10:

❖ Adam and Eve gave ear to the enemy they were supposed to rule over. ❖

Thinking on this statement, in what ways have you been giving ear to the enemy that you are supposed to rule over? (*Look back at your comparison list from Chapter Two if you need a place to start.*) What lies has he told you about God?

NOTES

TWO PATHS We have only two choices.

Path One
- Question God and His character
- ↓
- Cut yourself off from relationship with Him
- ↓
- Never discover who you truly are
- ↓
- satan wins

Path Two
- Trust God and His character
- ↓
- Experience God's goodness
- ↓
- Know your identity and purpose
- ↓
- Rule over satan

Which path have you been on and why?

SATAN'S TACTICS	HOW TO RESIST
Meet your own needs/become like God	Trust God to meet your needs
Question your identity	Know who God says you are
Take matters into your own hands	Trust God's ability to care for you

Describe a time that you have given into one of the enemy's tactics and what happened.

Which of the three methods of resisting the enemy (listed above) do you know you need to work on most?

The only way to live in our created identity is to

"WHAT YOU COMPROMISE TO GAIN, YOU WILL ULTIMATELY LOSE."

Know This:
The best way to lie-proof your life is to stay connected to Father God through relationship.

TAKE ACTION!

Your personal renovation project this week is going to require you to dig a little deeper. Don't just settle for your typical surface responses as you answer the following questions.

- Do you struggle to trust God's character and intentions toward you?
- If you do struggle with this in even the slightest way, where do you think that mistrust started?

If you've honestly answered those two questions, congratulations, you've taken a big step in your personal renovation project. You've pulled out your pry bar and started separating yourself from ugly, old, rotten beliefs.

Now, it's time to go to the Word of God.

This week, take time to read one of the accounts of Jesus' life found in Matthew, Mark, Luke, or John in the Bible. Keep record of anything God speaks or reveals to you as you read here in this study guide, on your phone, or in a journal.

Finally, be sure to also complete the Challenge at the end of Chapter Three in your book.

Prayer

This week, pray the prayer from Chapter Three of the book. Also ask God to show you more of who He is.

> Lord God, show me the lies I have believed about You and about myself. Reveal to me where those lies, attitudes, and misconceptions came from so I can bring them out into the light and get rid of them. I repent of trying to carry the weight of providing for myself, not trusting you to be my Father who cares for me. Today, I choose to trust You and place my life in Your capable hands.
>
> Show me who You are, and Your heart for me, more and more each day.
>
> Amen.

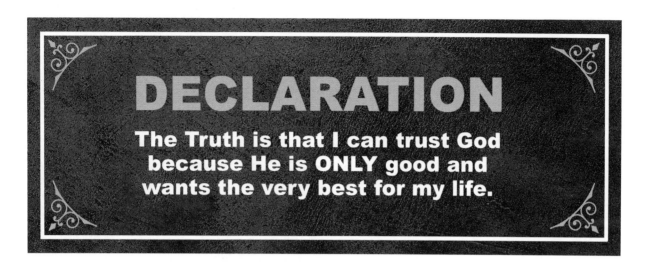

NOTES FROM THIS CHAPTER

> Look with wonder at the depth of the Father's marvelous love that he has lavished on us! He has called us and made us his very own beloved children. The reason the world doesn't recognize who we are is that they didn't recognize him.
>
> —1 John 3:1 TPT

> *We have become his poetry, a re-created people that will fulfill the destiny he has given each of us, for we are joined to Jesus, the Anointed One. Even before we were born, God planned in advance our destiny and the good works we would do to fulfill it!*
>
> —**Ephesians 2:10 TPT**

> For Jehovah God is our Light and our Protector. He gives us grace and glory. No good thing will he withhold from those who walk along his paths.
>
> —Psalm 84:11 TPT

04

Lie #2
"I AM NOT ENOUGH."

I praise you because I am fearfully and wonderfully made; your works are wonderful, I know that full well.
—Psalm 139:14

"What lies behind us and what lies before us are tiny matters compared to what lies within us." —Ralph Waldo Emerson

In Chapter Four of *The Truth About You: Overcoming Seven Lies You Believe About Yourself*, I ask you to grab a pen and paper and get ready to be honest with yourself.

Take just a few minutes to write down the things you like about yourself and the things you dislike about yourself.

LIKES	DISLIKES

Was one column easier to complete than the other?
☐ YES ☐ NO

Why or why not?

> ### Know This:
> You won't rise higher than your opinion of yourself.

Write out Proverbs 23:7:

NOTES

Describe a time when you now know that you let the voice of inferiority cause you to do something and what happened.

Of this list of symptoms of shame, which have you dealt with in your life? Circle all that apply.

Perfectionism	Keeping people at arm's length	Not inviting people to your house
Constantly saying, "I'm sorry"	Feeling out of place	Not wanting to attend events or gatherings
Not believing you deserve good things	Not being able to admit mistakes	Believing you'll never be able to "get it together"

If someone asked you right now what you don't have enough of, what would you say and why?

> **Know This:**
> If satan can make you feel like you are lacking something that God has already given you, he can replace it with his counterfeit.

God's love pronounces _____ and _____ to _____ situation.

List two things that encouraged you as you read this chapter:

1 _____

2 _____

This week's personal renovation action starts by requiring you to get someone else involved in the process.

First, complete the exercise in Chapter Four of your book that asks you to find a close friend or spouse and ask them to make a list of some things they like about you. (*Tell them Amy told you to do it for an assignment.*) Then, compare the list to the one you did in this study guide or on another sheet of paper. What do you see?

Next, complete the Challenge at the end of Chapter Four in your book. Choose at least two of the Scriptures from the Challenge, or other Scriptures that encourage you, and write them on sticky notes or paper and put them on your mirror(s) at home and/or in your car.

Prayer

This week, pray the prayer from Chapter Four of the book. Also thank God that He restores your life like a skilled, trained artist.

> *Father, teach me that I am enough because You are enough in me. You have fully equipped me with every tool I need to win in life, to enjoy my time here on earth, to accomplish that which you've called me to accomplish, and to love others fully.*
>
> *I am not lacking anything I need because Your Spirit is inside of me with every answer to my problems. You have given me Your ability (grace), so I will not listen to the deceiver's lies to me. I rebuke the lie of inadequacy.*
>
> *I thank You, Father, that You restore my life, brush stroke by brush stroke, removing the marks and blemishes, stains and damages put there by the enemy and by people.*
>
> *In Jesus' name, Amen.*

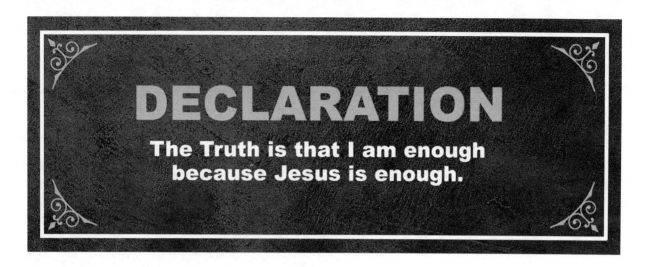

NOTES FROM THIS CHAPTER

> *Therefore, if anyone is in Christ, he is a new creation. The old has passed away; behold, the new has come.*
>
> —2 Corinthians 5:17

> *Yet you, LORD, are our Father. We are the clay, you are the potter; we are all the work of your hand*
> —Isaiah 64:8

> *What, then, shall we say in response to these things? If God is for us, who can be against us?*
> —Romans 8:31

05

Lie #2
"SIN WON'T HURT ME."

I praise you because I am fearfully and wonderfully made; your works are wonderful, I know that full well.
—Psalm 139:14

SIN:
Anything that hurts you or others, which breaks the Law of Love found in Matthew 22:37.

YOUR NEXT DECISION? FREEDOM

What is one thing you took from the story of Able at the beginning of this chapter?

___

Freedom is not a straight vertical line up, up, and away—it is often an upward spiral of _____ the same areas over and over to find another _____ of freedom.

Sin makes demands of your _____ and _____.

Write out Romans 6:23:

> ### Know This:
> The only reason any of us sin is because we get duped into living in the moment instead of looking down the road at the consequences.

"THE HEART IS LIKE AN INCUBATOR THAT WILL GROW WHATEVER YOU PUT INTO IT."

— Gary Keesee

NOTES

HOW DO YOU KNOW WHAT IS GROWING IN YOUR HEART? TAKE A FEW MOMENTS AND FILL OUT THIS TABLE. GO WITH THE FIRST THING YOU THINK OF WHEN YOU READ THE QUESTION.	
What is the last song you listened to?	
What is the last thing you looked at online?	
What is the last thing you looked at on social media?	
What is the last thing you talked about with a friend?	
What is the last thing you said about yourself?	

STOP What we _____ to becomes our inner voice.

STOP What we _____ with our eyes can set our future, because we will live out of the picture we see on the inside.

STOP The taste of what we _____ creates appetites.

STOP The aroma of the _____ we live in fills our spirit with either life or death.

STOP What we touch creates _____.

> **Know This:**
> It's fine to hang around sinners to minister to them, like Jesus did, but only to the point that you can keep your moral integrity.

Why is the sense of touch so powerful? _____

How is this chapter changing the way you think about your five senses? _____

God intended that our _____ and _____ would follow our _____ lead.

As you read Chapter Five in your book, what weeds did you discover hiding in the garden of your heart that need to be pulled out? _____

> Which works-based mentality have you been more likely to lean to in order to deal with sin in the past? Circle all that apply.

TRY TO BE "GOOD"	GIVE UP AND BE "BAD"
Comply	Give up
Perform	Rebel
Do all the "right" things	Fight against constraints
Judging others	Saying "I don't care."
Playing the role of a martyr	Taking on the bad boy/girl persona

A restored identity starts with receiving

_____

_____

Sin is a symptom of a soul sickness that we were all born with, but

_____

_____

Know This:
A true friend will speak Truth even when the other person doesn't want to hear it.

What are two things you took away from this chapter?

1. _____

2. _____

This week, go all in on your personal renovation project by pulling out your gardening tools and yanking the weeds from your flower beds and garden. Complete the Challenge at the end of Chapter Five in your book by reading the Scriptures and answering the questions.

Prayer

This week, pray the prayer from Chapter Five of the book.

Father God, I come to You through the wonderful name of Jesus, and I thank You for opening up the way for us to have a close relationship. I want You more than anything else.

Show me if there are lies about sin that I have believed.

Show me what weeds are in my heart that I need You to help pull out.

I repent of any sins that have come to try to pull me away from You. Wash me clean and create in me a clean heart. Restore in me a right spirit so that I can live this life with power and grace. I will not launch the weapons of blame or rejection against myself or against another.

Amen.

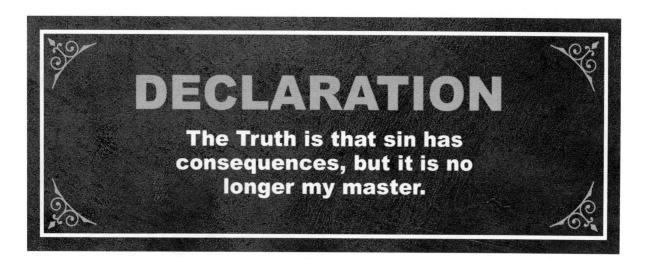

NOTES FROM THIS CHAPTER

> *I took you from the ends of the earth, from its farthest corners I called you. I said, 'You are my servant'; I have chosen you and have not rejected you.*
>
> —Isaiah 41:9

CHAPTER FIVE &/ "SIN WON'T HURT ME"

> *For it was always in his perfect plan to adopt us as his delightful children, through our union with Jesus, the Anointed One, so that his tremendous love that cascades over us would glorify his grace—for the same love he has for his Beloved One, Jesus, he has for us. And this unfolding plan brings him great pleasure!*
>
> **—Ephesians 1:5-6 TPT**

> *Instead of shame and dishonor, you will enjoy a double share of honor. You will possess a double portion of prosperity in your land, and everlasting joy will be yours.*
> —Isaiah 61:7 NLT

06

Lie #4
"I SHOULD BE ASHAMED OF MYSELF."

I praise you because I am fearfully and wonderfully made; your works are wonderful, I know that full well.

—Psalm 139:14

"You can't go back and change the beginning, but you can start where you are and change the ending." —C.S. Lewis

Chapter Six in *The Truth About You: Overcoming Seven Lies You Believe About Yourself* opens with a powerful story of freedom.

What is one thing you took from Wendy's beautiful story of triumph?

_____

_____

_____

God doesn't see what we _____; He sees what we can _____ in His hands.

Speak out this personalized version of 2 Corinthians 5:17:

> *Therefore, if I am in Christ, I am a new creation. The old has passed away; behold, the new has come.*

Know This:

If you call someone a name, expect them to start acting more like that name.

What does shame's voice sound like?

_____

_____

MEN AND SHAME	WOMEN AND SHAME
Coping mechanisms	Pressure to be perfect
Workaholics	Impossible expectations
Need to conquer everything	Retreat and shut people out
Gender dysphoria	Keep up perceptions
Despise perceived weakness	Lash out
Avoid vulnerability or emotions	Question relationships
No freedom to be unsure	Pretend to be tough, prove self
Try to do life in their own power	Reject womanhood
Try to control everyone and everything	Try to control everyone and everything
Lose all self	Lose all self

Look at the two columns above that list how shame affects men and women. Do you see yourself in those lists? Why or why not?

NOTES

CONDEMNATION	CONVICTION
Devil condemns us to life of shame	Holy Spirit convicts us to change
Makes us feel hopeless and worthless	Seeks to reconcile the relationship
Only satan condemns	Only God convicts
Satan says you're hopeless	God says what you did doesn't define you
Aim is to separate and isolate	Aim is to forgive and restore
There's no way out	Here is the way out
You *are* bad	You *did* something bad
You can never change	Turn from that action and don't repeat it

Take a few moments to study the differences between condemnation and conviction. Remember these descriptions the next time the deceiver tries to get you to listen to his voice.

What is one thing that really struck you as you read this chapter this week? _____

Know This:
God doesn't expect us to become perfect and then come to Him. Instead, He expects us to bring our imperfections and give them to Him.

In what ways might shame be keeping you in hiding or suppressing your true self? _____

TAKE ACTION!

This week's personal renovation action is about equipping you.

Ephesians 6:10-18 tells us about the Armor of God, the tools and weapons God has already given us to stand strong against the tactics of the enemy. Declare this personalized version of these Scriptures over yourself and your life.

> *I am strong in the Lord and in his mighty power. I put on the full armor of God, so that I can take my stand against the devil's schemes. For my struggle is not against flesh and blood, but against the rulers, against the authorities, against the powers of this dark world and against the spiritual forces of evil in the heavenly realms.*

> *I put on the full armor of God, so that when the day of evil comes, I may be able to stand my ground, and after I have done everything, I stand. I stand firm with the belt of Truth buckled around my waist, with the breastplate of righteousness in place, and with my feet fitted with the readiness that comes from the gospel of peace. I take up the shield of faith, with which I can extinguish all the flaming arrows of the evil one. I wear the helmet of salvation and I wield the sword of the Spirit, which is the word of God.*

> *I pray in the Spirit on all occasions with all kinds of prayers and requests. I am alert [to the tactics of the enemy] and always keep on praying for all the Lord's people.*

Be sure to also complete the Challenge at the end of Chapter Six in your book.

Prayer

This week, pray the prayer from Chapter Six of the book. Also thank God that He sees You as what you can become in His hands.

> Father, I ask You to set me free from shame. Help me step into the freedom to be myself without fear. Because of You, I am not condemned or hopeless. Instead, I receive your unconditional love for every hurt. I accept your forgiveness for every sin.
>
> I thank You that You always see me not as I am or as what I've done, but as who I can become in Your hands. I bring my imperfections to You and thank You for mercy and freedom. Amen.

DECLARATION

The truth is that I don't have to hide, because I have a good Father who has made me good, too.

NOTES FROM THIS CHAPTER

> *And so, dear brothers and sisters, I plead with you to give your bodies to God because of all He has done for you. Let them be a living and holy sacrifice—the kind He will find acceptable. This is truly the way to worship Him.*
>
> —Romans 1:21 TPT

> *Therefore, since we are surrounded by such a huge crowd of witnesses to the life of faith, let us strip off every weight that slows us down, especially the sin that so easily trips us up. And let us run with endurance the race God has set before us. We do this by keeping our eyes on Jesus, the champion who initiates and perfects our faith. Because of the joy awaiting him, he endured the cross, disregarding its shame. Now he is seated in the place of honor beside God's throne. Think of all the hostility he endured from sinful people; then you won't become weary and give up.*
>
> —Hebrews 12:1-3 NLT

> *You keep every promise you've ever made to me! Since your love for me is constant and endless, I ask you, Lord, to finish every good thing that you've begun in me!*
>
> —Psalm 138:8 TPT

07

Lie #5

"I DESERVE THE BLAME."

I praise you because I am fearfully and wonderfully made; your works are wonderful, I know that full well.
—Psalm 139:14

BLAME:
To find fault with, an expression of disapproval or reproach, a state of being blameworthy.

THE BLAME GAME

Human nature wants to _____ someone else—anyone else. That's because our sin nature makes us feel exposed.

Time to be honest with yourself, again.

What are two areas of your life or situations where you're afraid to be vulnerable or afraid of being "exposed"? (*This question alone might make you feel vulnerable, but please don't skip over this. Even though this is likely to make you uncomfortable, it's important to think about these things so you can conquer the lies of the enemy and live free.*)

1

2

> ### Know This:
> Shame tries to get us to cover our sins instead of bringing them into the light where they can be dealt with. Shame says, "If you admit you're wrong, then you're not worthy of love."

CHAPTER SEVEN — "I DESERVE THE BLAME"

We're about to do some more thinking. This time, think about some of the ways you use blame in your life and what the Truth really is. I've included some examples to help you get started.

ISSUE	BLAME GAME	TRUTH
My child misbehaved	I must be a bad parent	My child made a poor decision
Behind on a work project	Coworker didn't give info	I procrastinated

We should never shift the blame to someone else, because we can't receive forgiveness when we don't _____ _____.

> "ADAM AND EVE STARTED FIGHTING FOR SURVIVAL THE VERY MOMENT THEY BLAMED SOMEONE ELSE RATHER THAN FIGHTING TO PROTECT ONE ANOTHER AND OWN UP TO THEIR MISTAKES."

NOTES

What is one thing you took from Dawn's story in this chapter? _____
_____
_____
_____

Don't miss this! ⬇

Not all struggles or illnesses are caused by sin or by someone, but rather by
_____ or a
_____.

It is God's will that we are _____ from every form of pain, including soul sickness, mental illness, and emotional turmoil.

Write out Luke 4:18:

Jesus went about doing good, and healing _____ that were oppressed of the _____; for God was with him. —Acts 10:38

> **Know This:**
>
> Satan attacks the identity roles that matter most, the ones commissioned by God in Genesis 1-2.

The _____ should be the last place people feel blamed and hopeless.

Time for a heart-check. How frequently do you judge others? How frequently are you unfairly hard on yourself, as well?

Write out Hebrews 10:30:

NOTES

We should never talk about sin without also _____—which clearly _____ the sin from the sinner. Jesus is our _____, so no one is ever <u>hopeless</u>.

List two things that encouraged you as you read this chapter:

1 _____

_____

_____

_____

2 _____

_____

_____

_____

SHAME AND BLAME ARE TWINS THAT OFTEN COME TOGETHER, SENT STRAIGHT FROM THE DECEIVER. HE WANTS US TO HIDE, SO HE USES THESE TWINS TO COWER US IN A CORNER.

TAKE ACTION!

This week's personal renovation action will require you to step out of your comfort zone.

Since shame and blame make us want to hide, shun, and judge, we're going to purposely do the opposite.

This week, reach out to someone you know you need to hang around or to someone you know has been hurting. Refuse to isolate yourself from true friends, and also be on the lookout for someone who needs to feel loved by God.

Take some time to journal how it felt to take a sledgehammer to the walls of shame, blame, and self-righteousness.

Next, complete the Challenge at the end of Chapter Seven in your book. Choose one of the Scriptures from the Challenge that you need encouragement in the most and write it on a sticky note or paper and put it on your mirror(s) at home and/or in your car.

Prayer

This week, pray the prayer from Chapter Seven of the book. Also ask the Holy Spirit to show you ways in which you've judged others and how you can best love them instead.

> Holy Spirit, set me free from the lies of blame. Help me to identify them when they start speaking and to cast them down. Help me to receive the righteousness that you've paid for. Help me to overcome the voices of judgment or blame from others in my life. I replace those voices with Your voice.
>
> I also ask that you show me all of the ways that I have judged others. Reveal to me how harsh it is every time I do it, and help me to stop. Teach me how to best show Your great love to people instead.
>
> In Jesus's name, I am clean! Amen.

CHAPTER SEVEN // #5 "I DESERVE THE BLAME"

DECLARATION

**The Truth is that I am free from blame.
"Righteous" is part of my identity.**

NOTES FROM THIS CHAPTER

77

> *But Christ has rescued us from the curse pronounced by the law. When he was hung on the cross, he took upon himself the curse for our wrongdoing. For it is written in the Scriptures, "Cursed is everyone who is hung on a tree."*
> —Galatians 3:13 NLT

> *So keep coming to him who is the Living Stone—though he was rejected and discarded by men but chosen by God and is priceless in God's sight. Come and be his "living stones" who are continually being assembled into a sanctuary for God. For now you serve as holy priests, offering up spiritual sacrifices that he readily accepts through Jesus Christ.*
>
> —Hebrews 12:1-3 NLT

> *For God has not given us a spirit of fear, but of power and of love and of a sound mind.*
> —2 Timothy 1:7 NKJV

08

Lie #6
"I AM REJECTED."

I praise you because I am fearfully and wonderfully made; your works are wonderful, I know that full well.
—Psalm 139:14

"Be who you are and say what you feel because those who mind don't matter, and those who matter, don't mind." — Dr. Seuss

ONE OF YOUR ENEMY'S FAVORITE WEAPONS

How does the teaching at the beginning of this chapter change how you think about rejection?

_____

_____

_____

_____

THE IMPACT OF REJECTION
Keeps you from your created identity.
Distances you from good relationships.
Keeps you out of God's presence.
Causes you to turn on yourself, others, and God.

The very thing that makes you _____ or is part of your _____ _____ is the area in which you will receive the most rejection attacks.

> **Know This:**
>
> Satan often uses people to attack the thing in you that looks the most like God.

Satan loves to use the weapon of rejection because every time we reject ourselves, we _____ _____.

Rejection can enter our lives in many ways. What would you add to the list below?

HOW DOES REJECTION ENTER OUR LIVES?
generational influences and attitudes
bullying
racism
relationships with family
relationships with friends
relationships with significant others
word curses spoken

NOTES

Which of these six descriptions below sound most like how you have reacted to rejection in the past? Circle all that apply.

PRIDEFUL	**SHALLOW**
Build a fortress around your heart	Become the "class clown" and laugh it off
Try to control people or situations to avoid rejection	Try not to think about it or feel too deeply
Often talk negatively about people	Keep everything surface level
Won't admit mistakes or apologize	Wear the mask of lightheartedness
Try to prove worth through action	

PLEASURE SEEKER	**REBELLIOUS**
Try to cover pain with relationships, substance abuse, material things, positions of power, or attention, or recognition	Become the "bad boy" or "bad girl"
	Claim to not care what people think
Never satisfied or have enough	Hurt others before others can hurt or reject you

DEPRESSED	**CO-DEPENDANT**
Expect that no one will like you	Cannot function without someone else to bounce value off of
Look for rejection everywhere	
Try to guilt others into proving their love	One person is the "taker" and the other is the "fixer," wanting to be needed

> **Know This:**
>
> It's not wrong to want to help others and bring joy to their lives, but it is wrong to sacrifice your God-given purpose or identity on the altar of acceptance. The Bible calls this the fear of man.

Write out Proverbs 29:25:

How is an orphan spirit more than just a spirit of rejection?

It's an oppressive _____ stronghold that makes people feel like they don't belong anywhere.

It tries to make people _____.

It makes people focus on _____ instead of dreaming.

It makes people stop _____.

It makes people stop _____ to authorities.

It develops in _____.

It grows on a steady diet of _____ and _____.

It suspects rejection even where there is none.

The ultimate goal of a spirit of rejection is to _____ _____—both the love of _____ and love from _____.

Based on the descriptions below, have you been basing your identity based on what the enemy says or on what God says?

WHAT THE ENEMY SAYS	WHAT GOD SAYS
You are the sum of your actions.	You have a God-given identity.
You can keep working at it, but good luck.	You have God-designed potential.
Your identity is based on what you do.	Your identity is based on Who you belong to.
You have to try to earn love and approval and acceptance.	God already loves you. You don't have to earn His love.

The antidote for rejection is found in _____, which can only be found in _____.

In this chapter, I list seven ways that Jesus was rejected. In which of those ways can you relate to Jesus? How?

_____
_____
_____
_____

> *Know This:*
> God will complete every good thing that He has begun in our lives if we ask for His help and don't rely on our works.

When you read the list in Chapter Eight of how Jesus was rejected, did it open your eyes to realize He felt the same things you have felt? How? _____

_____

Whew! I know this was probably a deeply personal and intense chapter, but if you can truly live in this Truth, free from the opinions of man, you will be freer than 99% of the people around you. List two things that surprised you as you read this chapter:

1 _____ **2** _____

This week's personal renovation action has three parts.

#1 - Review the list of ways to be free from an orphan spirit that I listed in this chapter. Even if you don't believe you have ever battled this spirit, this list can still help heal any areas of rejection in your life. Is there one (or more) thing on that list that the Holy Spirit is prompting you to do?

#2 - Read all of Romans 8 in your favorite version of the Bible. Highlight and/or underline anything that stands out to you as you read.

#3 - Complete the Challenge at the end of Chapter Eight in your book.

Prayer

This week, pray the prayer from Chapter Eight of the book. Also ask God to show you any ways that rejection has entered your life so you can squash the lies of the enemy.

> God, I'm sorry for pleasing people or chasing after their approval instead of receiving Your full acceptance. I receive Your secure and steadfast love. I believe You will never leave me or forsake me, and You did not leave me as an orphan, having to make my own way through life.
>
> I ask that You show me any ways that rejection has entered my life that I'm unaware of so that, together, we can dig up those weeds from the roots. I thank You that You love me unconditionally, that I am accepted in Your Kingdom, and it's in You that I belong.
>
> I praise You, God! Amen.

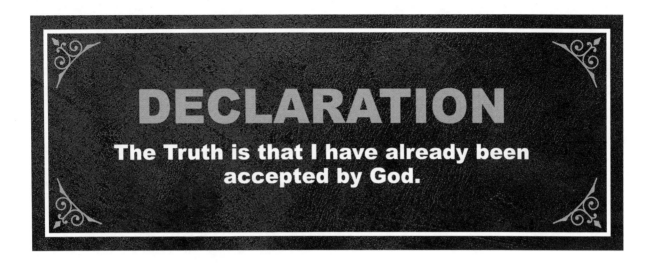

NOTES FROM THIS CHAPTER

> *For you did not receive a spirit of slavery that returns you to fear, but you received the Spirit of sonship, by whom we cry, "Abba! Father!"*
> —Romans 8:15 KJV

CHAPTER EIGHT *eye to* "I AM REJECTED"

> *And giving joyful thanks to the Father, who has qualified you to share in the inheritance of his holy people in the kingdom of light. For he has rescued us from the dominion of darkness and brought us into the kingdom of the Son he loves, in whom we have redemption, the forgiveness of sins.*
> —Colossians 1:12-14

> *God made Him who knew no sin to be sin on our behalf, so that in Him we might become the righteousness of God.*
> —2 Corinthians 5:21 NLT

09

Lie #7
"I AM A FAILURE."

I praise you because I am fearfully and wonderfully made; your works are wonderful, I know that full well.
—Psalm 139:14

God measures true success by how obedient you were to His calling on your life. You are not a failure if you keep saying "yes" to Him.

YOU ARE BIGGER THAN YOUR PROBLEMS

What is one thing you can take away from Olivia's turnaround story from this chapter?

_____
_____
_____
_____
_____
_____

Know This:

The results of the Curse have damaged mankind's identity, and surviving it has become mankind's purpose. But none of the effects of the Curse were God's will for our lives.

Which of the following ways that Adam and Eve lived in the Garden do you want most? Circle all that apply.

To be in close fellowship with God

To have a restored identity as God's child

To enjoy having my needs met without painful toil and slavery

To walk in authority over satan

To live out my purpose and giftings

To never experience sickness or pain

CHAPTER NINE ⋅ "I AM A FAILURE"

True or false? When someone gets delivered from the slavery of the kingdom of darkness, they instantly know how to live like a free person.

TRUE

FALSE

NOTES

> "TO LEARN THE NEW LAWS OF THE KINGDOM OF GOD, YOU MUST READ YOUR MANUAL FOR LIFE, THE BIBLE, IN WHICH YOU CAN DISCOVER YOUR FULL POTENTIAL AND START LIVING LIKE THE SUCCESSFUL PERSON GOD SAYS YOU ARE."

No one is hopeless unless they _____.

No one is a failure unless they _____.

The lie of failure not only tries to thwart your God-given genius but also tries to keep you from taking up your _____.

What is the driving force behind the lie of failure? _____
_____

In this chapter, I talk about fear being the language of the Curse and how we can end up speaking negative prophecies when we think we're just giving out innocent warnings.

Take a look at the table below and fill in your own examples of things you realize you say that are fear-based and negative and what you can replace it with.

LANGUAGE OF THE CURSE/ NEGATIVE PROPHECY	WHAT TO SAY INSTEAD
"Get down! You will fall and hurt yourself."	"Don't do that for your safety."
"You should take your vitamins or you won't have any energy."	"Vitamins boost your energy and help prevent sickness."

Fearful _____ lead to fear-filled _____, which open the door to _____.

Write out 2 Timothy 1:7:

What are two things you learned as you read this chapter that you'll implement in your life?

1 _____

2 _____

To keep your freedom from fear requires that you constantly feed on Truth and the language of faith, which is the language of Heaven's Kingdom. The language of fear surrounds us, so it's crucial that you up your intake of faith on a daily basis.

I challenge you, this week, to pay close attention to what you're feeding on. Is what you're feeding on—listening to, watching, touching, even speaking—from the earth-Curse and filling you up with fear or is it based on the Blessing and filling you up with faith?
Make changes where necessary.

Be sure to also complete the Challenge at the end of Chapter Nine in your book.

Prayer

This week, pray the prayer from Chapter Nine of the book. Also ask the Lord to set a guard over your mouth that keeps you from speaking fear-filled words.

> Thank You, Lord Jesus, that You have redeemed me and bought me out of the Curse due to Adam and Eve's rebellion. I no longer belong under that Curse. All the feelings of fear, rejection, and shame that came along with that Curse no longer belong in my life because I now live under the law of LIFE. You gave me a brand new way of living!
>
> I declare freedom over my mind now, in Jesus's name. Fear, I command you to take your hands off of my mind. SHUT UP and GET OUT! I don't belong to you. I belong to THE All-Powerful God who defeated you!
>
> And, Lord, I also pray Psalm 141:3, that You would set a guard over my mouth, and keep watch over the door of my lips so I speak only the language of Your Kingdom.
>
> I praise You, God! Amen.

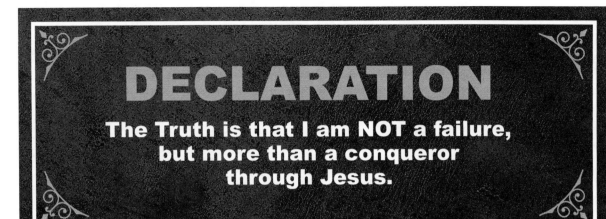

NOTES FROM THIS CHAPTER

> The Lord your God is in your midst, a mighty one who will save; he will rejoice over you with gladness; he will quiet you by his love; he will exult over you with loud singing.
> —Zephaniah 3:17 ESV

CHAPTER NINE // "I AM A FAILURE"

> *...bring my sons from afar*
>   *and my daughters from the end of the earth,*
> *everyone who is called by my name,*
>   *whom I created for my glory,*
>   *whom I formed and made.*
>   —Isaiah 43:6b-7 ESV

> *For God has not given us a spirit of fear, but of power and of love and of a sound mind.*
>
> —2 Timothy 1:7

10

I AM BECOMING

I praise you because I am fearfully and wonderfully made; your works are wonderful, I know that full well.
—Psalm 139:14

> "Can you tell me who you ARE without telling me what you DO? Your identity and assignment in the Kingdom of God are more than anything you own or even what you do." —Gary Keesee

IT DOESN'T HAPPEN OVERNIGHT

At the beginning of Chapter Ten of *The Truth About You: Overcoming Seven Lies You Believe About Yourself*, I share about the process of becoming Mr. and Mrs. Freudiger.

Think of one relationship you are in, and describe one example of how your relationship has grown or changed (for the better in this example.)

_____
_____
_____
_____

Through the parable of the lost son in Luke 15, Jesus paints a rich picture of Father God's _____ in bringing us back into the _____ and _____ our _____ as His kids.

> "ALTHOUGH OUR SPIRITS ARE REGENERATED AND ENTIRELY ALIVE TO GOD, OUR SOULS STILL NEED SOME WORK."

Write out Philippians 1:6:

104

How is this chapter changing the way you think about what you're becoming with God?

NOTES

THOUGHT

Good ⬇
Add value
Inspire you
Calm you
Help/warn you

Bad ⬇
Stronghold
Weigh you down
Trip you up
Imprison you

Know This:

Wrong thoughts will come from the enemy, friends, family, the media, and the worldly systems around us. We must learn to toss them away QUICKLY.

Good thoughts need to be _____, _____ on, and _____ on.

Write out your favorite Scripture version of Romans 12:2:

When we consciously decide to act on the Holy Spirit's thoughts, we become "established," which means _____.

Good thoughts can establish and _____ your _____, _____, and _____.

Bad thoughts can destabilize _____ good in your life.

We destroy arguments and every lofty opinion raised _____ the knowledge of God and take _____ _____ _____ to _____ Christ. - 2 Corinthians 10:5 (ESV)

Read over these two lists:

A WEAK MIND	A STRONG MIND
Is easily swayed	Stays focused and fixed on Truth
Allows thoughts to bombard	Only entertains thoughts that line up with what it knows is right, good, and true
Focused on self	Focuses on God and others above self
Entertains every thought	Intentionally shuts out strange voices and deceitful lures
Follows every voice	Follows the voice of God

CHAPTER TEN I AM BECOMING

Which of these two lists sound most like your mind before you started this study? _____

Has anything changed? Why or why not? _____

God's will for us is to give us _____ and _____. (Deuteronomy 30)

How can we know God's will?

1 _____

2 _____

3 _____

Truth doesn't care about our _____.

> **Know This:**
>
> God has chosen to reveal His ways to us. We have His mind (1 Corinthians 2), so we can make right decisions and judgments about *all things*.

107

How can we know God's will? (continued)

4 _____

5 _____

6 _____

Describe a time that you were either led by peace or did not follow peace. What happened.

_____
_____
_____
_____

_____ is put there by God to help us with our "blind spots," because we all have them.

Have you started to feel down on yourself this week? If so, stop and identify what that predominant thought is. Where did it come from? _____
_____
_____
_____
_____

"IF YOU WANT YOUR LIFE TO LOOK LIKE A HOLLYWOOD TABLOID DRAMA, BY ALL MEANS, FOLLOW YOUR EMOTIONS. BUT IF YOU WANT YOUR LIFE TO READ LIKE A NEW YORK TIMES BESTSELLER ON SUCCESS, THEN FOLLOW THE SPIRIT OF GOD."

What are two things that encouraged you as you read this chapter?

1 _____ 2 _____

As you continue to work on the most breathtaking renovation project ever—the masterpiece God made you to be, it's important that you start thinking about the next step in your journey. What will you do after you complete this study?

So, part of your challenge this week is to get a copy of the book *Better Than You Feel*, by my mom, Drenda Keesee. It's packed with wisdom on dealing with emotions, and it's a great next-step in your journey.

Be sure to also complete the Challenge at the end of Chapter Ten in your book.

Prayer

This week, pray the prayer from Chapter Ten of the book. Also pray the words of 2 Peter 1:5-8 from your favorite Scripture version. I've personalized the version I used in the book for you here as a part of this prayer.

> *Jesus, help me to walk with You each day. I submit my soul to You, and I ask You to mature me. Help me to become more like You. I want to serve You in everything I do.*
>
> *Jesus, I ask that You add to my faith goodness; and to goodness, knowledge; and to knowledge, self-control; and to self-control, perseverance; and to perseverance, godliness; and to godliness, mutual affection; and to mutual affection, love. For I will possess these qualities in increasing measure, and they will keep me from being ineffective and unproductive in my knowledge of You, Lord.*
>
> *Amen.*

NOTES FROM THIS CHAPTER

> For we are his workmanship, created in Christ Jesus for good works, which God prepared beforehand, that we should walk in them.
> —Ephesians 2:10 ESV

> *For I know the plans I have for you, declares the Lord, plans for welfare and not for evil, to give you a future and a hope.*
> —Jeremiah 29:11 ESV

> *Nevertheless the solid foundation of God stands, having this seal: "The Lord knows those who are His."*
> —2 Timothy 2:19a NJKV

11

I'M A MONA LISA MASTERPIECE

I praise you because I am fearfully and wonderfully made; your works are wonderful, I know that full well.
—Psalm 139:14

"Insecurity comes when we find our identity in anything but God." —John Bevere

DO YOU KNOW HOW VALUABLE YOU ARE?

Write out Ephesians 2:10:

LET'S TALK ABOUT JUST A FEW OF THE DETAILS OF WHAT MAKES YOU WHO YOU ARE, THAT WHICH GOD DELIGHTS IN. ANSWER THE FOLLOWING AND THINK ABOUT HOW GOD KNOWS THESE DETAILS ABOUT YOU, HIS VALUABLE MASTERPIECE. CONSIDER HOW MUCH FUN IT MUST BE FOR HIM TO KNOW UNIQUE AND WONDERFUL YOU.

What is your favorite color?	
What is your favorite activity?	
What makes you laugh really hard?	
What makes you cry happy tears?	
In what setting do you feel like you most sense God's presence?	

CHAPTER ELEVEN: I'M A MONA LISA MASTERPIECE

> ### Know This:
> "Loved" is who you are, not something you're trying to become.

Real joy doesn't rely on or come from _____.
It always has _____ as its root.

Absolute joy comes from _____.

Write out Galatians 5:22:

Who is someone in your life that you can be vulnerable with? _____
_____
_____
_____
_____

What is the most significant source of encouragement any of us have? _____

NOTES

What is the difference between courage and confidence?

Have you allowed other voices to paint over the real you, a masterpiece made in God's image? In what ways?

> "STOP GIVING PROBLEMS OR PEOPLE A PLACE OF HIGHER IMPORTANCE THAN GOD AND HIS WORD. WHEN YOU DWELL ON THOSE PEOPLE, SITUATIONS, OR PROBLEMS MORE THAN YOU DWELL ON JESUS, THEY BECOME THE RULER OF YOUR LIFE."

What are two things that encouraged you as you read this chapter?

1

2

TAKE ACTION!

It's time for a joy booster!

In this chapter, I suggested you start making a gratitude list daily. Do that this week. Purpose to focus on the positives and see all of the things you have to be grateful for.

While you're at it, consider shutting down the negatives of the world this week. Turn off the news, and don't listen to sad or angry music, television show hosts, or podcasts.

Instead, turn on some praise music. Watch some video testimonies, like the ones at faithlifechurch.org/real-experiences. Grow your joy!

Be sure to also complete the Challenge at the end of Chapter Eleven in your book.

Prayer

This week, pray the prayer from Chapter Eleven of the book. Also pray for Jesus to give you courage and to uncover your need for a Savior in every area of your heart.

> Jesus, I come to You and ask You to show me Your love. I surrender all fear of vulnerability and humbly say that I am in need. I ask You to heal me of all fear and sadness. I want to be deeply connected to You so that the joy of knowing You carries me to a higher place of living beyond what I see now. Deliver me from all depression and fear. Give me the confidence and courage to stand in victory today.
>
> I ask that You strengthen me and give me courage and that You uncover every area of my heart so I can let your love in.
>
> Thank You that I am Your masterpiece, and You are my Creator.
>
> Amen.

NOTES FROM THIS CHAPTER

> *God saw everything that He had made, and behold, it was very good and He validated it completely. And there was evening and there was morning, a sixth day.*
> —Genesis 1:31 AMP

CHAPTER ELEVEN: I'M A MONA LISA MASTERPIECE

> *I have been crucified with Christ and I no longer live, but Christ lives in me. The life I now live in the body, I live by faith in the Son of God, who loved me and gave himself for me."*
> —**Galatians 2:20**

> Submit yourselves therefore to God. Resist the devil, and he will flee from you.
>
> —James 4:7 ESV

12

I CAN BREAK FREE FROM DARKNESS

I praise you because I am fearfully and wonderfully made; your works are wonderful, I know that full well.
—Psalm 139:14

"When the devil puts a request across my desk, I say, 'request denied.' I deny satan a place of influence in my life." —Bill Johnson

FREEDOM STARTS WITH THE SPIRITUAL SIDE

At the beginning of Chapter 12, I share about how I stopped wrestling with oppression and started fighting back with God's Word, using my authority as His daughter to command evil spirits to leave, and they did.

What are you realizing that you have been "taking" or putting up with that you are going to start fighting back with God's Word and your God-given authority? _____

_____

_____

_____

_____

_____

Satan only has legal jurisdiction to work in _____.

We give satan "leasing rights" to our lives when we _____
_____.

The only power satan has is _____.

CHAPTER TWELVE: I CAN BREAK FREE FROM DARKNESS

How is this chapter changing what you've always believed about mental illness?

Write out Isaiah 53:4:

Does it surprise you to know that there are more instances in the Bible of Jesus setting people free from mental illness symptoms than from physical symptoms? Why or why not?

Know This:

Jesus healed people's minds, bodies, and spirits. He still does.

NOTES

What are two things you learned or discovered as you read this chapter?

1 _____   **2** _____

This personal renovation action is crucially important. (Not that all of them aren't, haha, but I really want to emphasize this one.)

First, have you been diagnosed with any kind of "soul sickness?" (ie. schizophrenia, extreme anxiety, ADHD, etc.) If so, I want to challenge you to take the following steps right now:

1. Write that diagnosis on a piece of paper.
2. Picture that piece of paper being nailed to the cross that Jesus died on. Why? Because when He died, *that thing died with Him*. And when He was raised from the dead, He raised YOU up with Him, totally FREE from that torment!
3. Tear up or burn that paper, and say, "Thank you Jesus that I am free and I am healed!"

Second, Proverbs 6:31 tells us that the thief must pay back all he has stolen and then some. He doesn't just get to mess with your life and walk away. He has to pay back all he took AND pay plenty of interest, and for damages while we're at it!

What has the devil messed with in your life? Make a list, and then demand the enemy that it be repaid, in the name of Jesus.

Finally, be sure to also complete the Challenge at the end of Chapter Twelve in your book.

Prayer

This week, pray the prayer from Chapter Twelve of the book.

Thank You, Jesus, that You have given me power over all the power of the enemy, and nothing shall by any means harm me. You have given me the ability to command any darkness to leave, so I do that now.

Devil, I command that you leave and take your oppression, fear, depression, shame, and everything else, and GET OUT, in the name of Jesus. I command you to take every symptom of mental illness or soul anguish and GO! I DEMAND that you must repay seven times what you've stolen. Put it ALL back!

Thank You, Lord, that I submit my life to You, and I resist every thought of the devil, and he must flee.

Amen.

> *And in keeping with what is written: "I believed, therefore I have spoken," we who have the same spirit of faith also believe and therefore speak, knowing that the One who raised the Lord Jesus will also raise us with Jesus and present us with you in His presence.*
>
> —2 Corinthians 4:13-14

CHAPTER TWELVE: I CAN BREAK FREE FROM DARKNESS

> *Do not be afraid; you will not be put to shame. Do not fear disgrace; you will not be humiliated. You will forget the shame of your youth and remember no more the reproach of your widowhood. For your Maker is your husband— the Lord Almighty is his name— the Holy One of Israel is your Redeemer; he is called the God of all the earth.*
>
> —Isaiah 54:4-5

> *Little children, you are from God and have overcome them, for he who is in you is greater than he who is in the world.*
>
> —1 John 4:4 ESV

13

I HAVE THE ANOINTING

I praise you because I am fearfully and wonderfully made; your works are wonderful, I know that full well.
—Psalm 139:14

"Fear of the devil is nonsense. Fear of demons is foolish. The Spirit of God anointing the Christian heart makes the soul impregnable to the powers of darkness." —John G. Lake

FREEDOM STARTS WITH THE SPIRITUAL SIDE

What is one thing you took from Mary's story at the beginning of this chapter?

_____
_____
_____

Let's break down Isaiah 10:27: *And it shall come to pass in that day, that his burden shall be taken away from off thy shoulder, and his yoke from off thy neck, and the yoke shall be destroyed because of the anointing.*

"YOKED"	ANOINTED
Not free to move about	Unbound and unhindered
Held in the same pattern of labor	FREE from patterns and ruts
Around and around in circles, getting nowhere	Empowered
Weighed down, carrying cares and worries	Lifted into the realm of the Blessing; healed, refreshed, and restored
Unable to see a vision beyond surviving	Have vision for the future
Hopeless	Hope-filled

Which list sounds more like how you've lived life up until this point, and why? _____
_____
_____

> ### Know This:
> When you were born again and received Jesus as your Savior, the Holy Spirit came into your house. He is there. But that doesn't mean you have gotten to know Him or are listening to His voice.

He (the Holy Spirit) has a gift for you in the form of the _____, which can change your life if you receive it.

How does the anointing come? _____
_____

Write out John 16:7 from the Amplified Bible:

NOTES

When you listen to the Holy Spirit, He leads you in _____ and teaches you what is right.

Galatians 5:22-23 list some benefits we receive by spending time with the Holy Spirit. Which of those benefits is most evident in your life? _____

_____

_____

_____

_____

Which of those benefits would you like more of in your life? _____

_____

_____

_____

_____

The anointing is a by-product of _____ _____ _____.

The anointing comes upon you for a _____, to bring heaven to earth in any situation.

> "JUST LIKE WE TAKE COFFEE OR SNACK BREAKS, WE SHOULD TAKE AN 'ANOINTING BREAK' THROUGHOUT OUR DAY!"

CHAPTER THIRTEEN: I HAVE THE ANOINTING

NOTES

> ### Know This:
> When you rely on God and not on yourself, He will empower you to become so much greater than you thought.

The anointing is _____.

I included this powerful quote from John Poole in this chapter:

> *We must remember that we fight on the foundation of a victory already won. Human wisdom cannot heal emotional wounds. Human knowledge cannot set free those who are spiritually bound.*
>
> *Traditions and church rituals cannot cast out a demonic spirit. Human wit cannot restore those who have emotional bruises (blows to his or her identity). However, the anointing that was on Jesus can heal all those who have been oppressed by the devil.*

How does this quote change how you think about us humans trying to do so many things in our own strength and power? _____

_____

_____

_____

I can do all things _____ which strengtheneth me.

— Philippians 4:13

What are two things that you learned, or that encouraged you, as you read this chapter?

1 _____

2 _____

TAKE ACTION!

This week's personal renovation action is more about ongoing "maintenance" than it is about tearing down walls or doing interior decorating.

In this chapter, I talked about taking an "anointing break," just like you might take coffee or snack (or even restroom, haha) breaks throughout your day.

This week, start that process.

One of the easiest ways to build a new habit is to habit stack—add a new habit to a current habit or before or after a current habit.

So, make your "anointing break" a part of your coffee, snack, and/or restroom breaks. Or add your "anointing break" just before or just after your coffee, snack, and/or restroom breaks. Take those moments to bring the Holy Spirit into your day. Talk to Him. Ask Him to give you love, joy, peace, patience, kindness, goodness, faithfulness, gentleness, and self-control. Ask Him to give you direction or help you. And thank Him for being with you throughout your day, and life.

Do this and watch what happens as you implement the anointing power throughout your day. (I'm excited for you!)

Be sure to also complete the Challenge at the end of Chapter Thirteen in your book.

Prayer

This week, pray the prayer from Chapter Thirteen of the book. Also pray for the anointing to infiltrate every area of your life.

> Holy Spirit, I invite You to come right now and anoint me to do Your will today. I receive Your help, wisdom, and power that frees me from all spiritual darkness, the lies I've believed about myself, or anything that holds me back. Baptize me in Your anointing! Help me to receive Your power on a daily basis so that I can stay free.
>
> I want to be the REAL me, seeing myself the way You see me. I want to live in the reality of Your Kingdom, realizing my full potential as Your child. I refuse to keep falling back into the pit of poor self image, allowing the devil to lie to me about myself. Thank you for Your anointing that breaks off all the lies I hear around me. I give You all the pressure I try to put on myself. I give you all of ME.
>
> Thank You for being with me all day every day, and for Your anointing infiltrating every part of my life.
>
> Amen.

> *And they have conquered him by the blood of the Lamb and by the word of their testimony, for they loved not their lives even unto death.*
>
> —Revelations 12:27 ESV

CHAPTER THIRTEEN: I HAVE THE ANOINTING

> *And hope does not put us to shame, because God's love has been poured out into our hearts through the Holy Spirit, who has been given to us.*
> —Romans 5:5

> *In you, Lord, I have taken refuge;*
> *let me never be put to shame.*
> —Psalm 31:1

14

HELLO, MY NAME IS _____.

I praise you because I am fearfully and wonderfully made; your works are wonderful, I know that full well.
— Psalm 139:14

"The one who calls you by name is trustworthy and will thoroughly complete his work in you."
—1 Thessalonians 5:24

Just for fun, what are three of your very favorite name brands?

1. _____
2. _____
3. _____

> "BRANDING IS A BIG DEAL. BRANDING IS WHAT DISTINGUISHES ONE COMPANY FROM ANOTHER. GREAT BRANDS HAVE CREDIBILITY. SO, WHAT IS YOUR "BRAND"? WHAT DISTINGUISHES YOU FROM EVERYONE ELSE? BECAUSE WE'RE ALL MARKED, WHETHER WE LIKE IT OR NOT."
>
> - Gary Keesee

CHAPTER FOURTEEN: HELLO, MY NAME IS

Now, think about what distinguishes you from everyone else—because you are a name brand, labeled by God.

What characteristics and behaviors do you have because of that? _____

_____

_____

Write out 1 Peter 2:9:

God calls us by our _____, not our present circumstances or past sins.

Know This:
Satan doesn't have to go after your talents, money, or time as long as you don't know who you are. He is after your identity and purpose.

NOTES

Do you believe you are a threat to the enemy? Why or why not?

Write out John 16:33:

Have you ever begged God for anything? If so, what was it?

What are some things that are natural and easy for you to do, but that others compliment because it's not easy for them?

Do you see those things as part of your purpose? Why or why not?

What is one thing that you took away from reading this chapter?

TAKE ACTION!

I can't believe we're almost to the end of this study. This is where your personal renovation action gets really fun. Consider it the "design" phase in the most breathtaking renovation project ever—the masterpiece God made you to be.

I gave you four hints at the end of Chapter Fourteen to help you "design" your life (figure out why God placed you on this earth).

This week, take a look at those four hints. Read through them a few times each day.

Be sure to also complete the Challenge at the end of Chapter Fourteen, noting your responses here in this study guide, on your phone, or in a journal.

Then, GO!

Prayer

This week, pray the prayer from Chapter Fourteen of the book. Also ask God to tell you all He has spoken over your life, His name(s) for you, and to give you a glimpse of the incredible future He has for you.

> Lord, I thank You for creating me for a purpose. I ask You to reveal to me the next steps you would have me take in this season of my life. I take off the old begging mentality and any victimhood that has kept me stuck. I thank You for the freedom to be who You've created me to be.
>
> Father, I ask that You show me all that You have spoken over my life, the name You call me by, and for a glimpse of the incredible future You have for me. I thank You for that, for Your encouragement, and for the constant reminder that You are faithful. I love You, Lord.
>
> Amen.

NOTES FROM THIS CHAPTER

> *As a father has compassion on his children, so the Lord has compassion on those who fear him.*
> —Psalm 103:13

CHAPTER FOURTEEN: HELLO, MY NAME IS...

> *For in Scripture it says: "See, I lay a stone in Zion, a chosen and precious cornerstone, and the one who trusts in him will never be put to shame."*
> —1 Peter 2:6

> *I can do all things through him who strengthens me.*
> —Philippians 4:13 ESV

15
STEPS TO RECLAIMING IDENTITY

I praise you because I am fearfully and wonderfully made; your works are wonderful, I know that full well.
—Psalm 139:14

> We are no longer trying to reach up to someplace and attain value. Instead, we are in a high place of worth, value, love, and acceptance, so we can reach down to help those around us.

What is one thing you can take away from Alexis's story at the beginning of this chapter?

Do you practice more self-care or more spirit-care? Describe how.

GOD-ESTEEM
high place of worth, value, love, and acceptance

SELF-ESTEEM

What's a practical way you can live more out of your "God-esteem" rather than just your self-esteem?

Sickness and pain can only remain where _____
_____ will require a fight against your old sinful nature.

YOUR CHEAT SHEET FOR CHANGE GOING FORWARD

Take a photo of this on your phone and keep it somewhere you can easily reference. Refer back to the details for each of these in Chapter Fifteen as often as possible.

Spot the Lies (John 10:10 Test)	Identify, resist, cast it out, and declare Truth
Renew Your Thoughts	Write and post Scripture that counters the lie
Connect with Others	Work on connections with encouragers
Turn Off the Triggers	Walk away, turn it off, avoid, DELETE
Forgive	Test: Can you pray for them without malice?
Repent and Renounce	Repent from sin, renounce what's not godly
Receive Love	Get with God daily, study His love for you
Speak with Authority	Ask: What assignment am I sending my words on?

What is one thing from this chapter that you will implement in your life right away?

TAKE ACTION!

We're here! You've arrived! It's the end of the study, the "renovation for your soul." It's my hope and prayer that, no matter how messy or chaotic this personal renovation process was, that you know it was worth it—that YOU are worth it. Inner healing brings such peace!

Here's to the most breathtaking renovation project ever—the masterpiece God made you to be!

Your ongoing renovation action is to keep referring back to the tools for change included in this chapter (use the cheat sheet you hopefully took a photo of!).

Also be sure to complete the Challenge at the end of Chapter Fifteen. (If you don't want to pass your book along, would you consider getting someone a copy and gifting it to them?)

I look forward to hearing your story!

Prayer

This week, pray the prayer from Chapter Fifteen of the book. Also go back and revisit the prayers throughout this study. Pray them again for yourself or for someone else that you now know needs the same Truth you have found.

> God, thank You for bringing me this far, but I know You're not finished with me yet! Keep changing my view of myself until others can see You through me. I stand on the scripture that says, '...being confident of this, that he who began a good work in you will carry it on to completion until the day of Christ Jesus.
>
> I refuse to believe any lies about who I am. I refuse to sit down, hide, or hold myself back. Through Your power, Your anointing, and Your love, I will be the freest, boldest, most courageous version of myself! I love and value myself because You say I am loved and valuable. Thank you Jesus! I love You!

> As Scripture says, "Anyone who believes in him will never be put to shame."
>
> —Romans 10:11

CHAPTER FIFTEEN: STEPS TO RECLAIMING IDENTITY

> *Those who look to him are radiant; their faces are never covered with shame.*
>
> —Psalms 34:5

> *Those who look to him are radiant; their faces are never covered with shame.*
> —Psalms 34:5

ABOUT AMY

As an author, speaker, worship leader, and songwriter, Amy Keesee Freudiger has a passion to see people encounter the presence of the Living God, just as she did when she was miraculously and instantly healed of a thirteen-pound tumor.

Since then, Amy has been on a mission to set others free from suffering in every area of their lives through teaching, writing, and prophetic worship. Her compassion, bold faith, and sensitivity to God's presence have resulted in many others being healed. Her books include *Healed Overnight: Five Steps to Accessing Supernatural Healing*, *The 30-Day Healing Dare Devotional*, *The Truth About You*, and *The Know-How Book on Birth*. Amy is the Worship Pastor at Faith Life Church in Central Ohio and leads their recording group, Open Heaven Band (www.openheavenband.com).

Amy and her husband Jason, along with their four children, enjoy traveling, hiking, playing board games, and finding ways to make each other laugh.

Catch up with Amy and explore more of her resources:
www.healedovernight.com
Youtube.com/amyshelaine
Facebook.com/amyfreudiger
Instagram: @amyfreudiger

Mailing Address:
Faith Life Church
Attn: Amy Freudiger
2407 Beech Rd.
New Albany, OH 43054

Made in the USA
Monee, IL
12 April 2024

56515765R00090